ALL TOGETHER
SINGING
IN THE KITCHEN

# ALL TOGETHER
# SINGING
# IN THE KITCHEN

## Creative Ways to Make and Listen to Music as a Family

Nerissa Nields &
Katryna Nields

ROOST
BOOKS

Boston & London

2011

Roost Books
An imprint of Shambhala Publications, Inc.
Horticultural Hall
300 Massachusetts Avenue
Boston, Massachusetts 02115
roostbooks.com

9 8 7 6 5 4 3 2 1

First Edition
Printed in the United States of America

♾ This edition is printed on acid-free paper that meets the
American National Standards Institute Z39.48 Standard.
♻ Shambhala Publications makes every effort to print on recycled paper.
For more information please visit www.shambhala.com.

Distributed in the United States by Random House, Inc.,
and in Canada by Random House of Canada Ltd

Designed by Carolyn Kasper & Dede Cummings, dcdesign

Library of Congress Cataloging-in-Publication Data
Nields, Nerissa, 1967–
All together singing in the kitchen: the musical family / Nerissa Nields &
Katryna Nields.—1st ed.
p.   cm.
Includes bibliographical references and index.
ISBN 978-1-59030-898-1 (pbk.: alk. paper)
1. Music—Instruction and study—Activity programs.  I. Nields, Katryna,
1969– II. Title.
MT10.N54 2011
780.854—22
2011006800

This book is dedicated to

Our parents, Gail and John Nields,

For the music then

And the music now.

# CONTENTS

# PART THREE:
# DEEPENING YOUR RELATIONSHIP WITH MUSIC

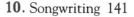
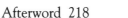

# FOREWORD

At the time of this writing it's fair to say that although we in the industrialized world consume music in record quantities, we are not living in the most musical of eras. For many of us here in this complex, frantic, and noisy society the idea of social music making, though still a way of life on much of the planet, is daunting and almost unthinkable. And yet these are times of great possibility! Imagine a day when the sound from apartment windows, parks, classrooms, loading docks, doctors offices, and auto repair shops is that of people singing and perhaps playing instruments with each other. It may seem like a pleasant yet remote fantasy, but there is a new generation on the rise and they have no reason to believe it would be otherwise.

The music that we make with our young people will have a positive impact on their lives and shape their worldview forever. Music making is proven to be a tremendous help in the socialization process; it provides a way for people of different cultural vantage points to find common ground; it stimulates the brain and helps establish the pathways that are crucial for learning during all stages of life; and, let's not forget, music is wildly enjoyable. So yes, making music changes lives. But how does it happen? How do we begin to do this with our young people? How do we help them become comfortable breaking into song when we ourselves aren't always willing to hum along with the chorus from the back of the room? In my experience, it starts at home with the family, with a new baby on day one, and it spreads through the neighborhood. From there the songs, the sounds, and the spirit go out to the world in concentric circles.

When my daughter was born I agonized over the first song she would hear in her lifetime. What record would I play for her? It never once occurred to me that I could sing that first one myself! I had been a professional musician for my entire adult life and, oddly enough, it didn't cross my mind to pick up my guitar and sing. Like most people that I knew at that time, my concept of a musical household was limited to choosing the recordings I thought might be best to play for her and yet my strongest early musical memories aren't of the records that were played around our house but of my father singing "Blue Tailed Fly" and "Danny Boy"—quite possibly his entire repertoire. Although he would never be considered a phenomenal vocalist when he sang, I knew that he was relaxed and that all was well in our world. It gave me a sense of peace and a connection with him that I needed as a child.

When music is made on the neighborhood level, more possibilities emerge. That's where the revolution takes off. I was visiting Musurgia Vintage Instruments here in Brooklyn recently and one of the luthiers said that when he was growing up there was a man on the block who would sit on his front steps and play guitar. Every kid in the neighborhood loved to listen to him and many of them were inspired to begin playing themselves. Some eventually became professional musicians. Years later my friend went back to visit the street he had grown up on and the guy was still there playing. As he put it, "I walked over to say hello and listen to my old guitar hero for awhile. After standing there for a minute I realized something . . . he was *terrible*!" When he was a kid, no one knew it and no one cared. Technical ability was beside the point. There was someone in the neighborhood playing music and that was all that mattered. The guy didn't wait to come out until he had his act down—he just came out. And he lit the fuses of a few imaginations. To any young

person experiencing music being made, right there in front of them for the first time, it doesn't take much to carry the message.

When we play music with each other and for each other the world begins to look like a different place. Petty cares and fears fall away. Priorities become shaken and realigned, jokes become funnier and there are more of them, food tastes better and more people are willing to help clean up, differences fade away and similarities appear in unexpected ways, and we begin to experience a new sense of life's best possibilities—musically, socially, creatively, and spiritually. Music remains the best deal in town.

My daughter is sixteen now and, although they're still meaningful, our musical interactions are different than they used to be. I'm grateful that when she was younger I found ways to fill the house with music. Now it's your turn. Thank you to the Nields for gathering all the ideas, hopes, stories, and songs that people share about family music making, and for putting them into this one generous, limitless, and inspiring book, which we can refer to when the snow is piling up outside, friends are coming over, and it's time to turn off the TV, clean up the house, cook some soup, and maybe have a wild party—one with plenty of food and friendship and laughter and, of course, running through it all, the sound of people singing and playing with each other.

—Dan Zanes

# PREFACE

*If you can walk, you can dance.*
*If you can talk, you can sing.*
—NIGERIAN PROVERB

MUSIC HAS ALWAYS BEEN A BIG PART OF our lives. We're sisters and touring musicians who set out to conquer the world in 1991 with a fifteen-passenger Dodge Ram van and a five-piece rock band named after our family, The Nields. We played on stages all across North America to audiences of tens of thousands. We garnered a lot of national airplay and watched in bemusement as record company executives and their lawyers haggled over us in bidding wars. We went to Grammy parties and rubbed shoulders with artists whose records had formed the soundtrack of our youth.

We have many great memories, not to mention sixteen CDs, as a result of our touring-musician path. The one thing we felt sure of was that once we became mothers, we would raise musical children.

But somehow, when we did start our own families, we drew a musical blank. We were too tired and distracted to even think of introducing our kids to music. Making and listening to music for ourselves was completely different than sharing music with our children. This was something new, something we had to learn to do.

So we started slowly. It has been said that as a new parent, you lose part of your brain when your baby is born. The version of this phenomenon for both of us was—in the moment of greatest need—to lose the memory of every song we'd ever known, with the exception of songs we had no interest in passing along, such as "The Farmer in the Dell" and "Old MacDonald Had a Farm." So we did what we could. Katryna started making up songs when she couldn't think of a lullaby, and she dusted off her old guitar. Nerissa made it a priority to create the space—away from chores—for sharing music with her children. Soon making music for our kids became a part of our lives. It didn't feel forced; it had become natural for us and our children.

To reinforce our dedication to making music for and with our kids, we decided to start Hoote-Nanny—a music class for children from birth to age five and their grown-ups—because if two musicians had a hard time bringing music to their kids, surely others must be having trouble too. We designed HooteNanny to give parents the songs, ideas, and inspiration they need to make music with their children. This book is largely based on those classes.

Other musicians who had become mothers warned us that motherhood would stall our writing and music careers, that all our creativity would be poured into our children and there would be none left for us or for our audience. Ironically, motherhood turned out to be a gateway to each of us rediscovering our music.

HooteNanny has given both of us an outlet to find a new musical voice, connect to our musical heritage, give our children a hearty dose of folk music, and learn how to hold a baby and a guitar at the same time. Even better, it has given both of us a community through which we can make and participate in music.

## NO MUSICAL BACKGROUND NECESSARY

We grew up in a musical household, attended musical schools, and became professional musicians as adults. However, none of that is necessary

for sharing music with your child or having your own musical family.

Our parents loved music, and they gave it to us in a very simple way. It was the early seventies, and they had been beneficiaries of the folk boom of the early sixties. It seemed to us (and to our aunts and uncles) that our father knew every word to every folk song ever written—or at least all those we wanted to know. Our mother had figured out how to play the guitar and taught our dad his first three chords. He figured out the rest on his own. He started with first position three- and four-chord songs—nothing fancy, just basic fingerpicking, no flat-picking. But he knew how to convey a song with his whole heart and being. He knew how to bring a song inside himself, make it his own, and then give it back to the world—or, at least, to us.

He also was fearless about learning new songs. He quickly figured out that most songs worth knowing have just a few chords and that once you learn those chords, you can play almost any song.

We most commonly heard music around the kitchen table. After dinner, our father would pull out his guitar while our mother did the dishes. While she sang a harmony, he would entertain us by playing the songs he grew up with, as well as anything he'd recently heard on the radio. He sometimes substituted simpler chords to the songs he wanted to learn, but he could usually pick out the core structure and approximate the song well

## Katryna

Six weeks after I gave birth to my oldest child, Amelia, a fan came up to me at the Falcon Ridge Folk Festival and commented on how lucky Amelia must be to be getting so much music in her life.

"Your house must be so magical," she gushed. As I smiled and demurred, I realized with some shock and sadness that I hardly ever sang to my baby. Sure, she came to our shows, and she must have been listening while we worked, but I wasn't giving her music in any kind of directed, personal way.

I decided to make more of an effort to sing to my daughter. But whenever I wanted to sing her a lullaby, I drew a blank. I couldn't remember a single appropriate song.

Someone gave Amelia this tiny music box that played "Over the Rainbow." So I would sing that, forgetting all the words and singing the verses out of order, but it made her happy.

This encouraged me to sing more. I actually began writing songs for the first time in my life. One day, while driving a wailing Amelia home from the grocery store, I was trying everything I could think of to console her. Finally, I made up a song whose only lyric was her name, repeated over and over to an upbeat neo-Baroque tune. It worked. Amelia stopped crying and was interested and soothed by the sound of my voice. Encouraged, I began writing songs about her stuffed animals: "I'm Amelia's little red dog, I'm Amelia's little red dog . . ." or "I'm a caterpillar and I squeak . . . ." I now had a whole repertoire of songs to sing to

my daughter. These animal songs also gave me a way to interact with her in the moments when I couldn't think of anything else to do.

When my son William was born, I suffered a polyp on my vocal chords (a not-uncommon occurrence as the result of childbirth, as it turns out). As lead singer for the Nields, I had barely picked up my acoustic guitar since college, leaving the guitar chores to Nerissa and the guys in the band. But because I couldn't sing to my baby, I dusted off my old guitar and started strumming. And once I started playing, William wouldn't let me stop. He would crawl over to the case and bang on it until I took it out and sang him a song.

William's first word? *Guitar.* Coincidence? I think not.

## Nerissa

By the time Lila was three weeks old, I was convinced I would never write another song. My guitar sat lonely and ignored in the corner of a room I barely visited. The one time I picked it up to play for her, she cried, as if knowing somehow that it might be competition for her mother's lap. This, I thought, was a disaster. I worried that if I didn't carve away specific times to make music just for my daughter, she might not get any music from me at all. I believed Lila needed folk music like she needed breast milk, and if we didn't give it to her, terrible things would happen. She would become a TV addict. She wouldn't be able to dance. Worst of all, she wouldn't love music. For me,

making music for my daughter was a priority and a way for me to care for her.

But I was tired. I was constantly breast-feeding. I was postpartum and weepy. And there was a part of me that felt resigned to my future life as a nonsongwriter. After all, I had the most beautiful baby on earth. How could I ask for more?

Like many new mothers I know, I wanted myself back. I wanted both to be consumed by my love for my daughter and to be me again. One morning when Lila was about three weeks old, as I was breast-feeding her and despairing about the permanent mess on our kitchen table, I picked up one of the toys my sister Abigail had handed down to us: it was a plush, black and white dog with a red collar affixed to a red and blue ball. I reflected on the wave of kid's toys made in

black, white, and red under the theory that these are the only colors infants can see. I shook the ball and something inside it made a jingle sound. Lila was intrigued. I animated the little dog and sang this song to my baby:

I'm a dog on a ball, and I
  chime.
I'm a dog on a ball, and I can
  rhyme.
I'm a dog on a ball, and you're
  compelled to look at me,
'Cause I'm a dog on a ball, and
  I chime.
They did studies to see what
  you could see;
What they came up with
  looked like me,
'Cause I'm black and I'm white
  with just a bit of red.
And I'm a dog on a ball, and I
  chime.
And you track me around the
  kitchen table,
'Cause your parents seem to
  be unable

enough to sing his own version. And that was
good enough for us.

We also went to schools where music was respected and given a lot of space and time, where
every child was taught to read music, just as they
were taught the alphabet. We took piano, recorder, clarinet, violin, and eventually voice
lessons. Later, Nerissa studied classical music,
voice, and guitar at Yale, sang in the glee club,
and started her own singing group. Katryna sang
with the acclaimed Trinity Pipes Concert Choir
and performed in every musical-theater production her college produced.

We are well educated musically. But when we
sing to our kids, and even when we write and perform our own songs today, we use almost none of
our formal education. Instead, we use the very
simple tools our parents gave us around the
kitchen table: three chords, two-part harmony,
and love and respect for the way a song can make
people feel.

Making music for or with your children
should be fun and heartfelt. It needn't be perfect.
Use your voice, use instruments, or even play a

recording—the simple act of engaging in music
with your child is enough. You don't need to
know a thing about music to get something out of
this book and successfully bring music into your
family life. If you're new to singing or playing an
instrument, we'll give you some guidelines in Part
One. Even if you're a classically trained violinist
or a teacher of elementary school music, you may
still learn some new songs or skills. We hope this
book provides you with songs and games that inspire your family. And if you're one of those
people who took piano lessons years ago or used
to sing in the church choir, we've also provided a
section on quick and easy theory to give you a
good refresher.

Parenthood provides a once-in-a-lifetime opportunity to begin again, to learn and/or relearn.
Perhaps as an adult, you've thought, "I've never
read *A Wrinkle in Time*! Oh, well. When I have
kids, I'll read it to them." In the same way, having
children may be the perfect opportunity for you to
pick up a guitar or refine your singing.

In many families we know, parents have taken up piano lessons or singing to support their child's musical efforts, but they have continued for their own pleasure. Any parent who ventures to a music classroom is soon called to learn (and practice) along with his or her child. If your kid is in the school musical, before long, you too will know all the words to *Bye-Bye Birdie* or *Once Upon a Mattress*. Music is a huge, elastic medium with plenty of opportunities for both beginners and advanced practitioners. Some families institute family practice time or family music time, and parents look forward to and get as much from the experience as their kids do. We hope this book motivates you to jump into music making with your family no matter how skilled you are.

There are countless music teachers who can show you or your child how to play an instrument and lots of music books—music philosophy, music education, Irish and Beatles songbooks, Carl Sandburg's famous *Songbag*—on the bookstore shelf. We're here to tell you that music is yours for the taking. You don't need a music teacher, a working knowledge of at least one instrument, or even that elusive substance called talent. Music is accessible for anyone. We are born musical beings, and the river that is music is always flowing along beside us. We only have to notice and dip our toes in at will. Our hope is that this book will teach you some songs and guide you into a lifetime of finding and making the music that will bring your own unique family together.

## Cast of Characters

For the sake of readability, we've written this book in the first person plural, even though we didn't (usually) write our pieces in the same room, looking over each other's shoulders. When we felt the need to include a personal story, we've done so in the sidebars throughout. Although we do share much and spend almost every weekend together in the forced proximity of Katryna's Corolla en route to a gig, we have separate lives with separate families in separate towns (albeit only twenty minutes apart). Our children play together, but they are different

GAIL JOHN DAVE KATRYNA TOM MARK
NERISSA ABIGAIL
AMELIA TRENOR
WILLIAM REESE EMMETT
LILA JOHNNY

ages, all born within a seven-year span. We thought it might be helpful to provide you with a cast of characters so you know to whom we are referring when we tell our tales of music and family.

• **John Nields, our dad.** Our father had the great good fortune of having John Seeger as a geography teacher, which meant that in the fifties, when Pete Seeger was blacklisted, he came to our father's school to inculcate the kids. Our dad sings and plays guitar on several of our CDs and is our hero. Incidentally, he is also a lawyer.

• **Gail Nields, our mom.** She taught our dad how to play the guitar and is a whiz at playing Christmas carols on the piano. She also taught Nerissa (by example) how to harmonize. She is a writer, historian, and teacher, as well as the world's best and most sane stage mother.

- **Abigail Nields, our youngest sister.** She sings and also plays the guitar. Mother to Emmett, Reese, and Trenor and wife to guitar-playing Mark, she is most famous (in this book) for being the world's number-one Bruce Springsteen fan.

- **Katryna Nields, our middle sister.** She is our lead singer and big-idea person. Though Nerissa spent most of our childhood bossing Katryna around, now the shoe is on the other foot. Katryna regularly calls Nerissa to tell her exactly what kind of song to write and sometimes convinces her to write a whole book.

- **Nerissa Nields, our eldest sister.** She is a songwriter, guitarist, and harmonizer. The philosopher of the group, Nerissa is also the one who makes us get stuff done. That is why you're holding this book.

- **Dave Chalfant, Katryna's husband and father of William and Amelia.** He is the bass player for the Nields and currently our all-around musical genius, producer, and guitar player extraordinaire.

- **Amelia Nields Chalfant, Katryna's daughter.** Age nine at the time of this writing, she is a budding pianist, guitar, bass, and clarinet player, and violinist.

- **William John Chalfant, Katryna's son.** Age five at the time of this writing, he plays a mean cardboard guitar and knows exactly which brand of guitar is played in any given Beatles song.

- **Tom Nields-Duffy, Nerissa's husband and father of Lila and Johnny.** He is an occasional djembe player and also plays the Muffin Man in our DVD.

- **Lila Nields-Duffy, Nerissa's daughter.** Age four at the time of this writing, she is the inspiration for most of Nerissa's songs since 2006. She plays Suzuki violin and has a passion for Freeze Dance.

- **Johnny Nields-Duffy, Nerissa's son.** Age two at the time of this writing, he is obsessed with "Peter and the Wolf." If you ask him, he will tell you he wants to play the piano and cello when he's four, but not the violin.

# INTRODUCTION
## Making Time for Music

Some of the most frequent utterances we hear from parents (and utter ourselves) go something like this:

It's going by so quickly!

I turn around, and she's a whole different person!

I can't believe he's already ten months/fifteen months/two years/eight years old. Just yesterday he was falling asleep in my arms.

Is there any way to freeze this, to hold this moment and make it stay like this?

I'm not paying enough attention! I can't believe I just spent forty-five minutes checking my Facebook status instead of watching my kid play on the floor.

Sadly, we all know there is no way to stop time, but we can decide how to use ours to be more fully present with our children. That's the whole point of this book: being more completely in the moment of this miraculous phase of life as parents; witnessing, nurturing, and being fully engaged with our growing children. There are myriad ways to do this—hiking, soccer, cooking, reading aloud, crafting, carpooling, doing chores together, playing kids' games. But music has an element that sets it apart from all other activities: its domain, its very essence, is time.

A piece of music played live and sung together lives only for the moment the notes are struck or uttered. We can record it and listen or watch it again, but that's not the same as experiencing it directly, just as seeing a video of our one-year-old walking for the first time is not the same as being present for that numinous moment. Nor is it the same as actually being that child in that first step.

Music is all about being in the present moment. In fact, music can only exist in the present moment. Otherwise, it's merely silent notes on a page, grooves on a CD or LP, abstract workings in a metal device, potential in a wooden instrument. For music to exist, we have to get out of our heads. We have to leave behind our guilt about yesterday, our worries about today, and our dreams about tomorrow. We can only be with that one note we're singing, that one beat we're shaking a maraca along with.

Remember, music is everywhere and everything from tapping on the table to clapping your hands to humming in imitation of a truck driving or to whistling like a bird. And when we make music with our kids, we're filling our precious family moments with exactly the element our children most crave from us: our time and attention.

## STARTING A MUSICAL FAMILY

You don't need any musical training to start making music with your family. Throughout this book, you'll learn tips on singing, playing, listening, and interacting musically with your children. You'll

### Nerissa

Those of us who follow any kind of spiritual tradition that involves mindfulness may be doubly tormented as parents by the difficulty we face in trying to stay present in our experience without judging it, blaming someone for its imperfections, or wanting it to stay the same forever. Though I'm ordinarily prone to wishing that things were other than they actually are, parenthood—a state I desired deeply and worked hard to achieve—has challenged me to the hilt in this respect. It seems the more I want to be present for my kids—the more I want to sit on the floor with them and make Emerald Cities out of wooden blocks, or make up stories with their stuffed animals, or watch them paint, or take video of them singing "Sidewalks of New York" and "Twinkle Twinkle"—the more I am drawn to tidy the puzzle pieces, make a cup of coffee, check my e-mail, call a friend, worry about money, write a thank-you note, or do any number of not necessarily unwholesome activities rather than just be a mother. A friend of mine once suggested that I look at sitting on the floor and playing with my kids as a form of meditation, which works as well as anything, providing I'm in a good meditative space. Making music with my children, however, is a much more effective meditation practice for me. When I'm making music with Lila and Johnny, we are—by definition—in the present moment.

find musical games, songs, and dances, as well as projects such as making instruments and songwriting. And you'll discover ways to take your family music to new levels if you so choose.

Sprinkled liberally throughout the book are songs we love; songs to fit specific times in family life, such as entertaining a new baby; first songs for little voices; rounds to let family members experiment with singing individual "parts"; songs to modify for any occasion; and so on. When we introduce a song, we include the chords, lyrics, and any other information we think might be helpful; we've also included these songs on the accompanying CD so you can learn the melody and sing or play along. Feel free to skip the songs and just read this book as a how-to. Or you can ignore the text, plunge straight into the music, and use this as a songbook.

We focus on folk music because we feel the genre is perfect for new parents who are picking up instruments for the first time or again after a long hiatus. Folk music welcomes newcomers, old-timers, prodigals, and prodigies all. Because so much is new to young children, most thrive on predictability and reliability; folk music is predictable in its chord changes and timeless themes, and reliable in its longevity. At any given time, children take in so much new information that it's comforting to know there are certain things in life they can depend on: breakfast, naps, bedtime routine, and so on. Folk music makes sense in the same way. The chord structures become familiar even to a young ear, and the resolution at the end

is dependable and comforting. Our favorite songs growing up are also favorites with the kids in our music classes and our own children. This book contains some of those favorites and describes how to make them more than just songs to you and your child.

This book is not about *creating* a musical family; it's about *discovering* the musical family you already have. All twelve-month-olds are drummers of sorts. Somewhere between twelve and thirty-six months, children acquire dancing feet. And any three-year-old is a budding songwriter, narrating his or her day via melody like a small Oscar Hammerstein. Our mission as a band back in the nineties was to write songs that kids would sing at the back of school buses (or the equivalent) a hundred years in the future. Our hope in writing this book is the same—that your children and ours will carry these songs with them, change some of the words, and pass them on to their own kids, who will claim them as their own. The songs change as you bring your own musicality and originality to them; some remain the same.

## YOUR FAMILY MUSICAL CANON

Throughout this book, we often refer to your family's musical canon, which we define as a group of musical works representing your family. In the course of writing, it became clear to us that the idea of such a canon is the bedrock to our whole vision for how music can uniquely enrich family life. In discussions with friends, many told us wonderful stories of songs that stayed with their families for decades or generations and how these songs acted as a kind of web, connecting family members over years and continents. One friend remembers singing UB40's "Red Red Wine" with her small daughters while her husband shot a video of them all dancing, and this video is a cornerstone memory for the entire family. Both girls, young women now, still adore that song. Another friend, who calls her family "nonmusical," still fondly recalls a pop song from the eighties to which she and her sister made up new words; they now sing it to each other whenever they talk on the phone. Other friends speak of seasonal songs their families sang at Passover and Christmas and how certain rituals couldn't occur until the songs were sung. And every family has some version of "Happy Birthday." Such songs and experiences make up a family musical canon.

Yet the task of establishing this canon now, when your kids are still young, is a little like planning your family vacations for the next twenty-five years. You may make some assumptions about those vacations—you'll spend some time with grandparents and some at a beloved summer locale—and entertain hopes and dreams of new places you might go, such as a cross-country road trip or a voyage to China or Italy. But the truth is you can't know what will happen until the time comes, and you won't really know until you look back and see where you've been what your family loved most.

That being said, we are inviting you to start a

wish list. You can add and subtract as you go, depending on your likes and dislikes, your child's predilections, and changing tastes. A song you love today might get stale. Or you might surprise yourself by growing fond of an old chestnut like "Auld Lang Syne."

First, take a look back at your own childhood, adolescence, and young adulthood and jot down what was in your family's musical canon. It might be small or voluminous. What do you want to pass down?

A sample of our family canon from when we were kids includes "Happy Birthday," "Row, Row, Row Your Boat," "Sur le Pont d'Avignon," "Sunny Days" (from *Sesame Street*), "Miss Mary Mac," "Yellow Submarine," "The Leaving of Liverpool," "Rattlin' Bog," and "The Fox." Later on, we added "Night Rider's Lament," "When the Saints Go Marching In," "There Is a Balm in Gilead," and "I'm So Lonesome I Could Cry."

Next, consider the music you listened to before you had kids and the music you listen to now. Your soul music. You might not be able to introduce everything to your children right now, but do you have a road map? Do you want to nudge them in the direction of jazz and away from alt-country? In that case, consider what contemporary children's music you could bring into your home. Be discerning, and choose artists whose taste matches yours.

A fun way to discover songs you might have forgotten is to contact your family. You can start a group e-mail to your parents, grandparents, siblings, aunts, uncles, and cousins and ask them what they remember. We did this when we began writing this book, and it brought back amazing and wonderful memories for all involved.

Your musical canon will evolve as you and your family learn what your favorites are. This book is full of songs that were or have become a part of ours, and we have listed additional song ideas in the appendix. You may want to use some of them as a starting point. You may also discover a Tom Petty song that makes a perfect lullaby, make up your own words to the introductory phrase of Mozart's Clarinet Concerto, or sing a Wilco song really gently.

When gathering music to share with your children, start off with what you like. Don't be guilted into playing a CD a friend gave you or your child if you don't like it. If the Baby Einstein collection of Mozart, Beethoven, and Bach played on what sound like Casio keyboards drives you insane, get rid of it. Instead, introduce your child to the music you love—try the Beatles, Dan Zanes, the B-52s, Louis Armstrong, Frank Zappa, or Willie Nelson, depending on your tastes. Your child will have opinions too and might not like what you choose. Lila and Amelia didn't like Bob Dylan. William loved James Taylor, and Katryna got to play his greatest hits over and over when her son was between two months and a year. Not bad.

In the beginning, you might have to refer to your list when you are attempting to create a family music time or just to infuse your daily life with

songs. In the latter case, you will often find situations or conversations that are conducive to bursting into song. (For example, if Monty Python's famous "I Hate Traffic Lights" is on your list, you'll have plenty of opportunity to sing it to your kids in the car.)

If you have a small child, you already know that kids like repetition. They are soothed by hearing the same book or the same song over and over. How often have you heard, "Again!" from the backseat—the directive to push the Repeat button on the car system and listen to one more round of "The Fox" or, in our family's case, "Sweet Rosyanne." Although this might be annoying and frustrating for you, it's actually good for your child. It creates a sense of confidence, comfort, and control. The child's brain is learning something from that particular song. This is another reason to be sure to select only songs that you like.

At the same time, if your child doesn't like a song at first, don't give up. We've heard that a child needs to try the same food fifteen times before liking it. Songs can be similar, and this is true for adults as well. Sometimes it takes several listens before you fall in love with a piece of music. If you really adore a certain song, play it judiciously but frequently. Your child might surprise you one day by humming a few bars of it. Amelia confided to Katryna when she was about three years old that she didn't really like the Beatles.

Katryna was crushed, but she didn't push it. Now, at nine, Amelia can play the riff to "Day Tripper" better than Nerissa can.

In HooteNanny, we give parents a CD of the twenty to twenty-five songs we sing during the ten-week session, and we encourage them to play the CD often to familiarize themselves and their children with the music. The more you hear a song, the more it insinuates itself into your mind and body, and the more pleasure you get from the experience. (The word-for-word translation of the German term *ohrwurm* for a piece of music that gets stuck in your head is "earworm." In his book *Musicophilia: Tales of Music and the Brain*, Oliver Sacks writes, "Many people are set off by the theme music of a film or a television show or an advertisement. This is not coincidental, for such music is designed, in the terms of the music industry, to 'hook' the listener, to be 'catchy' or 'sticky,' to bore its way, like an earwig, into the ear or mind; hence the term 'earworms'—though one might be inclined to call them 'brainworms' instead."[1])

Don't worry if your family canon isn't very big at first. This is actually a good thing. Focus on a few beloved songs. You might even have to stick with just one verse for some particularly stubborn kids who, like Lila, only want to hear the part about the unicorns drowning in "The Unicorn Song."

## Creating Your Canon

Sit down with a piece of paper, and write down every song you can think of. Think back to your own childhood: what do you remember? Perhaps there are some songs you'd rather forget. (For example, our neighbor taught us one that went "My gal's a corker / She's a New Yorker / I buy her anything to keep her in style / She's got a pair of hips / Just like two battleships / Yeah, boys, that's where my money goes!" Though this is memorable, we might not want to pass it down to our kids.) Write for ten minutes or until you've exhausted your memory. Then go to your CD collection (or iTunes library) to jog your memory further. Keep writing.

Now look at your list and think about the songs you've written down. Which ones speak to you? Which ones do you want to speak to your child at this age and in the future? Circle those. Can you hum their tunes? If not, forget about them for now. The songs that you can hum or whose words you can easily recall by looking up their lyrics once make a good starting place.

Write your list down in a notebook. If you're the organized type, find the lyrics to these songs on the Internet or at your library, or type them out from memory and make your own songbook. Alternatively, you can just jot down the titles on a scrap of paper, if that's all you need. Put this in your pocket, and when you need a song, pull out your paper.

You can also post your ongoing list in your kitchen on a dry-erase board or your refrigerator door so you can add to it or scratch off songs about which you might have second thoughts. As your kids grow older, they can add to and subtract from the master list, too.

Next, make a mix CD or playlist for your mp3 player that contains your chosen songs. Play your list every day. Familiarize yourself with the songs and begin to sing them yourself, with and without the CD. Start in the privacy of your shower or car, and then move on to singing to your child.

If you can play the guitar or piano, learn the songs and play them for your child. You can easily find the chords to many tunes with Google; just type in the title and "+ chords, lyrics." While our father's ability to remember so many songs is partially a natural gift, it is also a skill he developed through sheer practice. He knew the lyrics because he had a devoted audience in his daughters. He was simply telling a tale, making sure he conveyed *all* the details to his listeners with the retelling (and retelling and retelling).

## Nerissa

It took me some time to develop my family musical canon. Songs like "Heavy Metal Drummer" or "I Am the Walrus," which I had assumed—prepregnancy— would fascinate my kids, suddenly didn't seem appropriate for the bundles of newborn innocence in my arms. Though she sees it differently, I thought Katryna handled this transition seamlessly. She seemed to just segue from the Breeders to Elizabeth Mitchell with ease and good humor, embracing the music she and her children both loved. I, on the other hand, propped Lila in front of the *Concert for Bangladesh* when she was about six months old; although she tolerated George Harrison, she downright hated Bob Dylan. *That's okay,* I thought. *I'll just listen to Dylan when I'm alone.* But I really was not alone very often.

I also found, as a parent, that my own sensitivities were heightened. I was no longer able to watch edgy movies. I bought an album by the White Stripes, a band

I'm certain I would have loved before I had kids. But listening to it when Johnny was just a year and a half old, I found it too hard, too loud, too angry. My skin had become thinner. I wanted to retreat back to the music of the playroom.

Our friend Heather says, "For the last twenty years of my life, I've listened almost exclusively to indie rock and old country. My husband and I bonded over indie rock, went to shows on dates, and got excited about sharing really loud music together. Even now, when we get a babysitter, we mostly just drive around blasting the Hold Steady as loudly as we can. This isn't something I can share with my daughters at this point, and there's a part of me that has had to mourn that. Music doesn't have the same place in my life and marital relationship as it did before the kids. Making music with kids is an adjustment, and it's not as simple as just introducing them to music you love. I used to listen to my music all day long; now I look forward to time alone in the car or on a run when I can hear it."

Amen. We too had to mourn the loss of putting on our favorite music at top volume when we came home from work or first thing in the morning. Now and then, when I'm alone in the car and I put on music I loved in college or in my early days as a member of a rock band, I turn the volume up and cry with relief and nostalgia.

## Katryna

When my children were four and one, I found myself talking to a friend I know through the folk music world. I asked him what kids' music his seven-year-old twins enjoyed. He told me they mostly listened to Green Day now, and my heart sank. It felt like my kids would soon be insisting on pop music, and then there would be no more simple, innocent folk music. I felt determined to avoid pop music so my children would love folk music for as long as possible.

But by William's fifth birthday, he was as obsessed with the Beatles as typical five-year-olds are with dinosaurs, princesses, and superheroes. My husband kept saying,

"Zeppelin is next." I was filled with fear that my family would leave me and my folk music–loving ways behind. My kids have since discovered Cyndi Lauper, Beyoncé, the Who, and Coldplay. But they also still love a rousing game of "A Ram Sam Sam" (see page 113). I should never have feared that exposing them to many different kinds of music would limit them.

The other morning, we were waiting in the car at the bus stop because it was pouring. Amelia insisted on trolling the radio for songs. She was elated when she found Taylor Swift. I had a beautiful time in the car for those few minutes, listening to my kids sing along to the "poppiest" music imaginable. The next day, they couldn't stop singing "The Horse Went Around,"

which we sing in HooteNanny (see page 112).

There is room for it all. I just have to remember to enjoy their love for music even when I don't care for the music they love. So far, they've convinced me: Beyoncé rocks. As long as we keep the communication lines open, they're still willing to have me introduce them to some of the music I like.

## ADDING MUSIC TO YOUR EVERYDAY LIFE

Once you've set the foundation with your family musical canon, start thinking about how to include music in your everyday life. Just as children need to hear other people talking in order to learn to speak, they need to hear music regularly in order to get the most out of it. Making music can require focus and attention, and with the busyness of our lives, it can be hard to find this kind of time to spend with our kids. When we do find some time, we may be overwhelmed with the choices available: Do I take my child to a music class? Should I play Mozart while he's sleeping? Is it okay to mix classical with pop? How do I get started? Do I need props?

Here are some ideas to help bring more music into your family's life.

### Turn on the Radio (or iPod or Stereo)

This may seem obvious, but we forget it all the time. Turn off the news and turn on the music when the kids are in the car with you. It takes just half a minute to press a button and fill your space with music. A little preparation can help: have your stack of chosen music at the ready; make your family-friendly iPod mix ahead of time. Take a little time once a week or once a month to update it and make changes—remembering to keep favorites, as children like repetition and consistency.

## Sing during Everyday Routines

Everything goes better with a song. Sing through regular activities, such as preparing meals, driving to school or day care, going for a walk, bathing, cleaning up, brushing teeth, and going to bed. (Chapter 8 has more ideas for incorporating music into daily activities.)

As you will see, we have a soft spot for changing the words to well-known songs to suit the activity of the moment. (For example, "Going to the Zoo" may became "Going to the School.") Our friend Kate, who describes herself as "a lover of music but slightly intimidated by singing and songwriting," was inspired to rewrite "Three Blind Mice" for her one-year-old:

Three big steps, three big steps
Down off the porch, down off the porch
Then we'll go and all play outside,
I'll push the swing and you'll go for a ride,
Just three big steps.

## Make an Effort to See Shows

Take a break from your outdoor activities to take your children to a family-oriented concert or play. Watching others perform is magical for children, and as long as the show is shorter than forty-five minutes, you won't have to wrangle too much. Most kids can be entertained (by someone other than you) for that amount of time. Keep in mind that it's often cheap to watch other kids perform (and your child probably won't care that the eleven-year-old on stage is mangling a British accent). Scan the bulletin boards for local school productions aimed at kids.

## Find Local Music Classes

While seeing musical performances or art can be enriching, making music—participating in the act of creation—is transformative. Find a class that suits your own style. We are particularly fond of programs like Music Together or HooteNanny, where the whole point is for parents to learn along with their children so that the experience goes well beyond the actual class time.

## Keep Instruments and Props Available

Children are not masters of organization. If you buy a lovely collection of instruments but keep them tucked away on a top shelf in the playroom or spread out all over the house in obscure places, your child may not engage with them—or worse, not know what to do with them. We keep such items at floor level, in a box with an open lid, in a corner of the house designated for music and musical items. Our collection includes small instruments, a ukulele, a collection of hand drums, all sorts of percussion instruments, and dance wands and scarves for waving along to the beat.

And to solve our perennial problem of re-membering a song to sing in the moment of great-est need, we suggest a song basket. At both of the preschools our children attend, there is a version of Song Basket. Take any container—a basket, box, file drawer, desk drawer, or pretty bowl—and put cards with the names of favorite songs written on them inside. Pull it down from the shelf and let your child pick a card; sing whatever song happens to be written on it. Alternatively, you can use small toys or small objects to represent the songs. Katryna got this idea from her daughter's teacher, Lise McGuiness. There is a figure of a fish that de-notes "Slippery Fish." A small fox means "The Fox." A rainbow-colored Slinky represents "My Favorite Color," although it could also double as the rainbow for "The Unicorn Song." (Using toys gives you some leeway in choosing which song to sing.)

Another take on this is to have a Lullaby Bas-ket. If you have a dozen different lullabies for your kids, have a basket of little trinkets that symbolize each one. Choosing songs can then be part of your nightly ritual.

If you're a crafty type, you can go to town dec-orating the box and getting fancy with the design of the cards. If you're like Nerissa, simple index cards will do. If you can't afford instruments and props, or you just don't have any this minute but are dying to get started, don't fret! Chapter 9 tells you how to make instruments out of the contents of your recycling bin.

## Schedule It In!

You are what you put in your day planner, date-book, or iCal. If something is important to you, you'll make time for it. Parents need to create time for important things by carving out specific times during the week when they will happen. When it comes to music, even we need to do this, which is why Nerissa insisted on creating Hoote-Nanny. Katryna signed up for a Music Together class because she knew that without a prearranged time and place to make music with her baby, it would probably never happen.

Less is more, and routine is best. Put another way, reestablish your intention to be a musical family every day. Set aside a small amount of time each day to honor music, but don't necessarily ex-pect or demand "progress." If your child is learning an instrument, five minutes is better than nothing, and five minutes a day is better than thirty-five minutes once a week the day before the lesson (although that too is better than nothing). In the beginning, Lila's Suzuki violin practice time took only five minutes a day, but we created the daily space and believed we were becoming violinists. Katryna played a recording of Mozart's clarinet concerto at the same time every day when Amelia was a baby. Johnny usually gets a lullaby before bed; William makes a cardboard guitar. Once a week the kids go to HooteNanny. We frequently have music playing in our houses. We take the kids to see Dan Zanes when he comes to town or to see a Beatles tribute band, and we plan to see Cyndi Lauper (with whom Amelia and William fell in love while watching their parents' old VHS tape of Live Aid). But it's not as though our lives or our kids' lives are all music all the time.

Remember, it's as easy to sing as it is to talk. As we mentioned earlier, taking a minute before you start the car to slide a CD into the player or set up your mp3 player will accomplish your goal of reestablishing your intention. Listen to the CD provided with this book for songs you can listen to every day, such as "Time to Take a Bath" and "This Is How We Clean Our Toys Up." (We will use the following icon to alert you when a song mentioned in the text appears on the CD:

Even better, begin to make up your own words, tunes, or whole new songs.

Time, space, and intention. These elements are really all you need to be musical, no matter what you might believe about talent and skill. No matter where your family is in terms of its chronology—whether your kids are still in utero, babies, school age, or even teenagers—it's not too late to commit the time, make the space, and create the intention to be musical and give this gift to your family. With your family musical canon and an eye and ear to bringing music into everyday life, you're ready to make music.

# Part One

## MUSICAL BEGINNINGS

# SINGING

THE VOICE IS THE MOST BASIC OF ALL instruments. It's versatile, flexible, and best of all, portable. The voice is almost everyone's first instrument, and it's certainly the most intimate. Often, when we teach a song in HooteNanny or just to our kids, we find it practical and even preferable to sing a cappella (without accompaniment from the guitar or piano) so we can pass along the words and tune with as little distraction as possible. In this chapter, we encourage you to sing as much as possible to and with your child. Each time you sing to your children, you are strengthening your bond with them and offering yourself an opportunity for transformation. You are modeling participation for your kids.

Many of you already sing to your children. Hooray! We want to reiterate that there is no wrong way to sing to your kids. We know parents who truly cannot carry a tune, and watching them sing to their little ones with love, kindness, engagement, and attention—not to mention a big smile—is one of the great privileges of working with young families. We know plenty of parents who have discovered their voices as young mothers and fathers, sitting on the edge of the sofa, crooning into their baby's ear. We know many parents who used to sing regularly, gave it up for a while, and are now singing again with gusto as their kids egg them on.

As with any relationship, practice, book, hobby, or institution in the world, the more time you spend with it, the more you can come to love it. Also, the more you refine a skill, the more you understand a person, the more times you read a book, and the better you do your job, the more pleasure you get out of that activity, person, book, or job. For this reason, we are going to give you some ideas for ways to deepen your relationship with your voice by becoming a more skillful singer.

Our Aunt Elizabeth grew up thinking she couldn't sing. When we asked her about this recently, she said, "I mainly didn't sing because the notes didn't come out where they were supposed to. I think I sang a bit when I was by myself. I would try from time to time with people when they encouraged me, but they would soon mention that they saw what I meant, that there was a problem." Her brother (our dad) and her youngest sister, Jenifer, became terrific singers and players, and this might have reinforced her notion that she was nonmusical. (She instead gravitated to painting and drawing; she's now a professional potter.) When the family gathered to sing Christmas carols, she held the hymnal and listened with a smile.

Yet when she became a mother, something changed. Her son showed great musical promise, so she took him to lessons when he was still small. In the course of these lessons, she was called on to sing, to play a tape over and over, and to coach her son to practice. Before long, we noticed that she was singing the Christmas carols and also that she wasn't tone-deaf. All it took for her to become a singer was the courage to do it. Motherhood seemed to give her this courage.

For adults, singing is inherently vulnerable. It's ridiculously emotive, and unless you are at least somewhat trained, it's easy to feel out of control at some point during the song. But no matter how uncomfortable you may feel singing, the good news is that your voice is your child's favorite voice in the world (for now, until someday some pop star eclipses you). Don't be shy about singing even if you've never sung before. Your children love to hear you sing, and you will become more confident and relaxed as you move into your new role as troubadour and/or lullaby music box. So if

your voice is the most important sound your children hear for the first year, why not use it? Give them that gift.

As with any kind of play, when we sing with our kids, we're also letting them know that we're okay with ourselves, that it's okay to take risks, invite ridicule, or just do something less than perfectly. This is a priceless gift.

Nurturing gentleness and appreciation of what you do have (perhaps good pitch or sweet tone) and acceptance of what you don't (so what if you aren't Cecelia Bartolli or Bruce Springsteen?) can go a long way toward making peace with your voice. Your children don't know Cecelia Bartolli or Bruce Springsteen (unless you are one of them, in which case, thanks for reading our book!); they love you and the sound of your voice. They don't care if you're overweight, have acne, or are losing your hair; they think you're the most beautiful creature on the planet, just as you think that about them. And, of course, nurturing gentleness and appreciation in yourself is fabulous modeling for your children, so they can learn to accept their own gifts and limitations.

So when you're home with that little baby and can't think of a thing to do, sing him a song. When you're on that long car ride home from the grocery store and your child is screaming her head off about being in the carseat, sing to her. Even if your singing is confined to the car as you trade bits of songs back and forth via the rearview mirror, you are forging a powerful connection by singing to your child. (You might also be doing a lot to calm yourself down, as it's difficult to be tense while you're singing. And the calmer you are, the more likely it is that your squalling baby will calm down too.)

Unlike adults, children are inherently musical. Every baby starts to babble in a delightfully singsong way, and many children learn to sing before they learn to talk. If you listen closely, you may notice that when children first learn to vocalize, they basically sing. Listen to preschoolers talk, and you will hear musical notes. They also experiment with rhythm—banging on the table, on pots, clapping, dancing. They listen, taking in huge quantities of sounds and information, for months before they express themselves. Most babies love music and are able to feel a rhythm from the moment they enter the world.[1]

Music is undeniably good for kids. Besides experiencing enjoyment, children exposed to music and musical training have better memories, higher literacy rates, and better math scores.[2] And although singing is one of the easiest ways to engage your child musically, most kids need no coaxing when it comes to being interested in music. The story of the Pied Piper assumes that kids will follow a musician in a trancelike way, and this has been our experience as well. In our HooteNanny classes, it's not uncommon for little ones to toddle up until they are nose to nose—or nose to guitar hole—with one or both of us. Whenever we play a show for children, they inevitably move closer and

closer to the stage until, by the last song, they—or at least some of them—are actually on the stage.

You can help bring music to your children simply by singing to them throughout the day. Our mother sang to us all the time. She made up little songs based on variations of our names; she made up a small movement game to keep babies from flipping over and crawling away while she was changing their diapers. She created songs to get us, as preschoolers, to keep up with her fast pace as she navigated the streets of Manhattan's Upper East Side. Her voice was an ever-present guide, an adult hand holding our baby ones as we crossed the street.

Our father sang to us in a more formal way. Many nights, he would pull out his guitar as we sat around the kitchen table after dinner. He sang songs from his own childhood, African-American spirituals, Irish folk songs, and cowboy songs from the American West. As his sweet, high tenor wafted above the sound of water running from the sink, my mother joined in, singing harmonies in her familiar, featherlight contralto. They sang "The Blue Tail Fly," "Big Rock Candy Mountain," "Billy Boy," and "Irene, Goodnight." Nerissa learned how to harmonize from years of listening to our mother come up with lines more friendly to her vocal range, as well as standing next to her in church while she sang the alto line of the hymns. Modeling—be it a behavior or a skill—is the way kids learn to do anything, as any child expert will tell you.

## SINGING 101

It's helpful to remember that you don't need to be good at athletics to love sports. In fact, some of the most avid fans of the Boston Red Sox or the Pittsburgh Steelers are veritable coach potatoes. The same goes for music. Even if you're quite sure that neither you nor your child has any discernable talent, suspend your disbelief and proceed. Talent may well be a myth (brain scientists keep proving that talent is merely a combination of passion and practice).[3] At the very least, you may be predisposing your child for a lifetime of pleasure in listening to and appreciating all things musical. Not all kids will be Derek Jeters when they grow up, but they will still benefit from Little League.

That being said, we can offer you some concrete tips on better singing. Here is a condensed version of the singing lesson we would give anyone who wants to learn to sing. These tips are for you, not your kids; voices needn't be trained until after puberty. We hope that as you become more confident in your singing, you will have more fun with your voice and thereby sing more with your children. Parents singing with their kids is the Nields' vision for global salvation.

1. Relax! Relax your throat. Really, all of you should be relaxed, but for now, let's start with the throat. Relax your jaw. Let the sound come out on an exhalation, and try to imagine that sound coming from the deepest part of your core with as little obstruction as possible.

2. Your whole body, not just your voice box, is your instrument. Just as the piano is more than keys and the guitar is more than strings, your voice is more than those mucus membranes known as vocal chords. When singing, ground your feet and stand evenly, as if you were getting ready to return a serve in tennis. Imagine the sound coming from your belly and shooting all the way up your windpipe and out through your mouth. Raise your upper palate (the roof of your mouth) and imagine it's like the inside of a great domed cathedral. Keep your neck straight; if you lift your chin too high, you'll squeeze your voice box closed. If anything, your chin should be slightly tucked—but only slightly. Breathe from your belly, letting it expand on the inhale and contract on the exhale. Your voice needs a big bellyful of air to rest on.

3. Sing in the key that is the most comfortable for you or your child. Don't strain your voice to reach those notes that are too high or low for you. To sing on key or to "tune" your voice the way you would tune a stringed instrument, try raising your eyebrows. This lifts the pitch. Try it and see. Smile too; this works really well. Plus, people, especially your kids, like to see you smile. (To learn more about finding your key, see page 225.)

4. Use your ear to tune your voice. How? Practice! Sing in the shower, sing in the car, best of all, sing with other people. Match your voice to voices you know to be in tune, such as the recording of a professional singer or the voice of your best friend whom you sit next to in church, temple, or yoga class. See if you can get your voice to match hers, pitch for pitch. Remember, the voice is just a muscle. The more you use it, the stronger it gets.

5. Be fearless! If you're inexperienced, own that and don't be ashamed. Know that the only way to get better is to just do it. Remember, your child doesn't think you sing off-key or sound like a braying donkey. He won't stand up and walk out on you.

6. You may have already noticed that you have more than one "voice." In fact, if you're a parent, you probably have many voices. Your voice can imitate everyone from Cookie Monster to Mickey Mouse. Try singing "Born in the U.S.A." like Cookie Monster. Now sing it like Mickey. Sing "Happy Birthday" like an opera singer. Now sing it like Johnny Rotten. As a singer, you have what's known as a head voice (the upper register or falsetto) and a chest voice (that louder, Aretha Franklin-esque, belting voice.) Take care not to sing too high in your chest voice or you may damage your vocal chords. In general, take good care of your voice by not shouting or raising it above the din of the playroom. We know, good luck with that. But the reason voices can often betray a person's age is that habitual misuse of the voice leaves it hoarse, ragged, and lower in pitch. Protect it by limiting the number of times you yell at your kids—which is a good idea anyway.

7. Once you're singing, get your brain out of the way. Pick a song you're very familiar with, even if you have to resort to "Happy Birthday," "Row, Row, Row Your Boat," or the perennial "Twinkle, Twinkle, Little Star." We've noticed that it's difficult for people who are tense to match pitch. Try singing the song all tensed up. Then try singing it as if you were a rag doll. Take your cheeks in your hands and shake your jowls as you sing. Flop your arms around. Your kids will think this is hilarious. See if you match pitch better this way.

8. If you sing a song as if you wrote it yourself, really embodying the meaning of the lyrics, you will deliver it in a much more satisfying way. The song will come alive for you and your audience. Parents incorporate this method instinctively when they sing lullabies, because if they don't (if they're off stylistically by singing too loud or too fast), the child might not go to sleep.

9. One of the best tools a singer has is diction. Put the words right up in your lips when you sing. Spit the words out. Let them help your mouth to shape the notes. Singers use vowels for tone and consonants for shaping that tone. Try this: sing a line ("Oh, say can you see . . .") with lazy lips

and the tune in the back of your throat. Now sing the same line with the focus up-front.

**10.** When singing a line, don't break it up; take a breath where there is a comma or where a phrase ends naturally. Singers use that big bellyful of breath to sustain their phrases. Your natural inclination might be to fill up your chest to look like Superman, but you should really be puffing out your belly. You can lie on your back and practice this by watching your belly rise and fall. Again, do this with your kids. They'll love it.

## Nerissa

 As a child, I loved nothing more than to sing on my own, with the records I loved, in the shower, in the car, or going about my day. But I never liked music class or choruses. I couldn't exactly put my finger on why; the songs just seemed annoying. In fact, the entire experience seemed annoying until one day, when I was in seventh grade, my music teacher had me sing an alto part to a piece in two-part harmony instead of singing the soprano part that I was normally given. The notes felt different in my throat, easy and effortless. They sounded good to my ears. I began to like music class.

Around this time, I was teaching myself to play Beatles songs on the guitar my father had given me. I had a gigantic book called *Beatles for Easy Guitar,* and I had learned from my father, in a limited way, how to transpose a song from one key to another. I now happily rediscovered songs that I'd eschewed because they'd been played in too high a key and had made my voice hurt. What a difference it made to sing "Let It Be" in a comfortable key where I could belt out the chorus with gusto!

All this notwithstanding, I always figured a kid would sing where she was comfortable, but I notice that Lila will sometimes pitch songs so low that she rasps like a fifty-year-old blues singer. I think she does this because my voice is so low, and she wants to sing with me. When I catch her singing by herself, she pitches the songs in a much more comfortable (higher) place in her voice. Now when she introduces a song to me in her Bonnie Tyler imitation, I gently adjust the pitch so that she is more comfortable, even if I'm not.

## SINGING GAMES

Once you've gotten more comfortable with your own voice, play singing games with your child. Perhaps you're like our mother and sing your way through the day. You sing to coax your child up a hill, to ease a diaper change, and to lull your baby to sleep. Or perhaps you're more like our father and have a repertoire of songs, an instrument, and a happy audience in your children. But if you find yourself in neither category, you may find some ideas in this section. If you like a little structure in your music, choose one of these games to engage your child. You can do some of them anywhere. Some might get you through a traffic jam. Some require a piano. Keep them in mind as a spring-board to bringing music into your daily life with your child.

Remember that these are games; they're supposed to be fun. So if they don't feel like play, choose another game!

## Funny Voices

Explore your voices together. See what kinds of funny noises they can make. Can you make your voice go high and squeaky? Can you make it go low and deep? Can you make it very, very soft? Very, very loud? Can you say something—the alphabet maybe—very, very fast? Very, very slowly?

## Imitate Sounds

Imitate the sounds you hear around you: a fire engine, a police car, the sound of the refrigerator, a dog barking, birds singing, waves crashing against the shore, a voice on the radio or TV, a truck backing up, a mosquito.

## Musical Book

Next time you're reading a book, sing some of the lines. Make up your own tune, or see if you can match a popular tune to the words in the book. Any Dr. Seuss tale works really well for this. Just making the sounds the animals make in a story is a kind of music.

## Match the Note

Sit at the piano with your child; if you don't have a piano, you can use a guitar or a recorder. (If you have no instruments, you can still play this game using your voice or find a website that has an interactive keyboard. Myriad websites can give you tones—even guitar- or ukulele-tuning websites.) Play a note and sing it back. See if your child can do the same. Remember to keep this light and fun; the last thing you want is for your child to associate bad feelings with singing. Use a funny

voice. Hold your nose and sing. The sound will amuse your child.

Next, play three notes and see if your child can sing them back. Can you sing them back? If they are right next to each other—say C, D, E (the first three white notes in the middle of the piano with only two black keys between)—it will be pretty easy. But try C, F♯ (the third black key up from the C), and B♭ (the fifth black key up). Even we might not be able to sing that. If not, try singing "Say It Again, Cow!" (which follows) instead.

## Warm-up Song

Many music classes include simple tonal exercises. The idea is to have parents and kids hear pitches or rhythms and then repeat them, thereby learning a rudimentary way to match pitch. Katryna asked Nerissa to write a song that would serve that same purpose while simultaneously being more fun than singing, "la, la, la," because the singers would make animal sounds. Think of it as the version of "Old MacDonald" that Maria von Trapp might have taught all those kids in *The Sound of Music*, if she'd been so inclined.

You can substitute any notes for any of the animal sounds, but our CD provides some basic options.

# Say It Again, Cow!

C    Dm    F    G7

**C**
I am a cow.
**F    G7**
I am a cow.
**C**
I am a cow who says, "Moo, moo moo." [Repeat back] "Moo, moo, moo."
**F     C     Dm     C**
Say that again, please; I didn't hear you. Moo, moo, moo. Moo, moo, moo.

I am a sheep.
I am a sheep.
I am a sheep who says, "Baa, baa, baa."
   [Repeat back] "Baa, baa, baa."
Say that again, please; I didn't hear you.
   "Baa, baa, baa. Baa, baa, baa."

I am a chick.
I am a chick.
I am a chick who says, "Peep, peep, peep."
   [Repeat back] "Peep, peep, peep."
Say that again, please; I didn't hear you.
   "Peep, peep, peep. Peep, peep, peep."

I am a horse.
I am a horse.
I am a horse who says, "Nei-i-i-i-gh."
   [Repeat back] "Nei-i-i-i-gh."
Say that again, please; I didn't hear you.
   "Nei-i-i-i-gh. Nei-i-i-i-gh."

[minor key]
I am a snake.
I am a snake.
I am a snake who says, "Hiss, hiss, hiss."
   [Repeat back] "Hiss, hiss, hiss."
Say that again, please; I didn't hear you.
   "Hiss, hiss, hiss. Hiss, hiss, hiss."

# KEEPING THE BEAT

RHYTHM, LIKE MUSIC, IS EVERYWHERE. Rhythm is the bones of music; melody is the flesh and blood. Every kid has rhythm, because every kid has a beating heart and knows how to breathe. Rhythm is just an extension of the pulsation that is at the heart of the universe and, certainly, at the center of every human being. A six-month-old will perk up if you tap in rhythm on the table, and by nine months, most babies want to clap their little hands, either to show their pleasure or to explore the unique sound they can make by doing so. If you're a person who has been told you have no rhythm, we say, "Pah!"

## HOW TO KEEP THE BEAT, OR HOW NOT TO EMBARRASS YOURSELF WHEN EVERYONE ELSE SEEMS TO BE ABLE TO CLAP ALONG AND YOU CAN'T

The most basic element of music is the beat. Rhythm is created by the *tempo* (or speed of the beats) and the *meter* (the pattern of beats). While tempo is self-explanatory (a fast song has a fast tempo, and a slow song has a slow tempo), meter is more elusive.

In any piece of music, there are patterns of strong and weak beats. These patterns determine the feel of the song as surely as whether the music is in a minor or major key. Without knowing anything about music, you can tell the pattern of the beats by noticing when you are moved to clap

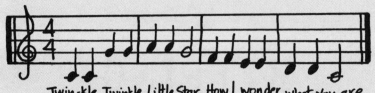

Twin-kle, Twinkle, Little Star, How I wonder what you are.

4/4 time

Rock-a-bye, Baby, on the tree-top

3/4 time

Hey Diddle Diddle the cat and the fiddle the...

6/8 time

**WHOLE NOTE**

**DOTTED HALF NOTE**

**QUARTER NOTE**

**EIGHTH NOTES**

**HALF NOTE**

**SIXTEENTH NOTES**

your hands or tap your feet: this determines the meter. The most common meters, also called *time signatures*, in Western music are duple and triple meter. Duple meter is represented by 4/4 or 2/4 time. Think about "Twinkle, Twinkle, Little Star." If you were to clap along, you would probably clap on each syllable, making four claps per line. On the other hand, if you were to try to clap to "Rock-a-Bye Baby," you would clap strongly on the *rock* and first syllable of *baby* and perhaps softly on *a* and *bye*. This is what we call triple meter, and it is represented most often as 3/4 time. Another common meter in Western music is 6/8, which can be felt as either duple or triple meter. The top number of the fraction indicates how many beats there are per measure. The bottom number indicates what kind of note is counted as one beat (an eighth note, a quarter note, a half note, and so on). Though the tempo of the music has an enormous effect on how the songs feels, the meter has an even stronger one. You can speed up or slow down "Row, Row, Row Your Boat" and it remains recognizable, but if you suddenly change it to triple meter, you have a very different song.

In 4/4 time, there are four beats per measure and the quarter note is considered a beat of one. The nursery rhyme "Mary Had a Little Lamb" is in 4/4 time. So are many of our favorite rock songs, such as "Twist and Shout," "I Love Rock 'n' Roll," and "Born to Run." In rock or blues, we tend to clap on the 2 and 4 of a measure. This is called the *backbeat*. The pattern would then be weak STRONG weak STRONG (as with "Twist and Shout" and "I Love Rock 'n' Roll"). You can also clap on the 1 and 3. The pattern would then be STRONG weak STRONG weak (as in "Born to Run").

There's a general feeling among musicians that clapping on the 2 and 4 is hip and cool, and clapping on the 1 and 3 is square. Squareness aside, for the purposes of making music with children, it may be best to clap on 1, 2, 3, and 4. Or even "1 and 2 and 3 and 4 and." This is considered clapping on the *microbeat*. Perhaps because of their faster pulses, babies and children have an easier time clapping or bouncing along to the microbeat, which is easier for them to feel. Rests are hard. When you clap more often, there is less waiting, and children, like adults, don't always like to wait (or rest).

Think of a waltz. That "oom pa pa" beat which is its trademark is formally described as "three-quarter (3/4) time." This means there are three beats per measure, and the quarter note is considered a beat of one. Three-quarter time makes you feel like each measure leads to the next, which is helpful for dancing because it has the effect of swaying and leading you on. "Rock-a-Bye Baby" is in 3/4 time.

You create a swingy feel with 6/8 time. It is both triple meter and duple meter at the same time. Some famous songs in 6/8 time are Bach's "Jesu, Joy of Man's Desiring," "Norwegian Wood" by the Beatles, and "Piano Man" by Billy Joel. The nursery rhyme "Hey Diddle Diddle" is also in 6/8 time. You can feel the song as a 123456, 123456, 123456, or you can feel it as a slow 1, 2, 1, 2. The 1 would fall where the 123 falls, and the 2 would fall where the 456 falls. Those sets of 123 and 456 are called *triplets*.

> Hey diddle diddle, the cat and the fiddle,
> The cow jumped over the moon.
> The little dog laughed to see such sport,
> And the dish ran away with the spoon.

Each line has the count of 123456, 123456.

Most of the time, the feeling of the rhythm or beat is intuitive. You have been listening to rhythm since you were in the womb and the windshield wipers beat the rain away, since you first heard nursery rhymes like "Mary Had a Little Lamb." Every band's driving force is the rhythm section—the bass and the drums. So why deconstruct it and learn the names of these beats? Why learn the science behind the beat? It's not completely necessary, but you will feel cool knowing it, and more important, you can rock your baby to the right beat, either swinging her back and forth in 3/4 time or up and down in 4/4. Taking anything we know intuitively and relearning it intellectually is enriching and makes us feel closer to the process and the art form.

## SMALL PERCUSSION INSTRUMENTS

Playing along to the beat or the rhythm of a song is also intuitive. You will see small children stomping, clapping, or swaying along before they can even form words. Though clapping is fun, many small percussion instruments have been created to enhance our experience of playing along. These instruments are perfect for young children. They are the right size for little toddler hands and make pleasing sounds. Some make a sharp sound, which accentuates the beat the way clapping does. Others make a looser sound that is fun for children who are too young to be able to follow a beat precisely.

We each have a basket of small instruments in our music rooms. In these baskets, we have rhythm sticks, claves, shaker eggs, maracas, nylon straps with Velcro closures and jingle bells attached, small hand drums, tambourines, small cymbals, a cabasa, and many others. These range from bought plastic, metal, and wood instruments to homemade drums and shakers to recycled oatmeal boxes. There are now instruments created for and marketed to kids: shakers in the shape of fruits and vegetables, clappers with faces on them, castanets with animals painted on. Whatever suits your child's fancy is likely available. Ultimately, your little one will probably be more taken with the sound than the shape. We had one child in

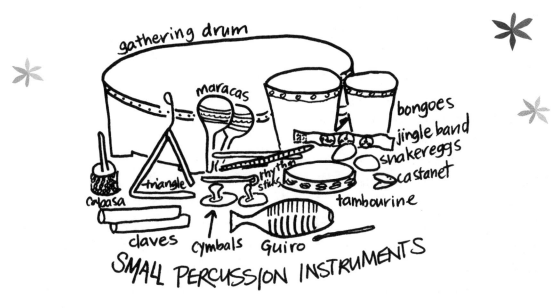

gathering drum

maracas

bongoes

jingle band

snakereggs

castanet

triangle

rhythm sticks

tambourine

calbasa

claves

cymbals

Guiro

SMALL PERCUSSION INSTRUMENTS

## Our Grandmother

Our grandmother, who died at the age of 103, suffered from dementia for the better part of the last decade. It is hard to know how to interact with an aging person who doesn't speak much. Grand-mummy had the good fortune of having a percussionist for a daughter. Our aunt, Sarah Tenney, brought tall Remo drums and a mallet to Grandmummy's apartment. After that, Grandmummy would play at drumming with anyone who cared to join her. It was the closest thing we had to conversation with her. We would tap a beat on the drum, and she would tap one back to us. Rhythm is such a basic, ancient skill. On the visits when this would happen, we all felt powerfully connected to her, as if we were finally able to communicate with her again.

music class who loved her maracas so much that she slept with them. Imagine waking in the morning to a toddler shaking along to her own cooing. (Of course, if you allow this, make sure the maracas are firmly sealed. It would be terrible if the child could get the maraca open and sprinkle choking hazards all over her bed!)

These instruments are so easy to use that anyone is drawn to play along when a basket full of them is placed on the floor. Of course, now that you've read this chapter on meter, tempo, and rhythm, you're a veritable expert. But even if you didn't understand any of that, you could still play along to your favorite CD. So put on some music, get out your basket or bowl of instruments, and shake along with your child. You might even feel inspired to stand up and boogie while you stomp your jingle-laden feet and shake your tambourine.

# RHYTHM GAMES

Even before children can identify pitches, they are able to identify rhythms. Try out these simple rhythm games with your family.

## Name Rhythm Game

Grab some wooden sticks or get ready to clap your hands. Go around the room and discover the rhythm of everyone's name. Here are some examples:

Jennifer would be "Ti ti Ta."
Nerissa would be "ti Ta Ta."
Mary would be "Ta Ta."
Dave would be "Ta."
Amelia would be "ti Ta ti Ta."

With a large group—at a birthday party, for instance—you can divide the players into teams by these rhythms. Thus, all the people with one-syllable names form a team (in our family, that would be John, Gail, Reese, Tom, Dave, and Mark); those with two-syllable names are another team (Johnny, Emmett, Trenor, and Lila). Then it gets more complex: Abigail and William ("Ti ti Ta") would be one team; Nerissa and Katryna ("ti Ta Ta") would be another; and Amelia ("ti Ta ti Ta") would be on her own, unless our Aunt Elizabeth came over for dinner.

## Rhythm Meditation

This activity is good for older kids and even better for Mama. Choose any small percussion instrument or a hand drum, put on your favorite music, and play along. Really listen to the beat, and try to synch up with it. The many become one when you play along with the beat.

This can be a deeply calming and soothing practice for you. Don't worry about your kid playing to the beat. Let him have fun and shake the maraca how he pleases. You just worry about you. Shake your own maraca in time, get into the zone, and enjoy the peace that comes from concentration. Your child will learn by example.

## Guess the Sound

Find four objects in your home that are made out of different materials, such as a metal pot, a plastic yogurt container, a cardboard box, and a pillow. Have your child close her eyes and hit each object; have her guess which item you struck. Then let your child have a turn while you close your eyes. You can make it more complicated by choosing two metal pots of different sizes.

## Tap the Sentence

Here's a game you can play anywhere, anytime. Simply say a sentence to your child and have him tap or clap the rhythm of it. In the following examples, *Ta* stands for quarter notes, and *ti* stands for eighth notes.

> Johnny's going to the playground.
> Ta Ta ti ti ti ti Ta Ta
> CLAP CLAP clap clap clap clap CLAP
> CLAP

> Where do you want to go today?
> ti ti ti Ta [rest] ti Ta ti Ta

If it is too tricky for him to figure out the rhythm on his own, do it with him for a while. Or have him say the sentence, and you tap it out. Of course, you could also do this backward. Have your child tap a rhythm, and you make up a sentence that goes with his rhythm.

## Rhythm Sticks Song

Rhythm sticks are one of our favorite props in HooteNanny. They are sticks that are about ten inches long and a third of an inch wide. One stick is ridged and the other smooth, so that in addition to simply tapping them together, you can scrape the ridged stick against the smooth stick to create a guiro-like sound. Like shaker eggs, rhythm sticks make ideal first instruments for babies, toddlers, and preschoolers. Older kids like to pretend they're drumsticks, and in fact, they function pretty well in that capacity.

We like to play rhythm sticks with this song. On the last line of each verse, we sing the word *chick* one fewer time and click the rhythm stick instead. So at the end of verse one, we sing *chick* five times and click our stick once; in verse two, we sing *chick* four times and click twice; and so on.

This song is a nice first encounter with counting down, a developmental milestone that, of course, succeeds counting up.

## Six Yellow Chicks

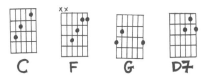

C      F      G      D7

six yellow chicks

    C                 F
Chick, chick, chick, chick, chick, chick
  C G7    C
Six yellow chicks,
   F     C   F      C
One ran off to seek her fortune,
D7            G7
Diving off the high dive.
     C               F
Chick, chick, chick, chick, chick [click stick]
    C  G7     C
Now there are five.

Chick, chick, chick, chick, chick [click stick]
Five yellow chicks,
One ran off to seek her fortune,
Opening a knitting store.
Chick, chick, chick, chick [click stick, click stick]
Now there are four.

Chick, chick, chick, chick [click stick, click stick]
Four yellow chicks,
One ran off to seek her fortune,
Growing spearmint tea.

Chick, chick, chick [click stick, click stick, click stick]
Now there are three.

Chick, chick, chick [click stick, click stick, click stick]
Three yellow chicks,
One ran off to seek her fortune,
Herding kangaroos.
Chick, chick [click stick, click stick, click stick, click stick]
Now there are two.

Chick, chick [click stick, click stick, click stick, click stick]
Two yellow chicks,
One ran off to seek his fortune,
Baking hot cross buns.
Chick [click stick, click stick, click stick, click stick, click stick]
Now there is one.

Chick [click stick, click stick, click stick, click stick, click stick]
One yellow chick,
She ran off to seek nirvana,
Sitting in the sun.
[click stick, click stick, click stick, click stick, click stick, click stick]
Now there are none.
Om

## Clap Your Hands/Old Joan Clark

This is a song that allows you to incorporate any and all of the small percussion instruments you may have around the house. It's one of those songs that borrows its tune from a traditional folk song called "Old Joe Clark." We retitled it "Old Joan Clark" because we already sing about "Old Dan Tucker," and we figured we'd shake up the genders for the twenty-first century.

This song comes from a tradition where banjos reigned supreme. As a result, it has a modal scale that is different from the typical major scale in much of Western music.

### Clap Your Hands/Old Joan Clark

③

**A**
Clap, clap, clap your hands.
**G**
Clap your hands together.
**A**
Clap, clap, clap your hands.
**G    A**
Clap your hands together.

*continued . . .*

**A**
La, la, la, la, la, la, la
        **G**
La, la, la, la, la
**A**
La, la, la, la, la, la, la
    **G**   **A**
La, la, la, la, la

Click, click, click your sticks.
Click your sticks together . . .
Click, click, click your sticks.
Click your sticks together . . .

La, la, la, la, la, la, la
La, la, la, la, la
La, la, la, la, la, la, la
La, la, la, la, la

Shake, shake, shake your eggs.
Shake your eggs together . . .
Jingle, jingle, jingle bells.
Jingle bells together . . .

This can also be used as a dance number (tap your toes, twirl up high, dance around). So clap, click, shake, jingle—whatever your heart desires. If you feel like expanding on this experience, you can sing the song as a mashup with "Old Joan Clark" as we do on the CD.

Round and round, Old Joan Clark,
Round and round, I say.
Round and round, Old Joan Clark,
I ain't got long to stay.

Old Joan Clark, she had a house
Eighteen stories high,
And every story in that house
Was filled with chicken pie.
Round and round . . .

I went down to Old Joan's house,
She'd invited me for supper.
Stubbed my toe on the table leg
And stuck my nose in the butter.
Round and round . . .

I went down to Old Joan's house,
Never been there before.
She slept on a feather bed,
And I slept on the floor.
Round and round . . .

# ADDING ACCOMPANIMENT

THE FIRST THING WE WANT TO SAY ABOUT instruments is that you absolutely don't need one to be a musical family. You don't need to play guitar, have a piano in your house, or start your children on Suzuki violin when they're toddlers. We firmly believe that music is everywhere: the sounds of traffic going by, the rhythm of waves against the shore, the twitter of birds in the morning, and the tap-tap-tap of Daddy cracking an egg against a ceramic bowl. (Of course, it's beneficial to emphasize the music of these sounds by singing along with or parroting them and by taking them into our bodies and reinterpreting them through hand clapping, whistling, and foot stomping.)

This said, having one or more instruments accompany your singing can be a fun way to enliven your family's musical experience. (Chapter 9 is all about making your own musical instruments and playing games with instruments.) In the last chapter, we introduced some small percussion instruments. This chapter introduces melodious instruments—namely the guitar and piano—and explores ways that you can bring instruments into your home or rediscover those that might already be there.

It almost goes without saying that the guitar is a fabulous accompanying instrument for a parent to learn (or relearn) for the purpose of discovering your musical family. It's beloved for a reason: although only a few people can achieve the mastery of Eddie Van Halen or Andre Segovia, almost anyone can learn to strum three chords in first position. If you're lucky enough to have a piano, congratulations. It's an extremely versatile and helpful musical teaching instrument, and it's hard to think of a more evocative object in terms of family musical memories. Your child has probably already spent a considerable amount of time exploring it, banging on it, or—if they're like our children—walking on its keys. With the right teacher or instruction, you can begin to demystify this behemoth in your family room and even begin to play it yourself. (See page 43 for easy piano games and Appendix 2 for a quick and easy piano lesson.)

# THAT OLD GUITAR (PIANO/OBOE/DRUM KIT) IN THE CORNER

Many of you probably used to play an instrument in a band or orchestra or sing in a choir or glee club when you were in high school or college. Maybe you deduced at some point that music was a good hobby but not something on which to build a career that would, as writer Robert Parker famously stated, put the tub margarine on the table. Maybe you continued to play here and there in your twenties, getting rustier and rustier as your life got busier and busier. Maybe that old guitar is actually in the attic or buried in the closet behind the equally unused sports equipment.

Never fear. One of the great perks of being a parent to young children is that even though you might not be excellent at something, chances are you will be a master compared to your three-year-old (maybe not your eight-year-old, but definitely your three-year-old).

So the first step in discovering your musical family may be for you to venture into the back of that closet or attic and dust off your instrument. Take some time to hold it, smell it, and put your ear up to the strings (which will almost certainly make you wince) and tune it. If your child is with you, tell him about how you first started to play. Tell him how it was hard to practice, but you're glad you did it because now you can still remember a little. Then show him what little you remember. Don't be embarrassed. It will almost certainly be more than he knows.

If you really don't remember anything, or if you never knew much to begin with, turn to page 227 in this book and review (or learn) the basic music theory we have provided. Find your key, and find your three or four chords. Then play along with one of the songs on the CD.

Depending on how old your child is, she will probably want to take the guitar away from you and start to play herself. Allow this to happen. Let her stand in front of you and strum as you finger the chords. Then explain that she needs to be careful and gentle with guitars. If she has a baby brother or sister, she will already understand this concept. The guitar will probably be too big, and you can explain that it is much easier to play when the size of the guitar matches the size of the person.

If you have no personal history with an instrument, now may be the perfect time to take one up! (Chapter 11 provides a list of ideas to help you find the perfect instrument to get started.) It's never too late to learn an instrument. Our father was given his first guitar as a college graduation present. (He says that, to this day, he has never been given a better present.) We know many other people who have taken up instruments as adults and find great satisfaction in creating their own practice time. All instruments have their own commendable characteristics. But in terms of incorporating an instrument into family music, nothing beats the piano or guitar. While a flute or cello can play lovely melodies, they can't play chordal accompaniment as guitars and pianos can. Plus, the world is set up to support guitarists and pianists, and books abound with chords and chord diagrams for these two instruments. Banjos, mandolins, ukuleles, and accordions can play chords too, but they are a little more obscure, and it can be harder to find books and references with chords for them. Still, if you feel drawn to one of these instruments, by all means, go for it!

## Nerissa

A fan named Mary Jane sent me a letter that I think illustrates that it's never too late to pick up an instrument. She didn't grow up with a lot of music, but one year, when she was in her late thirties, her father gave her mother a mountain dulcimer for Christmas. "Look what I can do!" her mother exclaimed to Mary Jane the next time she came to visit.

Her mother passed away several years later, and her father suggested that Mary Jane take the dulcimer home with her. "I was thrilled," she said. "This was something my mother had loved, and it was a beautiful object. I would hang it on my wall and remember Mom each time I passed it."

So she carried the dulcimer under her arm through the crowded Charlotte airport. A stranger came up to her and asked what she had in the case. "When I told him that it was a mountain dulcimer, he smiled and said, 'Oh, you play mountain dulcimer!' I replied, 'No, I just inherited it.' He said,

'Well, you're going to have to learn, aren't you?' and without waiting for an answer, he disappeared into the crowd.

Her letter went on, "I like to imagine that he disappeared entirely, having carried out his assignment. I stood there as though paralyzed amid all those hurrying people, my mouth hanging open. It had never occurred to me before. At forty-seven, I was going to learn to make music.

"A dulcimer has only three strings, and one can quickly learn to play tunes on it. With a little more practice, it begins to sound haunting and lovely. I rusted out the first set of strings from crying (it made me think of Mom), but soon I was doing fine. And I had an audience! Our twelve-year-old son would sit at my feet and listen intently. In his eyes was a look I hadn't seen before. It said, 'This is something special. I need to do this.' Pretty soon, he was perched on the sofa playing Mom's dulcimer. The next Christmas, he got his first guitar. Several years later, he very nearly went to Oberlin Conservatory but veered away from a career in music at the last moment. He was afraid if he had to make a living from it, it would lose the magic. He still plays beautifully.

"Then there is his little brother, six years younger, who grew up listening to us do our thing. With little training, just following his heart and his ear, he plays multiple instruments and composes. For him, there is no effort. Music pours out of him.

"Sometimes I think of that man in the airport and I wish I could tell him what a tremendous gift he gave to our family, just with an offhand remark. He probably has no idea."

I love this story because it begins with a moment to which many of us can relate: that moment in a store when we have an idea for a gift for a loved one, but we're not sure if the recipient will like it. In this case, the dulcimer was like the proverbial mustard seed, growing from a humble pleasure to a huge source of joy and strength for Mary Jane and her sons.

# STUFF THAT CAN MAKE GUITAR LIFE EASIER: YOUR GUITAR TOOLBOX

All guitarists need a few things to help them out. That's why a guitar case has a little compartment under the neck. After some intense research, we discovered that this is called the accessory compartment. You should keep the following tools in this compartment.

## Tuner

Small electronic tuners are now generally available at your local music shop for reasonable prices—between $17 and $100. You can get the kind that attaches to the end of your guitar (violin, banjo, or mandolin). If you just remember that the guitar strings are EADGBE, the tuner will let you know how close you are to that and allow you to tune.

*Capo*

## Capo

A capo is used to raise the key on your guitar. If the chords you're playing suit your fingers but not your voice, fear not. Simply apply the capo and you can raise the key until the tune feels comfortable to you. We're almost always able to avoid difficult fingerings by judicious use of the capo.

The capo needs to be placed in the middle of a fret. It should never touch the raised fret. Make sure it's nice and tight so the strings are pressed down firmly. Then pretend that the capo is the end of the guitar.

## Extra Strings

You never know when a string might break. It's a good idea to have extra strings in your case for emergency replacements. In general, it's a good idea to replace all your strings about every two months, unless you're playing constantly and hard. Then it's more like once a week. Many of our colleagues change strings before every show. If you're finding your fingers getting sore, try lighter strings. They're easier to press down, and some guitars actually require light strings.

## String Winder

This plastic item aids in changing strings. It allows you to wind the tuners quickly and with little effort. It's not essential, but it makes life a lot easier. It fits over a tuning peg and allows you to turn the peg continuously instead of one rotation at a time.

## Strap

If you have pegs for a strap, it's nice to attach one. You can then stand up and play the guitar. You can also tighten the strap when you're seated and place the guitar exactly where you want it on your body.

## Picks

There are many types of picks (technically named *plectra*, although one pick is a *plectrum*). They're cheap—usually about a quarter each, although Nerissa is partial to Mosay picks, which cost almost a dollar. Experiment with different weights (they come in light, medium, and heavy, just as strings do) and different kinds (flat picks, thumb picks, finger picks, and so on). You might end up just using your bare thumb or fingers as Katryna and our dad do.

## Extras for Electronics

If you can plug your guitar into a sound system or amplifier, and you plan to perform, you will also want to have a quarter-inch cable.

If your dream is to play electric guitar, but the idea of buying a monster-size amp makes your back hurt or gives you visions about the ire of your neighbors, there is an alternative. Several companies sell miniature amps the size of a deck of cards, and they can cost less than $50. This type of amp won't give you professional-level sound quality, but it will give you enough volume to play happily in your apartment or house, making it great for you and your kids.

## YOUR COLLECTION OF INSTRUMENTS

Starting a collection of instruments will surely invite music into your home. (You can, of course, sing anytime.) You can make an instrument out of any pot or pan or used yogurt container, but a piano in your living room begs to be played every time you pass it. A basket of instruments invites your children to conduct their own hootenanny whenever you call attention to it. One of the main tenets of the well-regarded educational philosophy called Reggio-Emilio is that children can use any number of "languages" to express themselves and learn. Languages range from paints to rocks to blocks to, of course, music. Offering instruments as part of the world you present to your children encourages them to express themselves in the language of music. In our music rooms, we have a piano, numerous stringed instruments, an old clarinet, and our basket of small percussion instruments (described in chapter 2). All of them are valuable. A

cardboard box with a couple of wire brushes entreats even the most timid to join in the music making.

## INSTRUMENTS IN THE HOME

In 1989, Nerissa graduated from college and invited Katryna to join her folk group, Tangled Up In Blue, on a cross-country tour. We started off driving from New Haven up to Brattleboro, Vermont, and then headed cross-country on Route 90 to Seattle. After following the west coast down to Los Angeles, we headed east again through Arizona, Kansas, Missouri, West Virginia, and Washington, D.C. Along the way, we stayed in the homes of friends, family, fellow alums and friends of friends. The homes ranged from modest to palatial. One friend who lived in Akron, Ohio, showed us her family's music room, a small crowded parlor filled to the gills with instruments of all kinds: a piano, of course, but also several stringed instruments on music stands. There was even sheet music on stands. The room was so full of musical instruments that our entire group couldn't actually fit in the room to sing, so we had to practice in the dining room.

In a suburb of San Francisco, we stayed with another family. At the back of the house, there was a room that felt like the most elegant treehouse we had ever encountered. Generous windows filled the room with light. The room was sparsely decorated, but everything in it was musical. There were glass shelves with classical music books. There was a baby grand piano and a brass music stand. The room was sophisticated. It invited you to practice music for hours, music that adhered to a staff with a complicated key signature. All this airy space was dedicated to the making of music. We imagined it as a place where a modern-day Mozart would go to court benefactors. It made us want to play Chopin.

We were brought up with the idea that you need to have a room saved especially for company. But one of the relics of our postcollege sojourn was the notion that it was essential to have a music room, so we both opted to designate one in our houses where the piano and all the other instruments live. It's wonderful, if you have the space, to dedicate an entire room to music. Musical instruments, especially a piano, can take up a lot of space, as can sheet music, CDs, LPs, and a stereo system.

Many instruments are delicate, beautiful objects that have been created (usually) with a deep intention to bring beauty and joy to the world, so while it's important to make instruments available to your children, it's also important that they know how to treat them. Owning and caring for instruments is a wonderful opportunity to teach your children about respect and honoring. It's never too early to encourage and model this kind of care. We live in an age where possessions are often treated as disposable at worst and easily replaceable at best, but a well-loved, well-made, well-used musical instrument is more like a work of art or a pet than a mere object. As we as a cul-ture and species become more conscious about our planet's limited resources and the need to consume less and preserve more, musical instruments provide a welcome invitation to practice these values and model them for our children. When Nerissa carefully takes her guitar out of its case and rubs it with a chamois cloth; when she pulls out its humidifier, fills it, and returns it to its place; when she changes its strings and disposes of the old ones, she is showing her children how to care for an object with love and respect. When she brings her guitar to our guitar doc, Ivon, to have the neck adjusted or realigned, she is modeling a behavior counter to the current culture that pushes the old out of the way to make room for the new, throwing away the broken because it's cheaper and easier to replace it.

Instruments are also made to be hit, which presents an inspiring paradox: treat this object with respect and also whack the heck out of it. Let your kid watch a video of Jerry Lee Lewis or Elton John flying full-bodied at the piano to show them how crazy they can get with an instrument (but trust us when we say you should save the images of Pete Townshend smashing a guitar for a later date—we know from experience). You don't want to keep instruments locked away as if they were sacred museum pieces, because that defeats their purpose. Instruments are made to be played, sometimes forcefully. Willie Nelson's guitar has that famous gouge to the southwest of the sound hole where his pick has repetitively struck. That guitar sounds all the sweeter for it.

Find that balance of gentleness and engagement. Again, instruments are rather like pets. At the age of fourteen months, Johnny understood what *gentle* meant because we had a dog (George Harrison, the chocolate Lab); when he would whack George, we'd say, "No, gentle. Like this," and take his hand and stroke it gently along the dog's back. When Nerissa brought her guitar out to play and he hit it, she'd take his hand and stroke it along the guitar while saying, "Gentle. Like this." Our children now know that guitars and even guitar cases are not to be stepped on or over but carefully walked around. Tambourines are for hitting but not destroying.

## INSTRUMENT GAMES

The following are some games that explore ways you can play (in all senses of the word) with instruments. They range from those that require little skill, such as Jamming with the Band, to those that require at least a familiarity with the instrument, such as the piano games that appear courtesy of the brilliant Maggie L. J. Shollenberger and her Modern Piano Fluency method. And we've thrown in one for your own practice time, just in case you were missing that.

### Jamming with the Band

Give your kids a homemade guitar or other instrument (see chapter 9 to learn about homemade instruments) and let them jam to their favorite

I like to keep my listening apparatus (a CD player) in the same space as my performing apparatus (a guitar), because I frequently learn songs straight off CDs. Likewise, I leave my guitars out on guitar stands rather than locked up in their cases. This encourages me (and my children) to play them—although it also leads to small objects, such as Lego pieces and shaker eggs, frequently winding up in the sound hole. I've set up a corner of our music room just for kids' musical instruments and musical toys. We have a series of drums and a box full of shakers and small percussion instruments that's easy for a one-year-old to open. We're partial to eggs because they fit nicely in the hand, are funny, and make a pleasing sound.

song on the boom box. Better yet, join in the fun. Your child already thinks you're a rock star, so why not go for it? Get dressed up together in your wackiest clothes from the attic, tie a ripped-off sleeve from your oldest, grooviest shirt around your child's head and play Jamming with the Band together. Give your child an overturned pot with a spoon while you play air guitar. Crank up whatever suits the two of you, and sing along at the top of your lungs.

By the time he was four and a half, William and his father would each strum their own instruments along to "Life Is a Highway," while William sang into a toy microphone that he jammed into the rungs on his bed.

## Finger Play

This is a good game for a beginning piano player. For some kids, the fine motor skills needed to play the piano are challenging. This is a great game for building those skills. Both you and your child place your hands on a surface—a table, a book, the top of the closed piano—with the fingers comfortably apart as if you were placing them on piano keys. Make sure to curve your fingers a bit, as if you have a small ball in the palm of each hand. Assign numbers to each finger: the thumb is one; the index finger is two; the middle finger is three; the ring finger is four; and the pinkie is five. Call out numbers at random one through five and tap with the appropriate finger on each hand until it feels easy for your child. This can be very chal-

lenging for young players, so have patience. Be sure your child doesn't change the shape of his hands and keeps all his fingers on the surface throughout the game. Kids are often tempted to pull back all their other fingers to isolate the one you called.

## Japanese Garden

The primary rule of this game is to stick to only the black keys on the piano. If only black keys are played, there will be no wrong notes. You and your child can play at the same time. You start the game by gently playing notes. The person on the lower notes (usually but not necessarily the more experienced player) can play chords, a few keys at a time. The person on the higher keys can play one note at a time, again at random. (You can choose your notes at random because you are effectively playing a pentatonic scale, and all the notes fit together.)

To expand the game and your child's notion of music, use imaginary cues from a garden to inspire different playing styles. For example, imagine there is a jumping frog and have your child play "jumpy" music. Think of water falling; she can start at the highest notes and move to the lower ones. Imagine a bird flying by; she might play smoother music on higher keys. If a large animal—perhaps a big bear—makes an appearance, the music might be slow and loud. Imagine that it starts to rain. What sound would that be? Use your imagination and your experience.

## Your Toddler Plays Your Guitar

The most natural thing in the world is for a toddler (or a child of any age) to want to strum on the guitar you have in your lap. This is excellent. When we were little kids, our father would change the chords with his left hand while we strummed. He would even sing along. This made us feel like we were actually playing (which we were).

Have your child stand in front of you while you're sitting with your guitar, and let him strum while you change the chords. He can use a pick or just his fingers, hitting all the strings at once, or just one at a time. At some point, perhaps age four or so, you can begin to introduce rhythmic elements, such as Down, down, down, down strums; Down, Up, Down, Up strums; or even triplets.

## Guitar/Piano Dance

Perhaps you already play the guitar or piano and parenthood seems to be an impediment to your own practice time. Try practicing with your child in the room and turn it into a game. Your child gets to dance while you play, but when you pause to work on a phrase, your child has to freeze. You might refine this by playing one particular phrase over and over again, giving your child a small movement to do along with the phrase (like waving one hand in a half-moon shape over her head, picking up one foot, and so on). This will help you practice while teaching your child to recognize musical phrases.

# LISTENING

LISTENING IS AS IMPORTANT A MUSICAL skill as singing or playing. In the end, it may be more important. Listening is to singing, playing, and composing what reading is to writing. At music schools and conservatories all over the world, fully half if not more of the curriculum is devoted to listening and understanding how and why music works. But beyond all that, listening—like singing and playing—is both a skill to be developed and a pleasure unto itself. Of all the elements we talk about in this book (singing, playing, songwriting, dancing, crafting), listening is the simplest. Not necessarily the easiest, especially for busy parents with a lot on their minds, but certainly the simplest. All you need for listening is a pair of ears that work, attention, some music you like, and a way to play it.

So if you're a budding musician or music lover, this chapter is for you. But even if your only role in your musical family is to be a receptive listener—if you've decided that you really don't want to sing (a decision we'll try to talk you out of) or play an instrument—this chapter is also for you. Being an active listener rather than a singer or player doesn't make you one iota less important to the whole than your cousin the first violinist or your sister-in-law the New Age vocal diva. To be a music aficionado and a music lover is to be a kind of musician. Although we come from a mostly musical family, our nonsinging/nonplaying relatives are great appreciators of music. Even though one of our grandmothers was (arguably) tone-deaf, it didn't stop her from encouraging us, applauding our efforts, and attending all our school performances. It also didn't interfere with her support of her own musical children, all of whom were given lessons, or her enthusiasm for listening to her children sing and play piano or guitar. She was always seated front and center in every audience, and she could tell very well when any of us were singing or playing with our full attention and when we were somewhere else or having an off day.

Moreover, the relative who did the most to light an enthusiastic musical fire in our family was probably our grandfather who, though he could sing and whistle (remarkably well) and play some French horn and violin, was most notably a music listener and appreciator. He would come home from work and stand in rapt attention facing the hi-fi speaker in his living room, often for an hour or two.

Your listening can take many forms—from listening to recorded or live music to attending large rock concerts or local concerts in the park. We're going to argue that live music is better than recorded music. Why? First of all, it's a full-body, full-sensory experience. Your whole family is together to witness what's happening onstage (if you're attending a concert) or from the group encounter (if you're part of a sing-along). Look back at your own memories; for us, the memories of experiencing music with our parents at church and on the lawns of outdoor music venues, as well as with our friends at school, are more indelibly etched in our minds than the important but more ordinary doses of Elvis, *Sesame Street*, Burl Ives, and the Beatles on our home stereos, car radios, or iPods.

Moreover, seeing a musician play in person seems to trigger something profound for a child. In our own experience and that of countless other musicians we know, kids are constantly saying that after seeing our show, they picked up a guitar for the first, second, or upteenth time because they want to be "just like you." Dan Zanes regularly encourages his audiences to start family bands of their own.

# A WORD ABOUT PROTECTING LITTLE EARS

Even as we encourage you to listen to music both on your stereo and at concerts, we heartily beseech you to safeguard your children's eardrums. One of the most common causes of hearing loss is exposure to loud noises. Noise-induced hearing loss can be avoided, and we want to do everything we can to protect our children.

A basic rule of thumb is to make sure you can speak and be heard easily over the music. If you have to raise your voices to be heard, turn down the volume. At a concert, it's a good idea to bring some headphones or earplugs for your little one, just in case. When Amelia was a baby and coming to all of our concerts, Katryna wouldn't let her in the room with a drum kit unless she had some protection over her ears.

We continue to protect Amelia's ears now that she has her own iPod. When she received it, she also got a small boom box with a dock for the mp3 player. We told her the earbuds were not to be used. She can listen to her music either on the player itself from the small speaker on the device, through the speakers on the dock, or from noise-canceling headphones when we're in the car on a long trip. It's hard for a child to regulate the noise level of these devices. Especially in the car when there is ambient noise, we're all more likely to turn up the volume to an unsafe level.

## CONCERTS

We are huge fans of attending concerts, bringing together two of our favorite things: music and community. We are sure that we ourselves became performers in part because witnessing live music with our parents was such a joyful, transformative experience. When we were teenagers, our parents began to take us to see Pete Seeger and Arlo Guthrie at the Filene Center at Wolftrap Farm Park in Vienna, Virginia—a lovely outdoor arena where we usually sat way up on the hill picnicking on sesame noodles, cold chicken, and cheese and crackers. Pete and Arlo seemed like family, Pete acting as the father figure to his old friend Woody's son. Their show was casual. They traded songs back and forth, Arlo lending his organ and harmonies to Pete's, Pete adding banjo to Arlo's or sometimes just lying on his side on the stage, tapping his foot along to the beat. They swapped stories and got the audience singing along with them, and we always left feeling warm, soft, happy, and hopeful again.

We recently had the pleasure of attending a Dan Zanes show in our hometown, meeting each other with our four kids in tow. All six of us enjoyed the experience immensely, sharing one cozy pew in the First Congregational Church. Johnny, the youngest, sat on Nerissa's lap, craning his little neck to see over the heads of the big people in front of him. Amelia, the oldest, sat quietly by her mother, taking in the chord changes and the lyrics. Lila and William stood up on the pew,

William strumming along on his cardboard guitar, Lila dancing up and down. We sang along, adding harmonies when appropriate, reveling in our family music experience made all the richer by our collective familiarity with the songs. (We have all of Dan Zanes's albums and know many of the lyrics, which really makes the concert-going experience more fun for the kids and, therefore, for us.)

Look in your local paper for concert listings; check out your favorite artists' websites and see when they will be playing in your area. You may want to ask other parents if they take their kids to see live music and plan to go together. Right now is a fantastic time for family music, with artists like Dan Zanes, Elizabeth Mitchell, Justin Roberts, They Might Be Giants, and Sarah Lee Guthrie (daughter of Arlo, granddaughter of Woody) touring and making CDs. These artists are a far cry from what you might have in your head as children's music. They don't talk down to kids; rather, they include children in a musical embrace. They set a place at the table for young people, but the whole meal is for everyone.

For young kids, stick to children's shows. Taking your child to a U2 concert may not be your best bet. For one thing, the volume will be too loud for his delicate ears. If you do choose to take him to a "grown-up" concert or even to a loud family show, bring along some noise-canceling earphones. Another drawback to grown-up shows is that they might not be friendly places for curious kids who like to wander and get up and dance during their musical experiences. Steep amphitheater stairs and fold-up chairs present hazards to containing and amusing kids. When we were a five-piece rock band, parents often brought their small children along to our loud shows, and those particular kids were fine with the experience, curled up in their mothers' coats. Today, our own children wouldn't do this.

So look for age-appropriate shows, if not "children's shows." Even better, look for outdoor venues where there are swaths of grass to lay down a blanket and picnic, or indoor venues where seating is on the ground. When we're the ones onstage, we almost always end up having a toddler mosh pit where the smaller kids can do their thing up front. Look for situations like this. It's an excellent twofer: you can relax and watch the show, while keeping an eye on your kid at the same time.

Keep in mind the time of the performance when planning a musical outing. Don't take your little one to a show when she usually naps, and by the same token, don't take her to a show that starts at seven in the evening or later. Most family shows are scheduled either midmorning or mid- to late afternoon to reflect kids' natural biorhythms.

## RECORDED MUSIC

As we mentioned earlier, our grandfather was a great lover of music though not necessarily a great musician. He had a gigantic stereo speaker the size of a large bookcase in his living room. When he wanted to listen to music, he would put a Beethoven LP on his turntable, close the door to the living room, and sit in a chair in the middle of the room with his head in his hands as if he were deep in prayer. He would sit like that, listening with his whole being, for the duration of one side of the LP. If it was a long piece, he'd get up to flip the record and then resume his position until the symphony or concerto was at an end. He didn't put on music and let it play as he went about his chores or paid his bills. Music was more like church.

Today, music can be a lot like wallpaper. You can program your iPod and let it play through Bose speakers to create a soundtrack to your life from the moment you rise until you go to sleep, seven days a week. We know people who can't fall asleep without their headphones on, playing Enya while they drift off.

There's something sad about the evolution (or devolution) of our miraculous entertainment systems. In the 1950s, the sound system took up huge amounts of space in our grandparents' home:

# Nerissa

When I go to a concert with my children or even my parents or grandparents, I experience the music partly from their point of view. Did they hear what I just heard, or were they paying attention to some other aspect of the experience? Did they catch that lyric, that intonation, the way the singer inflected that phrase? Did they just get the shivers too?

It is precious beyond words and somewhat rare to feel these kinds of musical shivers collectively. As disorganized as I was in the weeks after giving birth, music found a way into our new family life anyway. Just a few days before Lila's birth, Bruce Springsteen had released *The Seeger Sessions,* a collection of folk songs brought to the nation's attention by our family favorite Pete Seeger. That CD formed the soundtrack to my brand-new trio's initiation into familyhood. In addition, my extended family—my parents and our sister, Abigail, the world's most knowledgeable and faithful Bruce fan—egged each other on to see who could see the Bruce concert in more cities, partying it up at the concerts to support the CD.

It occurred to me, six weeks postpartum, that this would be a fine first outing for our nascent family. So we set out on our first road trip. My mother came along, and Tom and I hired our friend Stacia to watch baby Lila in a hotel in Saratoga Springs while the new parents and grandmother boogied it up to Springsteen's excellent band. I sat on the blanket, singing and listening and marveling, exhausted and weeping with postpartum joy, while Tom and my mother danced a few hundred yards in front, seemingly reenergized by the power and skill of the band. My mother certainly connected back to the music of her childhood. It's one of my most cherished memories: uniting with my mother through music as I was beginning to realize the enormity of the role I had just stepped into as a mother myself.

Lila was too little to be taken along, but we sang those songs to her when we got back in the car and played the CD, generally well refreshed by our musical outing and rejoicing that we could pass along our family favorites to our newest generation.

a stereo as big as the couch; a whole closet to house the Victrola, shelves and shelves of LPs. When we were kids in the 1980s, Nerissa's stereo system snaked around her bedroom, with the main components in one corner and the speakers taking up space on her desk and file cabinets. Katryna's boom box was the size and height of an entire shelf and bestowed rotator cuff injuries to those who tried to move it. Now all our music is housed in a tiny iPod played out of headphones the size of pennies or a small eight-by-eight-inch box with speakers. It seems to take a lot more focus to direct our children's attention to the noise coming out of those little speakers than it did for our grandfather to prove to his children how central the act of listening—really listening—to music could be to their edification.

This is why, as with everything, a little mindfulness must be applied to the act of listening to music. It's okay to interrupt the aural wallpaper and say, "Sh! Listen. Hear the way that singer just hit that note? Hear that guitar riff? A riff is a little piece of music that just the guitar plays."

Driving through town in the midafternoon, Nerissa recently turned on the radio and caught the end of "Bolero." "Lila!" she said. "Hear those drums?" The drums in Bolero turned out to be fabulous, at least for a four-year-old. Lila immediately beamed and began miming drumming in the air along to the piece.

By engaging with the music this way, we notice the wallpaper, see its minute designs and stories, and stop taking it for granted.

# CHOOSING YOUR SHARED MUSIC WISELY (YOU MAY HAVE TO LISTEN TO THOSE SONGS FIVE THOUSAND TIMES EACH)

One of the main reasons we created HooteNanny is because we wanted to encourage parents to toss out the notion of "children's music" in favor of "family music." There is absolutely no reason you or your children ever need to listen to music you don't find pleasing just because someone in a music company's marketing department has decided what children should like. Your kids might like Barney as Nerissa's do, or they might abhor him as Katryna's do (truth be told—we know you will find this shocking—we don't appreciate Barney either). So we both have Barney-free playlists, although Nerissa does give in once a week and allows her children to watch a TV show they like. However, Nerissa has not (and will not) download any Barney music, sing his songs, or include them in the family music canon because she doesn't like them and she'd rather share music the whole family enjoys.

When kids see their parents enjoying music, something magical happens. Listening to our family musical canon together gives us a shared reference point as a family. We all have the same earworms going at the same time, and we can cross-reference them in delightful ways. Lila will look up at Nerissa in the produce section of the grocery store and say, "Mama! There's a mango!"

*Musical Beginnings*

and then start singing "Mango Walk." While Johnny was still preverbal, he would hum the tune of the "ABC Song" whenever Lila pulled out her letter blocks.

As kids get older, they develop their own tastes. You might be horrified, and this is as it should be. If Nerissa's kids continue to love Barney (a half-hearted fear, because, let's be honest, how many teenagers love Barney?), she certainly won't stop them from blasting his hits on their boom boxes or the twenty-first-century equivalent. Our parents were not Beatles fans and were quite dismayed when we fixated on the Beatles when we were tweens in the late seventies. From their point of view, the Beatles were commercial, bubblegum. (We always said, "It could be so much worse! We could like KISS!" But they didn't know who KISS was, so they weren't impressed.)

Even if your musical tastes diverge, listening to music can remain a way to connect with your child. In our desire to get our parents to appreciate our tastes in music, we began to make them mix tapes of songs that we thought might help them cross over to loving the Beatles and our favorite bands. Even early on, our father enjoyed "Ob-La-Di, Ob-La-Da"; in fact, he learned to play it on his guitar, and it was one of the first songs he taught Nerissa to play. Slowly, over time, we figured out what the common musical ground was with each of our parents. Noticing what another person likes, how we are all different but have these points of similarity, is part of becoming a mature, healthy adult. This is the higher octave of listen-ing. It has become a tradition for each of us to make our father a mix CD for holidays and his birthday, all of his daughters vying to come up with the song he will choose as his new favorite.

Katryna's husband, Dave, and his father, Henry, found a great connection in listening to music together. Henry would find music he loved and bring it home to play for his son. They would sit hunched over the turntable and marvel to-gether at Jimi Hendrix's guitar on "The Star-Spangled Banner" or Paul McCartney's bass lines on "With a Little Help from My Friends." Listen-ing so carefully together taught Dave how to listen for what he loved most in a piece of music and forged a bond with his father that probably helped them navigate the alienating years of adolescence.

These are just some examples of how music knits us together, strengthening the natural family bonds we already possess. Start listening to music with your children when they're young, and it could create a connection that lasts a lifetime.

## YOUR CAR, YOUR VOCAL BOOTH

The humble automobile is where our children most likely spend a great deal of their time. We may bemoan this or choose to look on the bright side. Forget for the moment the car seats and seat belts, the arguing over where and when to stop for dinner, the bickering in the backseat, the unrelenting boredom of Highway 80, the smell of ancient fried chicken emanating from the creases in the seats. Car trips are the absolute

## Nerissa

Whenever I can, I put on music in our house. I try for variety, but I insist on choosing music I like. What would be the point of sharing music I don't honestly appreciate with my daughter? There will be plenty of opportunity for that when she's a teenager. But for now, I stick with what was beloved to me. So today we listened to *The Wizard of Oz* soundtrack. She danced around the island in the kitchen singing, "We're Off to See the Wizard" and "Ding Dong! The Witch Is Dead." As we were eating breakfast, I used my cereal spoon to conduct with. Lila thought that was interesting and copied me. I took the opportunity to explain, "When people put on a show, sometimes there's a whole orchestra performing in a secret pit in the stage. A person called a conductor has the job of directing all the other musicians by waving around a stick like I'm waving this spoon. See how I'm following the beat?"

Lila nodded and waved her spoon back and forth. At that moment, some horns swooped in to take the melody of "Ding Dong! The Witch Is Dead."

"Hear that?" I said. "That's a trombone."

My hunch is that, besides having fun and experiencing a work of art together, we're learning how to listen.

best arena for making and listening to music as a family.

Why? First of all, you have a captive audience. Second and perhaps more important, though certainly less satisfying, you are a captive audience.

A car stereo is the number-one best place to really listen to music. We're not alone in this opinion. When we worked with Grammy Award–winning recording engineer Ed Thacker (who has also worked with Bruce Springsteen, George Harrison, Ray Charles, 10,000 Maniacs, Tori Amos and many others), he told us that he and every great engineer he knew listened to each and every one of their mixes in the car before playing them for their clients. A car is like a small vocal booth—you hear everything as long as the windows are rolled up and it's not raining too hard. But more important for our purposes, a car trip provides a fabulous opportunity for listening to music together and introducing music (stealthily once the kids become teenagers) to your progeny.

Start when they're babies, and as we keep reiterating, be sure you choose music you like! Find that common ground early. You don't have to play them "children's music" just because it's there. We listened to Dan Zanes because he made us all happy.

As your children get older, treat the iPod with caution. For those of us born in an era of CDs and cassettes (or even vinyl), iPods are miracles of technology. What's not to love about having your entire music collection—organized and alphabetized, no less—in the palm of your hand? What's not to love about a device that can instantly demonstrate to your children what "classic rock" or "baroque" means? What's not to love about a wallet-sized machine that can play videos for your kids in the middle of a traffic jam and save everyone in the car from the piercing wails of an impending meltdown?

Nothing. We Nields love our iPods. But the danger of the iPod is that music, which is an inherently communal art form, loses something intrinsic when it is enjoyed in isolation. We can all individually appreciate Jimi Hendrix or Itzhak Perlman, but it's so much more meaningful to experience music in the same time and space as another person.

Consider this scenario: Four family members set off on a summer trip to the beach. The driver plugs her iPod into the car stereo system and plays the Dixie Chicks. The front passenger grunts, puts on his own iPod, and listens to a Moth podcast. The ten-year-old daughter in the backseat fires up her iPod with some Taylor Swift. The seven-year-old son, who is too young for an iPod, puts on his child-friendly, noise-blocking headphones and watches *Cars* on his portable DVD player. The trip may be more peaceful than those our generation recalls from similar summer trips, but something is lost. Does this family miss the corny sing-along to old show tunes? Do they even know any shared show tunes?

We're not proposing that all music should be homemade, organic folk music; we love *American Idol* as much as the next family, and we would no sooner leave for a road trip without our iPods than we would our toothbrushes. But as parents, we need to balance this trend with providing more venues to experience music together as a family. We can have both the iPod and the hootenanny. On your next summer vacation, leave some space for yourselves to participate in music; bring a guitar, or see if there is a family-friendly concert to attend. And if cars still have CD players by the time this book goes to press, bring along the *Oklahoma* soundtrack, the Beatles' *Hard Day's Night* album, anything by Dan Zanes, or something embarrassing from your childhood.

Better yet, do what our friend Mike does with his family of six. They have a rule for long car trips: every family member must make a mix for the occasion. "That way, everyone gets to show off their musical taste," he says. Even a preschooler can put in his requests for the family mix. When his song comes on, point it out. If your kids are teens, this is your golden opportunity to practice your newfound musical-connection-making skills.

## Nerissa

When Katryna and I were little, we rode around in the trunk of our parents' 1967 Barracuda convertible. Those were the days when car seats were optional, and my parents opted out. Just a swath of canvas separated the backseat from the trunk of the car, and we hurled our little selves from backseat to trunk at will, often at fifty-five miles per hour. Often, we would hide from our parents below the rim of the backseat and then pop up, puppet-theater style, and sing them a song that they would watch via the rearview mirror.

We all live in the green submarine,
The purple submarine,
The red submarine.

Or

Miss Mary Mac, Mac, Mac,
All dressed in black, black, black.

As we grew older, our repertoire expanded. We learned "I've Been Working on the Railroad." To make it last and last, when we got to the part that goes "Fee, fie fiddle-e-i-o," we sang through the entire alphabet—"Fee, fie, fiddle-e-i-A,""Fee, fie, fiddle-e-i-B," and so on. When we discovered "Ninety-Nine Bottles of Beer on the Wall," my parents rationed it to a one-time-only singthrough, once a year, for the fifteen-hour trip up to Bar Harbor, Maine.

## SILENCE

The opposite of music is not silence; it is cacophonous chaos. Though we are certainly not experts in this field, we have a sense that children today are overstimulated, and as providers of family music, we have no wish to contribute to that trend by insisting that kids be exposed to music at every juncture. Part of our job as parents is to protect and nurture our children's delicate and growing nervous systems, to say nothing of their ears, and not overload them with noise.

This is why we're skeptical about claims that our children would somehow become little geniuses if we played them Baby Einstein CDs 24/7. Better, perhaps, to listen to the same beloved piece of classical music at the same time every day.

Silence can be rich and full, and for would-be musicians, it's vital to transmit respect for silence.

Just as from an atomic point of view, we are mostly composed of space, so music is mostly composed of silence. In this crowded and cluttered world, it's important to give your family a good dose of silence at least once a day, clearing a space for future sonic delights. Honoring silence can be as simple as merely not playing music in the car or at home. Or, you might even note the silence and stillness in a more formal way. Thich Nhat Hanh, the Buddhist monk and author, suggests designating one room of the house as the "Peace Room" where family members may go to meditate or just be still. No one may fight or argue in the Peace Room.

# LISTENING GAMES

For a nice balance to all the active games we play with our kids, here are some more contemplative ones. Listening is a great skill we can all stand to develop, and it's a wonderful activity to do with your child. When kids feel "listened to," they almost immediately calm down, open up, and relax. How better to honor your relationship with your child than by showing her that you too are practicing your listening?

## Breathing Game

Listening can be an excellent way of helping an overstimulated kid calm down and focus, and this game facilitates that. It's great for kids three and older and helps with both breath work and listening skills.

To play, the person who is "It" breathes in and out slowly. With the first breath, he lifts one finger and counts, "One." Second breath, second finger, and "Two." Third breath, third finger, and "Three." On "three," he points his first finger to another player, who then takes a turn counting and breathing.[1] In addition to helping kids calm down, this game also tends to sync up their breathing, which is a great precursor to playing together in a band or an orchestra.

## Family Listening Time

Instituting Family Listening Time can be a great way to fit some music listening time into your day. It's like putting money away in that other kind of CD or taking out an insurance policy on your family's emotional health. We have a friend who used to lie down on the floor of the living room with his young son at night after bathtime. They turned on one of those dome lights that makes the ceiling look like a starry sky and pretended they were out on the prairie in late summer. They would choose a piece of music to listen to together, sometimes singing along and sometimes just letting the music fill up the space.

To be more intentional about listening time, we suggest you pick a time of day that works for your family. Maybe turn off the TV news or National Public Radio in the morning and make seven to seven-thirty your Family Listening Time. Maybe bathtime or right before bed works well. Perhaps you have a lengthy commute to school;

if an older child isn't into the concept, you can play your desired music on the drive home or on the way to day care with a younger child.

At least for a while, you may want to play the same thing every day—a favorite piece of classical music; your Suzuki, Music Together, or Hoote-Nanny curriculum CD; or a special mix you and your partner make. (Remember, kids love familiarity and predictability.) As your children get older, let them choose the music for Family Listening Time. You will already have established a space and time for this practice. And as with any mindfulness practice, the purpose is to bring awareness to "everyday life." As you go about your day, remark to your children on what you're hearing, be it actual music or the music of the world passing by.

## LISTENING AND DRAWING GAME

Music can evoke all kinds of visions and emotions. An activity that we have tried with groups of kids and in our own family life is to draw what music makes us feel. It's kind of an abstract idea, but kids always seem to respond to this mixing of their senses and emotions.

Choose three different kinds of music to listen to. Make them as varied as possible; Vivaldi's "Spring" from *The Four Seasons*, "Pinball Wizard" by the Who, and Pete Seeger's "This Land Is Your Land," for example. Get out some paper and markers or crayons, and have everyone use the color each song makes them think of to draw the shapes and images they hear. It's amazing to talk about the pictures when you're done and notice how each family member may have heard something different in a piece of music.

*Nerissa*

We arrived at the house where we were staying on vacation in the Adirondacks. I set up the mp3 speakers and plugged in my iPod. When Lila heard her familiar Suzuki violin playlist wafting through our new surroundings, she exclaimed, "Hey, it's my music!" She often says the same thing on regular days when I remember to stick that CD into the car player. Sometimes she's silent, but when I turn to back out of the driveway, I see her face beaming, and she's swaying back and forth in time to "The Happy Farmer" by Schumann.

*Musical Beginnings*

# Katryna

In the waning days of summer, my kids start to get antsy. I'm at a loss for new, creative ways to fill their days while still getting my work done. One of my solutions was to play the Listening and Drawing Game. My daughter was the deejay. She chose "Real Gone" by Sheryl Crow from the soundtrack to the movie *Cars*, "Supercalifragilisticexpialidocious" from *Mary Poppins,* and "Country Roads" sung by Nerissa and me. Amelia called this game Drawing Noise.

Both kids were completely engrossed in the activity and wanted to show me what the music made them feel. Sometimes they were literal in their drawing; sometimes they were abstract. William even relied on his memory of the *Cars* movie to draw the Sheryl Crow song. But the value of the exercise was that the three of us were spending time together. There were no wrong answers. They felt seen and understood as I looked at what they had drawn. They wanted to explain what the music felt like to them. The bounciness of the *Mary Poppins* song made Amelia draw polka dots. The rolling nature and perhaps the road images of "Country Roads" made her draw long swirls all around the paper. All I know is that, in that moment, I was able to make both of my kids feel competent and important while having a great time myself.

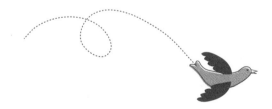

# Part Two

## THE MUSICAL FAMILY

# 5

# SINGING SONGS

ONGS ARE OUR FAVORITE ART FORM because they're portable, malleable, emotional (they run the spectrum from silly to sad to scary to exhilarating), motivational (more effective than wheedling for getting your kid to do what you want), and memorable. Songs can be as lofty as Homer's *Iliad* or Beethoven's "Ode to Joy," or as humble as the three-note "Hot Cross Buns." A song can unite the world or get your kids to eat broccoli. Not bad.

## Nerissa

There is *nothing* that brings me more joy as a parent than hearing my children singing. The particular sound of children's voices—especially my own and especially when they're straddling that preverbal-verbal chasm—warbling along to songs they've learned either from me or from school is my favorite sound in the world. Equally wonderful is the way we parents begin to pick out the words or phrases our child is forming, also known as "mondegreens" (the unintentional mangling of a lyric). Lila has been singing, "We wish you a Merry Christmas / We wish you a Merry Christmas / We wish you a Merry Christmas, and a happy to you!" Johnny now sings, "Wish ki-ma and haa ta ya!"

## SONGS WITH CHORUSES

Choruses are really wonderful for children—and adults—because they repeat and invite you to join in. A chorus can be as short and simple as "town-o" or as complex and integral to the song as the six-line chorus to "When the Saints Go Marching In."

## The Fox

WHEN WE WERE KIDS, OUR FATHER HAD a well-loved and quite worn copy of Pete Seeger's songbook *American Folk Ballads*. We loved "Yankee Doodle," "Big Rock Candy Mountain," and of course "The Fox." When our father would sing us this last song, we would join in on the last lines of each verse with "town-o, town-o, town-o."

In this song, the chorus is really only one word with *o* at the end, repeated three times. For some kids, this is their first invitation to sing on a song. Even the littlest family members can join in on the words in the chorus. We have a cherished family recording of our dad and Abigail singing "The Fox" together when she was about four years old. Her scratchy morning voice comes in at the end of every verse, "town-o, town-o, town-o," getting louder and more confident with each repetition.

# The Fox

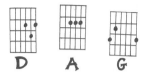 

D A G

      **D**
Well, the fox went out on a chilly night,
              **A**
Prayed for the moon to give him light.
       **D**       **G**
He'd many a mile to go that night
 **D**     **A**     **D**     **A**    **D**
Before he reached the town-o, town-o, town-o.
  **G**        **D**       **A**           **D**
Many a mile to go that night before he reached the town-o.

The fox he ran 'til he came to the pen,
The ducks and the geese were kept therein.
He said, "A couple of you are gonna grease my
   chin
Before I leave this town-o, town-o, town-o."
A couple of you are gonna grease my chin
Before I leave this town-o."

He grabbed the gray goose by the neck,
Swung the little ones over his back.
He didn't mind the quack, quack, quack,
And the legs all dangling down-o, down-o,
   down-o.

He didn't mind the quack, quack, quack,
And the legs all dangling down-o.

Well, old Mother Flipper Flopper jumped out
   of bed,
Out of the window she stuck her head,
Crying, "John, John, the gray goose is gone,
And the fox is on the town-o, town-o, town-o.
John, John, the gray goose is gone,
And the fox is on the town-o."

*continued . . .*

Well, John he ran to the top of the hill,
Blew his horn both loud and shrill.
The fox he said, "I better flee with my kill,
Or they'll soon be on my trail-o, trail-o, trail-o."
The fox he said, "I better flee with my kill,
Or they'll soon be on my trail-o."

The fox he ran 'til he came to his den.
There were the little ones, eight, nine, ten.
They said, "Daddy, better go back again,
'cause it must be a mighty fine town-o,
    town-o, town-o."

They said, "Daddy, better go back again,
'cause it must be a mighty fine town-o."

The fox and his wife, without any strife,
cut up the goose with a fork and a knife.
They never had such a supper in their life,
and the little ones chewed on the bones-o,
    bones-o, bones-o.
They never had such a supper in their life,
and the little ones chewed on the bones-o.

# Hi, Ho the Rattlin' Bog

"RATTLIN' BOG" IS A STAPLE IN OUR FAMILY. In springtime—or even right before spring, when we feel like winter will never end—we sing this song to prepare for the season. Our kids love it. As small children, they would mutter their way through the verses and sing full force on the chorus, but as they get older, they want the challenge of remembering, along with the grown-ups, all the different parts of nature that are found in this rattlin' bog.

*The Musical Family*

# Hi, Ho the Rattlin' Bog

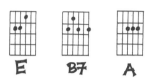

5 ♪

CHORUS:

E        A              E             B7
Hi, ho, the rattlin' bog and the bog down in the valley-o.
E        A              E             B7 E
Hi, ho, the rattlin' bog and the bog down in the valley-o.

Now in this bog there was a hole, a rare hole,
    a rattlin' hole.

Hole in the bog and the bog down in the
    valley-o.

CHORUS

E   B7      E   B7   E      B7
In this hole there was a tree, a rare tree, a rattlin' tree.
E        B7     E      B7                   E
Tree in the hole and the hole in the bog and the bog down in the valley-o.

CHORUS

On this tree there was a limb, a rare limb, a
    rattlin' limb.
Limb on the tree and the tree in the hole and
    the hole in the bog
and the bog down in the valley-o.

CHORUS

On this limb there was a branch, a rare branch,
    a rattlin' branch.
Branch on the limb and the limb on the tree
    and the tree in the hole
and the hole in the bog and the bog down in
    the valley-o.

CHORUS

*continued . . .*

On this branch there was a twig, a rare twig, a
    rattlin' twig.
Twig on the branch and the branch on the
    limb and the limb on the tree
and the tree in the hole and the hole in the
    bog and the bog down
in the valley-o.

CHORUS

On this twig there was a nest, a rare nest, a
    rattlin' nest.
Nest on the twig and the twig on the branch
    and the branch on the limb
and the limb on the tree and the tree in the
    hole and the hole in the bog
and the bog down in the valley-o.

CHORUS

In this nest there was a bird, a rare bird, a rat-
    tlin' bird.
Bird in the nest and the nest on the twig and
    the twig on the branch and
the branch on the limb and the limb on the
    tree and the tree in the hole
and the hole in the bog and the bog down in
    the valley-o.

CHORUS

Now, 'neath this bird there was an egg, a rare
    egg, a rattlin' egg.
Egg 'neath the bird and the bird in the nest
    and the nest on the twig and
the twig on the branch and the branch on the
    limb and the limb on the tree
and the tree in the hole and the hole in the
    bog and the bog down in the
valley-o.

CHORUS

Now in this egg there was some hope, rare
    hope, and rattlin' hope.
Hope in the egg and the egg 'neath the bird
    and the bird in the nest and the
nest on the twig and the twig on the branch
    and the branch on the limb
and the limb on the tree and the tree in the
    hole and the hole in the bog
and the bog down in the valley-o.

CHORUS

*The Musical Family*

Once you've got the song down, it's fun to sing it really fast. Alternatively, you can let every person in the room come up with a crazy, incongruous rattlin' thing to find in your bog. The song might turn out with an elephant on a chick pea and a chick pea on a lawn chair and a lawn chair on a dinosaur and a dinosaur on a baseball and a baseball on a Les Paul and a Les Paul on a banana and a banana on a car and a car in a hole and a hole in the bog and the bog down in the valley-o. You can also do related items: cheese in the sauce and the sauce on the meatball and the meatball on spaghetti and the spaghetti in Rebecca's mouth.

### Katryna

Truth is, as my brain gets older and weaker, my kids' brains are getting older and stronger. So when we're singing our crazy version of this song, sometimes they remember better than I do. What's more fun than outsmarting your parents?

## Mango Walk

WE HAD THE GREAT FORTUNE OF benefiting from the song-gathering efforts of Jack Langstaff, the music teacher at the Potomac School, which we three girls attended several years after he'd left. Even after his departure, the school kept up many of his traditions. He unearthed many gems and passed them on to students and teachers; some of his protégés became our elementary school music teachers. One such gem is "Mango Walk."

While mangos originated in India, this song comes from Jamaica. A *mango walk* is a grove of mango trees, an orchard for people who grow and sell mangos, but the term also conjures up the image of a mango physically walking.

If you rated mangos by size and beauty, "number 'levens" would be the largest and best, so stealing all of them would be selfish and ill-advised. See? Folk music teaches science and civic-mindedness.

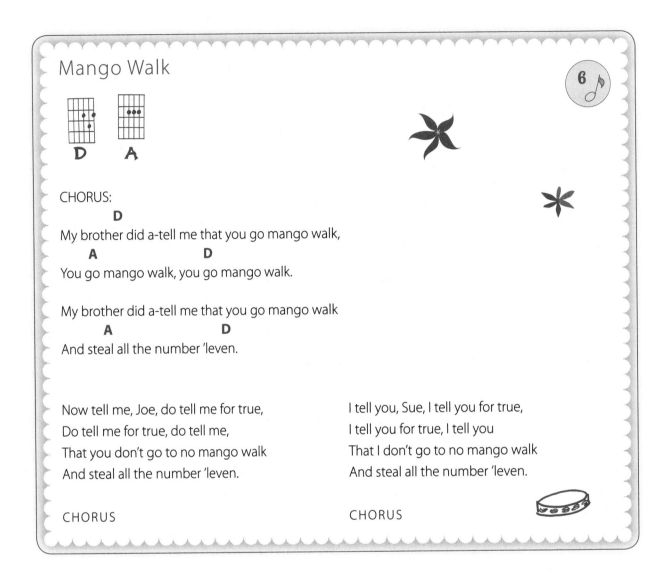

## Mango Walk

**D  A**

CHORUS:

     **D**
My brother did a-tell me that you go mango walk,
  **A**           **D**
You go mango walk, you go mango walk.

My brother did a-tell me that you go mango walk
      **A**           **D**
And steal all the number 'leven.

Now tell me, Joe, do tell me for true,
Do tell me for true, do tell me,
That you don't go to no mango walk
And steal all the number 'leven.

CHORUS

I tell you, Sue, I tell you for true,
I tell you for true, I tell you
That I don't go to no mango walk
And steal all the number 'leven.

CHORUS

Jack used this song to teach polyphonics through rhythms. It's really fun to sing it in four parts, with one person each singing one line.

Another alternative is to sing the chorus and verses at the same time. Or you can have people singing or clapping different beats at the same time—it sounds like the cacophony of an open-air marketplace where you might find one of those perfect number-eleven mangoes if you were very lucky.

## How to Eat a Mango

Enhance this song by eating some mango! The first thing you need to know is that the pit of a mango is huge. It's thick and wide, shaped like a fat surfboard, and flatter than the pit of an avocado but no less dense. Use a sharp knife to cut it: imagine it's a football; stand it on its longest, thinnest edge, and cut from top to bottom along the side of the pit. On the half without the pit, cut a crosshatch pattern through the flesh and scrape it off the skin into a bowl. Cut the pit out of the other side of the fruit, then remove the flesh in the same way. If you're really greedy, you can suck and chew the remaining fruit from the pit. We don't recommend eating the skin.

Choose mangos that are soft to the touch like a peach or an avocado, not hard like an apple.

## CALL-AND-RESPONSE SONGS

Our parents' musical canon was informed by the folk revival of the mid-twentieth century. From the Weavers to Odetta to Peter, Paul and Mary, the folk revival brought many traditional songs to American radio and thereby into our parents' living rooms.

We were the beneficiaries of all that great music, and spirituals were a huge part of it. "Swing Low, Sweet Chariot," "Down by the Riverside," "Oh Mary, Don't You Weep, Don't You Mourn," and "When the Saints Go Marching In" all have a significant place in our family canon.

Spirituals are often call and response, as in the case of "Swing Low" and "When the Saints." For call and response, only one person really needs to know the words; everyone else can just follow the leader vocally. When Africans were first brought to America as slaves, they were separated from others who spoke their language. Music was a way they could communicate. The call-and-response song style originated in the fields as work songs. One person would sing a line, and others would respond with another line.

Eventually, this style worked its way into African-American church services and to what we now think of as spirituals. Gospel music is so often a call and response, inviting even a newcomer to join in the singing. These songs were often revived for the civil rights movement. They're all about salvation and, at first listen, seem to be about heaven and an afterlife. Having the twenty-twenty vision of hindsight and history, we now know they were also about salvation in this life and freedom here on earth.

As kids, these songs were the ones that taught us we could sing, but they simultaneously taught us about history, spirituality, pacifism, and hope.

## When the Saints Go Marching In

Ｗｅ ｒｅｗｒｏｔｅ ｔｈｅ ｌｙｒｉｃｓ ｔｏ "Ｗｈｅｎ ｔｈｅ Saints Go Marching In" to reflect our changing world and current challenges for a performance at the 2006 Falcon Ridge Folk Festival.

You can sing our words, or revert to the ones you may have known growing up. Or, best of all, make your own up!

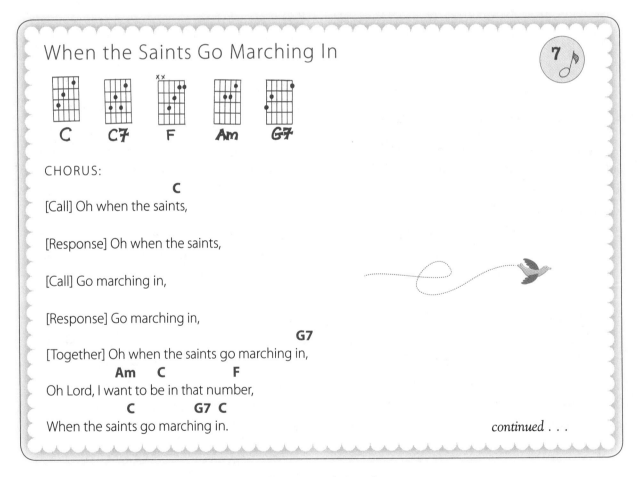

When the Saints Go Marching In      7

C    C7    F    Am    G7

CHORUS:
                          C
[Call] Oh when the saints,

[Response] Oh when the saints,

[Call] Go marching in,

[Response] Go marching in,
                                                    G7
[Together] Oh when the saints go marching in,
              Am    C              F
Oh Lord, I want to be in that number,
                      C          G7  C
When the saints go marching in.

*continued . . .*

*The Musical Family*

```
        C      C7      F
We are traveling in the footsteps
     C                      G7
Of those whose hands we took.
           C                F
If we can learn from all their traveling,
       C        G7      C
We'll see saints where'er we look.
```

CHORUS

Some say this world's in trouble,
Full of greed and evil, torn.
But if we all will rise together,
Then a new world will be born.

[Call] Oh when the new,
[Response] Oh when the new,
[Call] World is reborn,
[Response] World is reborn,

[Together] Oh when the new world is reborn.
Oh Lord, I want to be in that number,
When the new world is reborn.

If you can't play guitar like Arlo,
If you can't write a song like Dar,
You can listen, you can dance, you can sing,
    sing, sing,
And find heaven wherever you are.

CHORUS

# ROUNDS

Rounds are the simplest and easiest way to sing "parts." Everyone sings the same line of music, but different groups start at different times. This creates a kind of harmony that almost anyone can do, because all that's required is the ability to sing a melodic line (whereas singing an isolated harmony part can seem strange and untuneful).

# Row, Row, Row Your Boat

ONE OF THE MOST FAMILIAR ROUNDS IS "Row, Row, Row Your Boat." The entire song is mostly one chord, so all the lines of the song can be sung simultaneously and sound lovely together.

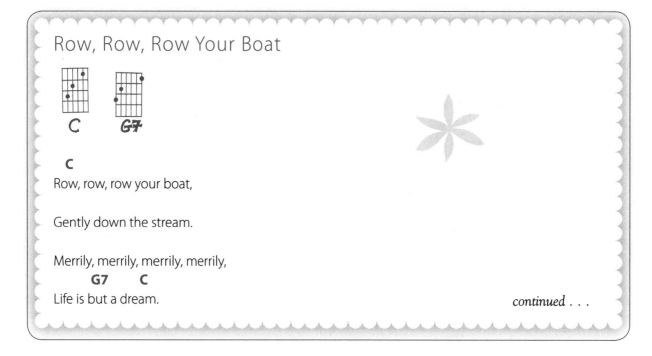

## Row, Row, Row Your Boat

**C**      **G7**

**C**
Row, row, row your boat,

Gently down the stream.

Merrily, merrily, merrily, merrily,
**G7**        **C**
Life is but a dream.

*continued . . .*

It's easy to overlook the beauty of the message in this simple song, as common as a sparrow in the lexicon of kids' songs. But the lyrics are really pretty cool and profound. Don't we all ultimately row our little boats down the stream? Doesn't it tend to go better when we row gently and merrily? (Our friend Karen points out that you get four "merrilys" for every three "rows.") Yet we do have to row and not just drift. As for the last line, it can be helpful in the middle of some parent-toddler conflict or tantrum to remember that all of this drama is really just that—a tissue-thin dream. (We know, tell that to the spilled milk.)

If your family is feeling a little adventurous, you can sing this song in groups, with strong singers—parents, perhaps—captaining each group. The first group starts, and the second group comes in on the first line as the first group sings the second.

This particular round is quite malleable if you want to write your own lyrics. You can sing about rowing a boat, driving a car, flying a plane, riding a bike, and so on. You can simply change the first line and sing the rest as is, but if logic is essential to your enjoyment, change the words to all the lines. Here are some examples:

Drive, drive, drive the car,
Gently down the street.
Merrily, merrily, merrily, merrily,
Faster than your feet.

Fly, fly, fly your plane,
Gently through the air.
Merrily, merrily, merrily, merrily,
Try it if you dare.

## Katryna

I remember, as a kid, trying to stick to my part during long family car trips. I'm sure I was unsuccessful at first, but eventually I could hold my own. Holding my hands over my ears helped me hear myself and hang on to my part. Sitting next to someone who is a strong singer and is singing the same part helps, too.

# Sugar Snap Peas

A VARIATION OF A ROUND IS CALLED A canon. In a round, every voice starts on the same note and sings the same part. In a canon, voices can start on different notes and might sing different parts. The song "Sugar Snap Peas" is a canon. It is easy in that each "verse" has a different tune, but when all the verses are sung at the same time, the result is a nice medley or, if you will forgive the metaphor, a fabulous musical salad.

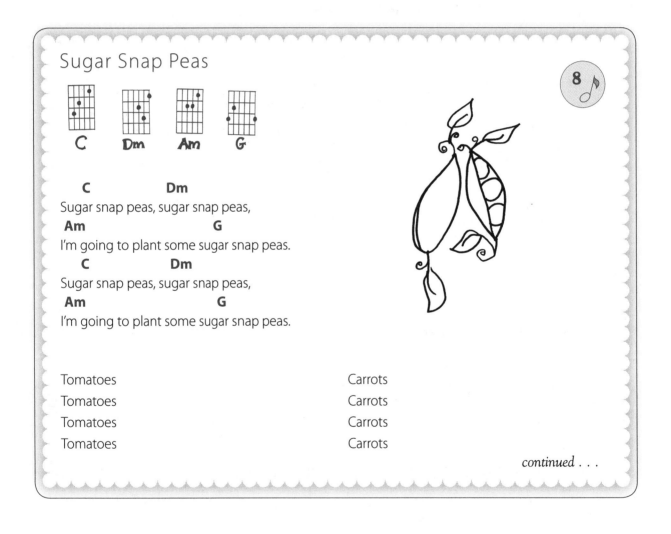

## Sugar Snap Peas

8 ♪

C    Dm    Am    G

    **C**           **Dm**
Sugar snap peas, sugar snap peas,
**Am**          **G**
I'm going to plant some sugar snap peas.
    **C**           **Dm**
Sugar snap peas, sugar snap peas,
**Am**          **G**
I'm going to plant some sugar snap peas.

Tomatoes              Carrots
Tomatoes              Carrots
Tomatoes              Carrots
Tomatoes              Carrots

*continued . . .*

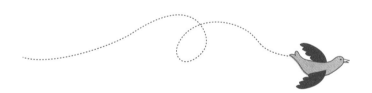

| Beets | Asparagus |
|-------|-----------|
| Beets | Asparagus |
| Beets | Asparagus |
| Beets | Asparagus |

This song is easier than a round because singers need only know their own vegetable part. Each verse employs one word with a different number of syllables (*asparagus* has four, *tomatoes* has three, *carrots* has two, *beets* has one), and each vegetable gets a different tonal acre, if you will. *Tomatoes* is an ascending triad, *carrots* is lower, *beets* is the bass, and *asparagus* is the descant (the highest part). You don't need to know or think about any of this while you sing, but you'll be teaching your children (and yourself) the rudiments of how four-part harmony can turn chaos into balance. Easy and fun as a summer salad! This song is also a great one to sing in the car.

## SONGS FOR LEARNING

From basics like letters and numbers to science and social studies, songs have been used throughout history as a way to teach children about the world. We first learned about the Titanic and the Civil War first from the songs our parents taught us. Lila knows about white blood cells through They Might Be Giants' "The Bloodmobile" from Here Comes Science. In this section, we've included three songs for younger kids that go over some basics: letters, numbers, colors, and body parts.

## Katryna

The musical logic of the tune that most of us know as "Twinkle, Twinkle, Little Star" is unmistakable for toddlers. I've heard so many preverbal children sing it; whether they're babbling sounds similar to the words from "ABC," "Twinkle, Twinkle," or "Baa, Baa, Black Sheep," they're able to grasp the pattern inherent in the tune.

The song is in three parts. The first and third parts are identical. In musical terms, the tune goes from the tonic to the 5, to the 6, back to the 5, and then walks down the scale back to the tonic, or 1. (The *tonic* is the first note of the scale, and it's the same note as the name of the key. So in the key of C, the tonic is C; in the key of D, the tonic is D; and so on.) The second, or middle, section walks down from the 5 to 2 twice. It makes sense. There's nothing surprising about the tune, and you feel comfortable when you get back to that tonic at the start of the third part.

My one-year-old niece came to visit and sang us this tune several times. She's not enrolled in a music class, and no one sings to her all day, every day. Yet this simple melody makes sense to her growing brain, so she sings her ABCs.

## ABC Song

Y OU PROBABLY LEARNED THE "ABC SONG" before you could even recognize the letters. We noticed that Johnny, when less than a year old, would point at letters and know they were connected to the song. Even though he certainly couldn't identify the letters individually or sing all their names, he somehow knew these funny symbols were related to that familiar tune.

We've created our own "ABC Song," which includes a counting portion and a directions section. The first verse is just the alphabet, pure and simple. Then we count to twenty. (Many parents have told us that the first time they heard their children count this high was to this song.) It seems so obvious that music and counting should go together. There are counting songs in almost every language. This one is as easy as they come. To play in the same key as the recording, place the capo on the second fret and use the chord fingerings indicated.

# ABC Song

G   D   Em   C

**G        D**
A, B, C, D, E, F, G,
**Em   C        D**
H, I, J, K, L, M, N, O, P,
**G**
Q, R, S,
**D**
T, U, V,
**G Em   G   D G**
W, X and Y and Z.

| | |
|---|---|
| 1, 2, 3, 4, 5, 6, 7, | Up, down, in, out, |
| 8, 9, 10, and then 11, | Forward, back. |
| 12, 13, | Over, under, |
| 14, 15, | On and off the track. |
| 16, 17, | North and south, |
| 18, 19, 20. | East and west. |
| | Near and far, and |
| | Right and left. |

For this last verse, we made up a simple dance, just acting out the following movements with the words we're singing:

**Up:** Stretch way up, feet together on the floor, arms together reaching to the sky.

**Down:** Crouch down to the ground, with your hands on the floor.

**In:** Hop forward into an invisible circle in front of you.

**Out:** Hop backward out of the invisible circle.

**Forward:** March forward and pump your arms.

**Back:** March backward and pump your arms.

**Over:** Stretch one hand out in front of you at about shoulder height.

**Under:** Stretch your hand out at about chest height, and crouch down so you can look up at the underside of your hand.

**On and off the track:** Hop sideways into an invisible circle, then sideways out of the circle.

**North:** Point north (or straight ahead) with your right hand.

**South:** Point south (or straight behind you) with your left hand.

**East:** Point east (or to your right) with your right hand.

**West:** Point west (or to your left) with your left hand.

**Near:** Stand with your feet together and your arms in to chest, fists touching at your heart.

**Far:** Stand with your feet apart and your arms stretched out to the sides.

**Right:** Lean to the right and stretch out your right hand, palm up.

**Left:** Lean to the left and stretch your left hand out, palm up.

# My Favorite Color

"M y Favorite Color" not only introduces color recognition, but it's a great way for kids to express their own ideas and preferences.

This song is infinitely expandable. Let your children come up with what each color makes them feel. Maybe red seems like the color of a strawberry and not a fire engine. Maybe it makes them feel like jumping instead of running. You don't need to maintain Nerissa's alliteration in every verse. This song has a structure that makes it easy for kids to find playful ways to make it their own.

We're constantly being asked to sing about colors that don't have a verse yet—light blue, magenta, turquoise, orange, and of course "rainbow." So we make up verses. Kids often have better ideas than we do. When we sing this song to kids, the older ones come up with sophisticated colors like tangerine, buff, and teal. Get creative with the colors and don't bother with rhyming. (As you can see, we didn't!)

# My Favorite Color

C  G  Am  Em  F

**C**           **G**
My favorite color is red.
**Am**         **Em**
Red is the color of a fire engine.
   **F**         **C**
It makes me want to run.
         **G**
Run and red, they go together, and
**C**     **G7**   **C**
My favorite color is red.


My favorite color is blue.
Blue is the color of the deep blue ocean.
It makes me want to breathe.
Breathe and blue, they go together, and
My favorite color is blue.

My favorite color is green.
Green is the color of a summer forest.
It makes me want to grow.
Grow and green, they go together, and
My favorite color is green.

My favorite color is yellow.
Yellow is the color of the sun in daytime.
It makes me say, "Oh, yay!"
Yay and yellow, they go together, and
My favorite color is yellow.

My favorite color is pink.
Pink is the color of a pretty flower.
It makes me want to play.
Play and pink, they go together, and
My favorite color is pink.

*continued . . .*

My favorite color is brown.
Brown is the color of an autumn mountain.
It makes me want to bow.
Bow and brown, they go together, and
My favorite color is brown.

My favorite color is white.
White is the color of falling snow.
It makes me wonder why.
Why and white, they go together,
And my favorite color is white.

My favorite color is purple.
Purple is the color of the sky at sunset.
It makes me very proud.
Proud and purple, they go together, and
My favorite color is purple.

My favorite color is black.
Black is the color of the sky at nighttime.
It makes me want to be.
Be and black, they go together,
And my favorite color is black.

## Katryna

"What's your favorite color?" is one of those questions children get asked all the time. As a child, I was annoyed by this question. Unlike my older sister, Nerissa, who was absolutely clear about loving purple and green, I was more fickle. I never could settle on a favorite. It depended on my mood and still does.

Colors are evocative. So when we thought about singing a song to teach our children their colors, we wanted to sing about how those colors made us feel. We especially love to sing this song while dancing with or just waving different colored scarves. You can also use cloth napkins or flags made out of construction paper and taped to a pencil.

# Alouette

IN QUEBEC, CHILDREN ARE OFTEN TAUGHT about body parts through the old folk song "Alouette." The real words refer to the body parts of a bird, so we've changed them to be about human body parts. We figure that since we're singing in French and that's already a leap, we might as well learn the French names for our noses and eyes and neck instead of a bird's beak.

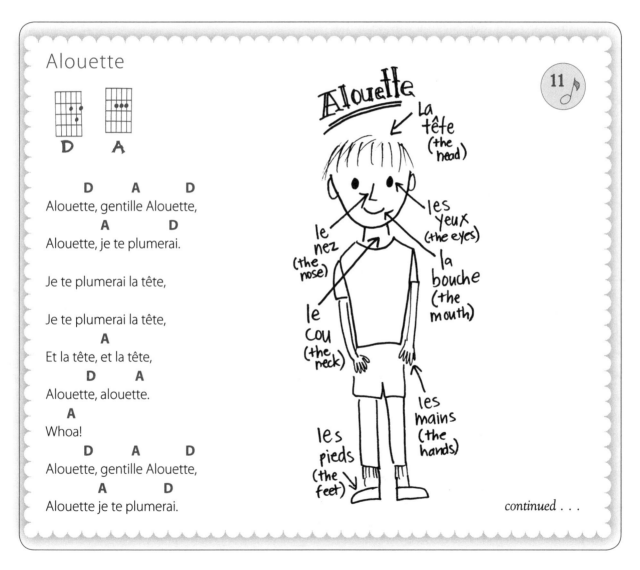

## Alouette

D    A

    **D**     **A**     **D**
Alouette, gentille Alouette,
       **A**     **D**
Alouette, je te plumerai.

Je te plumerai la tête,

Je te plumerai la tête,
     **A**
Et la tête, et la tête,
    **D**    **A**
Alouette, alouette.
   **A**
Whoa!
    **D**   **A**    **D**
Alouette, gentille Alouette,
      **A**    **D**
Alouette je te plumerai.

La tête (the head)

les yeux (the eyes)

le nez (the nose)

la bouche (the mouth)

le cou (the neck)

les mains (the hands)

les pieds (the feet)

*continued . . .*

Je te plumerai le nez,
Je te plumerai le nez,
Et le nez, et le nez,
Et la tete, et la tete,

Alouette, alouette.
Whoa!
Alouette, gentille Alouette,
Alouette je te plumerai.

Keep adding parts and then backtrack through the
parts already mentioned, as in:

Je te plumerai la bouche,
Je te plumerai la bouche,
Et la bouche, et la bouche,
Et les yeux, et les yeux,

Et le nez, et le nez,
Et la tête, et la tête,
Alouette, alouette.
Whoa!

We often end with *le cou* ("neck"), but sometimes we go on to *les mains* (hands), *les pieds*
("feet"), and so forth.

This is a wonderful way to sing to your baby
about the parts of his body. We always find it
amusing to sit the child on our lap facing us. As
we sing the first "et la tête," we place our hands on
our own head, and then on the "et la tête" response, we put our hands on the baby's head.
When you get to the nose verse, it is funny to
hold your nose when you sing, "et le nez," and
make a nasally voice. For a serious challenge, you
sing the song in French but switch to English
when you name the body parts:

Alouette, gentille Alouette,
Alouette, je te plumerai.

Je te plumerai the neck,
Je te plumerai the neck,

| | |
|---|---|
| Et the neck, et the neck, | Alouette, alouette. |
| Et the eyes, et the eyes, | Whoa! |
| Et the mouth, et the mouth | |
| Et the nose, et the nose, | Alouette, gentille Alouette, |
| Et the head, et the head, | Alouette je te plumerai. |

Being silly is always a good choice when singing for a toddler. No one can see you when you're in your own home—no one but that cute baby. Even if people could see you, they would be blown away by how willing you are to make a total fool of yourself in the name of entertaining and connecting with your child.

# 6

# MOVEMENT AND DANCE

THE SISTER ART TO MUSIC IS DANCE. WE can explore music directly by moving our bodies to its rhythms, echoing what we hear with our arms, legs, torsos, heads, fingers, and toes. You need absolutely no skill to incorporate dance and what we call "big movements" into your family music routine. And nothing is more effective in "teaching" a child rhythm than helping her to experience it in her body through movement.

As you know (probably all too well), babies love to be rocked. Though we always preferred the glider chair, many babies insist on being rocked, swayed, or jiggled by a standing person. A lot of parents we know had to pace the halls with their newborns. The reason for this is that babies like to move, and they are limited for a long time, dependent on their caregivers for their mobility.

Dancing with a baby is easy. Start by putting on your favorite music. Just move your weight back and forth from one foot to the other in time

to the music. (You probably already do this; we're just pointing out that it's as effective a "dance" to your baby as a ballet would be.) Lift your baby up and down in time to the music. Put her on your lap and move her arms or legs gently in time to the music. Gently turn her forward and backward. Smile and sing along. Of course, just picking your child up and holding her free hand with yours and boogying away is easy, popular, and our personal favorite. What is sweeter than waltzing with a baby? Twirl her, and she'll be even more delighted.

When your child is older, simple dance steps like up-down squats, and holding hands to skip around in a circle are great ways to engage with the music. Lila and William are partial to clown kicks, which their ballet teacher, Kelly, taught them; here, you keep your legs straight as you kick along to the music.

Try putting your child on the floor and dancing him under your arm in a simple twirl as he holds your hand. If you have two kids the same age, teach them how to hold both hands and do a double twirl under.

Or yell out, "Free dance!" and shake your thing. Kids love to watch their parents having fun, and what's more fun than dancing to your favorite music? The rest of this chapter provides some more ideas for incorporating movement and dance with your family's songs.

Songs with specific movements are a fun and active alternative to free dancing. If we have three people, "London Bridge" is always a great hit with our clan. You can substitute a different song, such as "Mango Walk" (see page 68), for "London Bridge," but the basic game remains the same. Two people hold both hands and face each other with their arms raised to make a bridge; the bridge then comes down to catch a third player. We play "Mango Walk" with the kids pretending to be mangos, and on "steal all the number 'levens," we catch the thief. Or we invent different ways a mango might move and have a contest to see who can do the best impersonation of a "mango walk."

## LAP GAMES FOR BABIES AND TODDLERS

We love lap games. We loved them as babies, and we loved them as kids who were too big to ride on a grown-up's foot. As young adults with no children, they were our go-to way of bonding with our small cousins, nieces, and our friends' children. They combine music and movement, involving the whole body and brain. Plus they're cuddly and fun. Their only drawback is that kids love them so much you might become a "Ride a Cock Horse" machine, like the mechanical bull in *Urban Cowboy*.

## Babar the Elephant

"B ABAR THE ELEPHANT" IS A WONDERFUL song/game that Nerissa made up. It tends to delight the under-one set and calms fussy babies.

## Babar the Elephant

12 ♪

Babar the elephant rides the elevator up, up,
    up, up, up!

Babar the elephant rides the elevator down,
    down, down, down, down.

Hold your baby in front of you—facing toward or away from you—and slowly lift her up as you sing the first line, then lower her back down on the second line. With a bigger child, you can each start out squatting on the floor and slowly rise to standing, arms outstretched to the sky, on the first line, then sink back down to the floor on the second.

This is a very rudimentary way of teaching the concept of notes getting higher and lower.

# The Noble Duke of York

IF YOU WANT A SLIGHTLY MORE ADVANCED ride for your child than "Babar" allows, "The Noble Duke of York" could be just the thing. This will take him on a ride and teach him directions like up and down and left and right. It will also delight almost any child. Be prepared for him to squeal, "Again! Again!" after this one.

## The Noble Duke of York

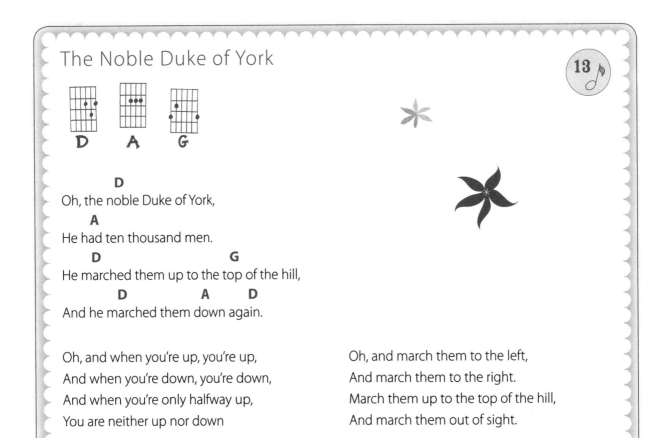

D
Oh, the noble Duke of York,
A
He had ten thousand men.
D                           G
He marched them up to the top of the hill,
D          A          D
And he marched them down again.

Oh, and when you're up, you're up,
And when you're down, you're down,
And when you're only halfway up,
You are neither up nor down

Oh, and march them to the left,
And march them to the right.
March them up to the top of the hill,
And march them out of sight.

You start this game sitting on the floor with your legs straight out in front of you. Place your child on your lap—his back to you and his legs on yours—and bounce him for the first two lines. On the second two lines, raise your knees up and then down, giving your child a ride in the process.

On the second verse, you bring your knees up quickly on "up" and down quickly on "down." Then halfway up on "halfway up" and even more quickly up and down on "You are neither up nor down."

On the third verse, you sway your child left and right, then bring your knees up one more time for the "top of the hill." On "march them out of sight," flip your child over your head, landing him on his feet behind you. (This is always our children's favorite part.)

The entire game can also be done with you lying on your back with your knees bent into your chest and bouncing your child on your shins.

## Katryna

When I was nine months pregnant with my first child, my best friend from college came to visit me with her two-year-old. Jenn and I shared a great love for discovering and listening to music, but I had never once heard her even sing along to the radio in college. Somehow motherhood had coaxed her into getting over her shy, quiet ways so she could communicate with her daughter in every language possible. This included singing to her child. It was Jenn who taught me my first singing games as an adult. I often think back to that visit and laugh at the irony.

Jenn showed me "The Noble Duke of York." It works best with a child who's at least a year old. It can be done with a smaller baby, but it has to be done very carefully. I still played this game with Amelia when she was eight, though I sometimes refused to really march her out of sight.

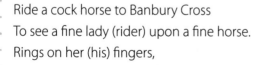

# Ride a Cock Horse

**O**UR AUNTS PLAYED THIS GAME WITH US when we were little. We loved the part where we got tossed in the air. When they were between the ages of one and two, both of Nerissa's kids would run over to her if they saw her sitting in a chair with one leg crossed over the other (which was often). This game works wonderfully with a baby who can hold her head up, and it continues to work until the child gets too heavy to toss with your foot.

## Ride a Cock Horse

14

Ride a cock horse to Banbury Cross
To see a fine lady (rider) upon a fine horse.
Rings on her (his) fingers,

Bells on her (his) toes,
(S)he shall have music wherever (s)he goes!

For this song, your child sits on your foot, which you need to hold strong to make a bicycle-like seat for her. Once she's aboard, hold your child's hands and bounce her up and down in rhythm to the rhyme.

On "Rings" and "Bells," kick your leg up high so your child flies a bit in the air. And on "goes," lift the child up until she's sitting on your lap.

Then, inevitably, do it again.

## *Crazy Rider*

"Crazy Rider" is sort of "Ride a Cock Horse" meets the B-52s.

---

### Crazy Rider

**15**

Crazy rider, crazy rider,
Riding in the west.
Riding in the west.

Whoop! There's a rattlesnake.
Whoop! There's a prairie dog.
Whoop! There's the Grand Canyon!

---

Put your child on your lap facing you. Your child needs to be strong enough to sit up by himself. Now hold on to his feet (if he's able to balance; if not, just hold him by the waist) and bounce him gently up and down like he's riding a horse. When you get to each "Whoop," bounce him a little higher. On "There's the Grand Canyon," drop him through your legs, catching him by the armpits.

Older kids like to sing this song standing up and pretending to ride a horse. On "There's the Grand Canyon," they fall down on their backs and wiggle their legs in the air.

*The Musical Family*

## SMALL HAND MOVEMENTS AND SIGN LANGUAGE

We've noticed that it is often helpful to involve more than just a child's sense of hearing in order to tap her musical interest. We often pat our children on the back while listening to music together. Engaging with your child using more than one of her senses at the same time can intrigue, distract, or console. While this is certainly developmentally helpful to your child's brain, we're more curious about its efficacy in entertaining a bored baby.

These days, many parents are intent on communicating with their children through sign language. Babies are often able to sign their desires before their mouths and throats have developed enough for them to speak. We had signs for *more*, *all done*, *up*, and *nursing* in our households, but a lot of parents we know have taught their children dozens of signs and can have whole conversations while their babies are still preverbal. This movement inspired us to consider learning American Sign Language (ASL) signs for some of our favorite folk songs.

There are myriad websites where you can learn ASL, and we've listed the official one in the Resources section at the back of the book. If you want to try signing a song, choose one in which the lyrics are sung slowly enough that you have time to sign along. If you want something less formal, numerous songs have been written with small hand movements in mind, or you can always make up your own signs to a song you like. Eventually you may notice how fluently your child can sign right back to you!

## Katryna

My four-month-old niece looked at me askance when I sang to her, but when I started showing her my fingerplay to "The Itsy Bitsy Spider," her interest was piqued. She wanted to touch my fingers as they made the cool shapes, and she was curious about the new sounds and sights she was experiencing.

# The Itsy Bitsy Spider

THE BASIC HAND MOVEMENT FOR THIS song starts with your right index finger touching your left thumb and your left index finger touching your right thumb. Flip them over each other, back and forth, like they are walking upward, and keep your other fingers spread out to resemble spider legs. This is referred to as "walking fingers up."

## The Itsy Bitsy Spider

The itsy bitsy spider went up the water spout
Down came the rain and washed the spider
    out

Out came the sun and dried up all the rain
And the itsy bitsy spider went up the spout
    again.

Here's a description of the hand movements to make while singing this song:

On "up the water spout," walk your fingers up.

The itsy bitsy spider went up the water spout

On "Down came the rain," move your hands from above your head to your waist, palms facing down, fingers separated and wiggling to indicate rain.

down came the rain

wiggle fingers

On "washed the spider out," cross your hands in front of you palms down, then uncross them and spread them to the side to indicate a washout.

and washed the spider out

On "Out came the sun," raise your hands over your head with fingertips touching in order to make your arms an oval to indicate the sun.

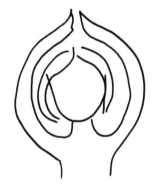

Out came the sun

On "dried up all the rain," separate your fingers and let your arms go out to the side and down to your waist.

and dried up all the rain

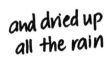

On "went up the spout again," walk your fingers up again.

# Three Craws

THIS IS ANOTHER ASL-INSPIRED NUMBER. We do it with our HooteNanny class.

The surprise at the end always makes the kids giggle.

## Three Craws

**16** ♪

Three craws sat upon a wall, sat upon a wall,
   sat upon a wall.
Three craws sat upon a wall on a cold and
   frosty morning.

The first craw was looking for his Ma, looking
   for his Ma, looking for his Ma.
The first craw was looking for his Ma on a cold
   and frosty morning.

The second craw was looking for her Pa,
   looking for her Pa, looking for her Pa.
The second craw was looking for her Pa on a
   cold and frosty morning.

The third craw found his Ma and Pa, found his
   Ma and Pa, found his Ma and Pa.
The third craw found his Ma and Pa on a cold
   and frosty morning.

The fourth craw wasn't a-there at all.

three    crows    SAT    upon    wall

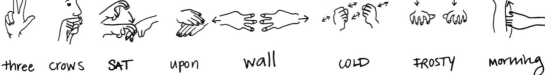

three   crows   SAT   upon   wall   COLD   FROSTY   morning

First crow looking for Ma

First crow looking for Ma COLD FROSTY morning

Second crow looking for pa

Second crow looking for pa COLD FROSTY morning

Third crow Find Ma pa

Third crow Find Ma pa COLD FROSTY morning

Fourth crow wasn't there at all

STEP 1: STEP 2:

## DANCING

We have been encouraging you throughout this book to sing with your children, whether or not you believe that you have "talent." The same goes for dancing, and we can speak directly to any feelings of inadequacy here. Neither of us has much formal training in dance, and it wasn't an activity in which we excelled. (We got yanked out of ballet class because the teacher spanked Nerissa for her bad form. As far as our mother was concerned, that was the end of our dancing career.) However, it's so much fun to dance with our children that we simply don't care how well we do it.

Just as singing is pleasurable in its own right, the act of moving your body intentionally to music forges a plumb line to joy. Think Snoopy—throw your head back and kick your legs in the air. Grab your child and whirl him around in a faux ballroom maneuver. Lie on the bed with your kids and say, "Everyone point one leg up to the ceiling! Now the other leg!" Make a bunny hop line of two or three.

In this section, we include songs and activities that range from organized (such as songs for a spe-

cific dance) to impromptu (such as Freeze Dance) to in between (such as Dancing with Props, which requires some preparation). It's never too early to demonstrate to your child (or let your child demonstrate to you) the joys of moving your body.

Not to be discounted is the healthy amount of exercise you will likely get if you dance with your child, especially if you let her lead the way. Don't forget, you can always just have a big dance party. Put on the music and turn your living room into a discotheque.

### Songs with a Specific Dance

What's more fun than a song with its own dance? We grew up learning simple choreography to all sorts of songs our music teachers taught us, and we made up our own dances to everything we heard on the stereo, from Elvis to *Peter and the Wolf*. So while songs can always work on their own and you can certainly dance to any song you hear, linking the two together can make the entire experience quite memorable. Our "ABC Song" (see page 77) and "Hal An Tow" (see page 148) both have specific dances that go with them. Here is another.

*The Musical Family*

# Sur le Pont d'Avignon

THIS FRENCH SONG DATES FROM THE fifteenth century, and the lyrics are about a dance, but we have added variations to this. The original song tells of soldiers and musicians, but we like to sing about children and babies. We have some simple suggestions for movements noted in brackets alongside the lyrics.

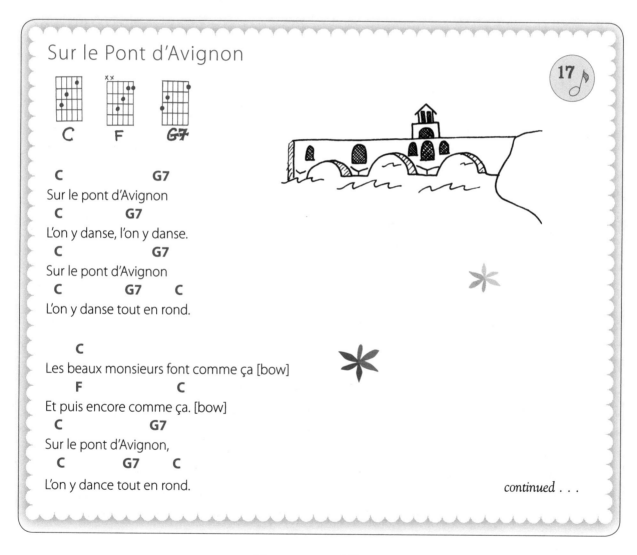

## Sur le Pont d'Avignon

C / F / G7

```
C              G7
Sur le pont d'Avignon
     C         G7
L'on y danse, l'on y danse.
     C              G7
Sur le pont d'Avignon
     C         G7      C
L'on y danse tout en rond.


          C
Les beaux monsieurs font comme ça [bow]
        F              C
Et puis encore comme ça. [bow]
     C              G7
Sur le pont d'Avignon,
     C         G7      C
L'on y dance tout en rond.
```

*continued . . .*

Les belles dames font comme ça [curtsy]
Et puis encore comme ça. [curtsy]
Sur le pont d'Avignon
L'on y dance tout en rond.

Et les enfants font comme ça [jump]
Et puis encore comme ça. [jump]

Sur le pont d'Avignon
L'on y dance tout en rond.

Et les bébés font comme ça [wave]
Et puis encore comme ça. [wave]
Sur le pont d'Avignon
L'on y dance tout en rond.

To add movement to this song, you can make a circle as in "Ring Around the Rosie" and walk counterclockwise as you sing the chorus. When you get to "tout en rond," turn in place, then face center and sing a verse. Each verse has a different action that you can act out as you sing.

Another way we like to dance to this song is to stand in a circle and, for every chorus, do a different kind of dance. Try ballet, the cancan, the Charleston, tap, the Hustle, the Electric Slide, or disco à la John Travolta in *Saturday Night Fever*—the sky's the limit. Be creative!

## Dancing Games

The most natural, instinctive reaction to music is to move to its beat. Children often dance before they can even walk. Watch a six-month-old who has just learned to sit up alone when he hears music. He bounces to the beat and sways to the sound. We see this every day in our HooteNanny classes. Toddlers who are new to walking will plant their feet when the music starts and move their whole bodies to the tune. As their skills broaden, we see them stomping, waving, and bouncing to the beat. Children's relationships to their bodies should remind all of us to pay attention to what our bodies want to do. When we hear those melodies, we want to move. We want to relate to the music with every part of our physical and emotional selves. So don't be shy. Sway with your child, bounce with your baby, jump with your preschooler, dance with your spouse. Family dance parties paint smiles on everyone's face.

You can work these dancing games into almost any situation, but our favorite is the post-dinner cleanup in the kitchen, with our current family mix playing on the iPod in the background. March around the kitchen with utensils. Tongs make great castinets. Wave a dish towel over your head.

Kids love contrast. Try dancing slowly and then quickly; or dance all stretched out, reaching to the sky, then all scrunched up in a ball on the floor. Dance with smooth movements, then try jagged, jerky movements. Anything you can think of that has an opposite will delight your children, because they will enjoy anticipating the opposite movement. You can make an iPod mix specifically suited to this kind of opposites dancing. Play a piece from the *Nutcracker* followed by a Bee Gees disco cut and then some U2. Imagine what it means to dance quietly and loudly. Remember, there are no limits. Just don't tear the ligaments in your knees and you'll be fine.

## Mirror Dance and Follow the Leader

In HooteNanny, we'll often notice a movement a preverbal child is making and pause to say, "Oh, look what Simone's doing. Let's all follow her." Or "Do what Ezra just did. Let's make that into a rhythm." Mirror dancing can happen naturally, as it often does with our own children when they say, "Mama, do this!" All we have to do is imitate, though sometimes that's easier said than done. If your child is older, she can mirror you.

Babies love to imitate. Try waving, stretching, and crouching with your baby. Start out as simply as possible. Put your hands over your face. Put your hands on your hips. Put your hands over your eyes, your ears, your cheeks, your knees. Try balancing on one foot. If you have an older child, you can try slightly more complicated steps. Start with easy moves and develop them into patterns; perhaps a heel and then a pointed toe brushed on the floor can turn into a heel/toe, heel/toe. Maybe elbows in/elbows out follows, and eventually, you put it all together.

For an older child—perhaps post-kindergarten—you can create a tighter version of this game. See how exactly you can imitate your nine-year-old's every move. This will require going very slowly and deliberately (which might have the added bonus of calming down an overstimulated child). Get into a kind of mind-meld with your child. Look her deeply in the eye as you follow her movements.

Either you or your child can be the leader. Don't be afraid to take turns leading. The attention span of toddlers can be short. They may not entirely understand what you're doing, but it will work anyway. The feeling of control they'll get from watching you do what they do is delightful for them. And what more precious gift can you give an older child than the feeling of being deeply seen and understood?

When you're with more than one child, Follow the Leader is a great dance game

that can go on for hours. Let each child take a turn being the leader, though if you have a family with kids of different ages, there may well be one dominant leader. This can be a fun way to go for a walk in the woods. It can also be a fun way to get through a rainy day. You can follow the leader while standing in a circle and imitating movements or while moving around the house. If, for example, you're playing in the living room, one child can put his hands on his head, balance on one foot, touch the floor, do a yoga tree pose, clap his hands three times, twirl, and pass leadership to the next person. Everyone else copies each leader's moves.

Alternatively, you can march around the house in a line, and the "following" can be more about where you go than how you move. A variation on this might be to pretend that you're moving through something, such as water. Are you swimming? Are you wading? Pretend to be walking through honey. Your feet stick to the floor with every step. Have the youngest person tell you what you're walking in—tall grass, peanut butter, fields of butterflies, stinky mud, glue, hot sand—and move accordingly.

Of course, Mirror Dance and Follow the Leader can be played without music, but it's twice the fun with musical accompaniment.

### Dancing with Crazy Rules

Play this game when you need to release some energy! Put some music on, then make some rules while you're dancing. Here are some examples:

Your feet are stuck to the floor, so you have to dance without moving them!

Your fingers have Crazy Glue on them and are stuck to your thighs, so you have to dance without moving your arms!

Your whole body was turned to stone by Medusa, but for some reason your face still moves. You have to dance using *only* your face!

Your body is made out of wood, so you have to dance stiffly!

Your body is made out of cooked spaghetti, so you have to dance all wiggly!

Take turns making rules about dancing. Anything goes.

### Balloon

The more people you have for this game, the more fun it is. Hold hands in a circle. Start very close together and pretend that, as a group, you are a balloon. Blow up the balloon very slowly. As you do, make the circle bigger and bigger until you are barely able to hold on to each other's hands. Then let the air out of the balloon and rush back to the center.

### Freeze Dance

Freeze Dance is a classic because it involves nondoing, which is such a refreshing break for kids. The basic idea is to dance until the music stops. Then everyone has to freeze. If you want to play it as a competitive game, the person who successfully holds the frozen position the longest without toppling over or fidgeting wins. But we usually play it noncompetitively.

To play, select someone to be "It" and have this person stand near the pause button or hold an instrument. This person plays the music and everyone dances; when she stops the music, everyone has to freeze.

Our kids love to play this game with the grown-ups dancing and freezing and the kids stopping the music. The more silly and wild we are, the funnier the frozen positions are and the more delightful and entertaining the game is. We're big believers in the notion that there are few things kids enjoy as much as adults—especially serious ones—acting silly.

## Dancing along with Props

Any dance can be enhanced with scarves of all sizes. Choose a scarf the size of a hanky, and you become morris dancers, snapping the hanky on the most important beat and waving it above your head. Choose a larger scarf and you have less control, but you can make more graceful, airy movements. If you have a large group, you can get a big tablecloth. Kids love to be under a giant piece of material that rises and falls. A sheer one allows them to see through as they feel the cloth go up

and down. They also love to be part of the team, making the material rise and fall.

You can buy dance wands, which have a nylon handle with three-foot-long ribbons of all colors hanging off them. You can also make a dance wand by covering a paper towel tube with duct tape and affixing the ends of some fancy ribbons to the inside. Stuff the rest of the ribbons inside, and when you flick the wand, they will fly out to delight your child.

Get a few hula hoops and pretend they're steering wheels as you sing "The Wheels on the Bus." (The bus might travel all over your house.) Get some peacock feathers and pretend you're birds while singing "Three Craws" (see pages 94–95) or "Six Yellow Chicks" (pages 32–33).

### *Three-Prop Dance Game*

Have everyone take some time to hunt for something in the house to bring to the game. For example, you may have a pillowcase, a pan, a stuffed animal, and a paperback book. Put all the items into a pile. Take the first item from the pile and hand it off to each person in turn. When handed the item, everyone has to think of a song that goes with it. They can then make up a dance that the rest of the family has to copy.

# 7

# MUSICAL GAMES AND PLAY

WHENEVER WE ASK OUR KIDS WHAT THEY did in preschool or at their play date—or what they would most like to do at any given moment—the most common answer is simply, "Play." This can be the best way to approach music for some children. How can a musical encounter be fun?

Music is naturally playful, and it has elements of a game. For some adults, music was presented as a dry academic subject with lots of rules, scales, structure, and expectations of performance. Yet it's natural to bring gamelike elements into music for children, and there are many wonderful musical games out there. One of the surefire ways to get Lila to engage with her Suzuki lessons is through a card game called Blue Jello,[1] in which different rhythms are notated through simple glyphs and then the child imitates them by hand. Games can take the mystery out of music, and let's face it, music can be an elusive process. Why is it that

one day you sing or play perfectly, while another day your voice is off or the notes just sound small and tinny?

This chapter will explore this topic in two ways. First, we'll look at how to incorporate music into your children's regular play. Second, we'll discuss how to introduce music in a playful way so it doesn't come across as yet another academic subject.

## GAMES FOR IMAGINATIVE PLAY

When we were growing up, our most frequent playmates were each other. We did a lot of imaginative play with dolls, small toy mice, and Smurfs, as well as regular old playacting. Nerissa used to scan the horizon for opportunities to lasso other sister duos into a game called Beatles, which consisted of the four of us pretending to be a four-piece rock band. Whoever got to be Ringo played pots and pans; the other three mimed guitar and sang into "mics" (spoons). We would set up our dolls in the same way. (We didn't have bona fide Beatles dolls, but in a classic situation of giving our kids what we were deprived of, our children do.)

When we play with our kids, we often pretend to be animals. The music cues us as to what kind of animals we might be. If it's a song about water (such as "Bamboo," in which you "take a stick of bamboo and you throw it in the water"), we might be salamanders or minnows or whales or sharks or lobsters or eels. If the song is "I Had a Little Rooster" or "Organic Farm," we might be pigs or chickens or cows or sheep. Then again,

we might be tigers or dragonflies or elephants or mosquitoes.

Every song has a million different applications and uses. We tend to think of "Whatever I'm Feeling Now Feels Just Fine" (see pages 121–22) as a "cheering up" kind of song, but it would work beautifully as a game to act out all the feelings. See how dramatic you can be acting happy, sad, angry, and scared. You may want to stick to the literal, and at a certain developmental stage, so will your child. You might both get anxious if monster trucks invade your organic farm. On the other hand, you might explore all the myriad ways you can sing one song, imagining unusual or fantastic alternatives in the lyrics.

## Organic Farm

THOUGH WE TOTALLY ESPOUSE BEING silly, we don't recommend singing songs you can't stand. Case in point, we don't really get "Old MacDonald Had a Farm." The tune is flat and hurts our voices. It's been overused. Plus, where's Mrs. Old MacDonald?

We caved in once on a long car trip and sang "Old MacDonald" to Lila when she was almost a year old. Through this experience, we did come to see the efficacy of farm songs as a genre: kids love

animals, and farms are a hot topic these days (especially polycultural farms like Old MacDonald's, which grow more than one crop, or have both crops and livestock, as opposed to monocultural farms that grow only one thing). Also, farm songs are infinitely expandable—just keep adding animals. So we vowed to write a more melodious version.

Around this time, we both joined local, organic, community-supported agriculture (CSA) farms. Almost nothing compares to the joy of spending a summer afternoon picking sugar snap peas with our kids. So Nerissa wrote this song to teach kids about the animals on a farm, the beautiful gifts they bring to it, and the sounds they make. And, of course, the names of their offspring.

## Organic Farm

**18** ♪

**D**
Living on a farm,
**Em**      **A**
An organic farm.
                              **D**
And on that farm, there was an organic cow,
                **G**
And the cow said, "Moo!"
            **D**
And the cow made milk.
            **A**
And the cow had a baby.
            **D**
And we called it a calf.

Living on a farm,
An organic farm.
And on that farm, there was an organic chicken,
And the chicken said, "Bawk, bawk!"

And the chicken laid eggs.
And the chicken had a baby.
And we called it a chick.

*continued . . .*

Living on a farm,
An organic farm.
And on that farm, there was an organic sheep,
And the sheep said, "Baa!"
And the sheep made wool.
And the sheep had a baby.
And we called it a lamb.

Living on a farm,
An organic farm.
And on that farm, there was an organic pig,
And the pig said, "Oink!"
And the pig made compost.
And the pig had a baby.
And we called it a piglet.

And on and on it goes, with a dog, cat, duck, turkey, horse, donkey, and so on. Go for obscure animals like llamas to learn what their young are called (a cria).

When we sing this song, we always pause after "and we called it," so the kids can fill in the answer of what the baby animal is called.

To introduce imaginative play, let each kid choose and act out the animal in each verse. Depending on how many participants are handy, have them take turns being the animal, or maybe let the children boss the parents around and have the parents impersonate the animal. In Hoote-Nanny, we make two rows with an alley down the middle, and kids take turns ambulating like their chosen animal down the aisle.

Parents have told us that this song has saved them on long car rides. Each member of the family comes up with a new farm animal to add to the flock. Thinking up their job on the farm and learning the names of their offspring are half the fun. We even occasionally sing about vegetables or tractors.

Living on a farm,
An organic farm.
And on that farm, there was an organic
    tractor,
And the tractor said, "Vroomgaga,
    vroomgaga!"

And the tractor plowed the fields.
And the tractor had a baby.
And we called it a lawnmower.

*The Musical Family*

Take away any of the cornerstone words of "Organic Farm," and you have a whole new song or game. Here are some options, but you will certainly come up with fun ideas of your own:

Living on a planet, / A big green planet.
Sleeping on a farm, / A sleepy lullaby
    farm.

And on that farm, there was a girl named [insert your child's name].

Or you can set up a farm in your playroom and animate the stuffed animals.

## Allee Allee O

THIS SONG IS POPULAR WITH THE CARS-and-trucks constituency, otherwise known as two-year-olds. We sing this song standing up and moving around in a big circle in HooteNanny. We act out what each kind of ship does with our whole bodies, as well as how we use our voices (such as loud, soft, slow, and quick).

## Allee Allee O

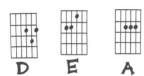

**D E A**

**D**
O the big ship's a-sailing on the allee allee O,
    **A**        **E**   **A**
The allee allee O, the allee allee O.
    **D**
O the big ship's a-sailing on the allee allee O
**A**            **D**
All the ding-dong day.

O the loud ship's a-sailing on the allee allee O,
The allee allee O, the allee allee O.
O the loud ship's a-sailing on the allee allee O
All the ding-dong day.

O the quiet ship's a-sailing on the allee allee O,
The allee allee O, the allee allee O.
O the quiet ship's a-sailing on the allee allee O
All the ding-dong day.

O the fast ship's a-sailing on the allee allee O,
The allee allee O, the allee allee O.

O the fast ship's a-sailing on the allee allee O
All the ding-dong day.

O the slow ship's a-sailing on the allee allee O,
The allee allee O, the allee allee O.
O the slow ship's a-sailing on the allee allee O
All the ding-dong day.

O the big ship's a-sailing on the allee allee O,
The allee allee O, the allee allee O.
O the big ship's a-sailing on the allee allee O
All the ding-dong day.

Once you finish with these lyrics, move on to colors, varieties of boats (such as sailboats, motor-boats, houseboats), and more. You can try other types of transportation and machines as well:

The motorcycle's driving on the allee allee O          The backhoe is digging on the allee allee O
The race car is racing on the allee allee O

This song can take you all the way from the Hudson River to the Massachusetts Bay!

## AUDIATION

*Audiation* is an academic-sounding word for something that could just as easily be seen as a kind of game. It is the ability to recall, or "hear," a song in your head without having to sing it out loud. It's the musical equivalent of being able to think in another language. At first, you may sing along when you recognize a song on the radio, or you can sing along with your parents, but eventually, you can conjure up the song all on your own. You will know you're audiating when you sing a song a cappella (all by yourself, no accompaniment) and find yourself pausing at the end of the verse and waiting to start singing again because, in your head, you "hear" the instruments playing that in-between music that comes before the chorus.

The songs in this section use audiation as a type of play. Kids love it when a song speeds up until it's out of control. They also love it when we leave bits out. When you play with a song by clapping a rhythm for a missing word or doing a full-body dance in place of a line of the song, you're engaging your children's brains on a whole new level. Kids enjoy the challenge of remembering when to sing and when to clap. Each of these three songs offers a slightly different take on audiation and how you can use it to play. "Molly" has a set pattern reminiscent of "B-I-N-G-O," always leaving out the same letter in the same order and replacing it with hand claps. "The Horse Went Around" uses whole-body movement while systematically leaving out more words with every verse until finally you're only dancing, not singing at all. "A Ram Sam Sam" is more malleable than the first two. There are hand movements for each set of words. You can leave out as much or as little as you like. The results are exciting for children because you not only have to remember the song and the hand movements while audiating, you also have to remember whatever pattern you choose. This, of course, leads to the greatest fun of all—hearing the grown-ups make a mistake!

# Molly the Donkey

THE QUINTESSENTIAL EXAMPLE OF A SONG that uses audiation is "B-I-N-G-O." As the song progresses, we leave out letters, replacing them with hand claps. Nerissa rewrote "B-I-N-G-O" in honor of Molly the donkey, who lives across the street from her at Smith Vocational/Agricultural School. With each repetition of the chorus, you clap in place of a letter.

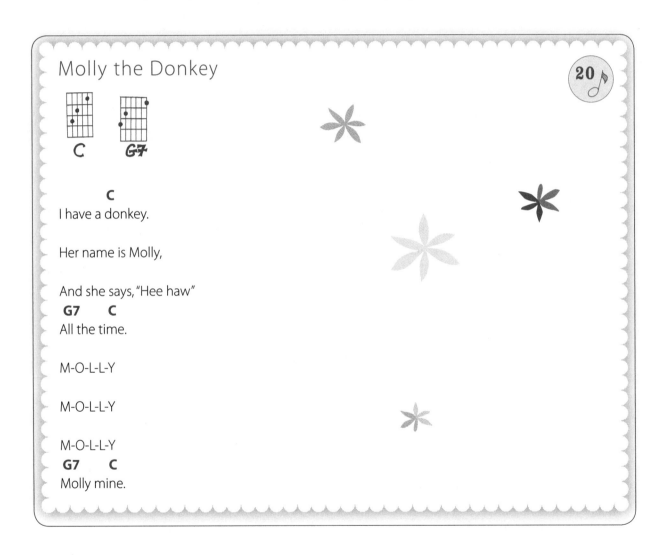

Molly the Donkey                              20

C
G7

     **C**
I have a donkey.

Her name is Molly,

And she says, "Hee haw"
**G7**    **C**
All the time.

M-O-L-L-Y

M-O-L-L-Y

M-O-L-L-Y
**G7**    **C**
Molly mine.

*The Musical Family*

I have a donkey,
Her name is Molly,
And she says, "Hee haw"
All the time.
[clap]-O-L-L-Y
[clap]-O-L-L-Y
[clap]-O-L-L-Y
Molly mine.

[Continue replacing one letter with a clap
each round until all the letters are clapped in
this last round.]

I have a donkey.
Her name is Molly,
And she says, "Hee haw"
All the time.
[clap-clap-clap-clap-clap]
[clap-clap-clap-clap-clap])
[clap-clap-clap-clap-clap]
Molly mine.

# The Horse Went Around

ON A RAINY DAY, WHEN EVERYONE desperately needs to move around, try this one. It is sung to the tune of "Do Your Ears Hang Low?"

Start singing this song relatively slowly. With each repetition, sing a little more quickly until you're singing as quickly as you can by the last line. The first time through, you sing all the words. Each time you sing through the four lines, leave off one word, leaving the space there. We always find it fun to stomp in place of the word.

The second-to-last time you repeat the song, you sing no words at all, and the last time, you sing all the words as fast as you can.

# The Horse Went Around

E        B7

           **E**
Oh, the horse went around with his foot off of the ground.
                   **B7**
Oh, the horse went around with his foot off of the ground.
           **E**
Oh, the horse went around with his foot off of the ground.
                 **B7**           **E**
Oh, the horse went around with his foot off of the ground.


Oh, the horse went around with his foot off of
    the ———.
Oh, the horse went around with his foot off of
    the ———.
Oh, the horse went around with his foot off of
    the ———.
Oh, the horse went around with his foot off of
    the ———.

[Continue dropping one word each round
    until you get to this last round.]

Oh, _____.
Oh, _____.
Oh, _____.
Oh, _____.

Oh, the horse went around with his foot off of
    the ground.
Oh, the horse went around with his foot off of
    the ground.
Oh, the horse went around with his foot off of
    the ground.
Oh, the horse went around with his foot off of
    the ground.

The cool thing is that you really will hear the words you're not singing in your head, as you sing, walk, or dance around the room—or the whole house. As you stomp around, you will all hear the crazy sound of the horse going around the room. Stop moving for the last repetition, because you'll need all your energy to sing the song as fast as you can.

## A Ram Sam Sam

THIS MOROCCAN SONG IS WELL LOVED BY children all over the world. The words are nonsense sounds and are accompanied by hand movements. The folk process has made room for many different hand signs, so if you know others, feel free to use them. The idea is to have the same movement with the same words every time.

You can sing this song as a round, or you can sing it slowly and then speed up until it's totally out of control. For the purposes of this section, we're interested in using it as an audiation game.

Try leaving out the words "A ram sam sam" but singing all the other words. Or try leaving out all the words except "A rafi, a rafi." Do the hand movements to every line whether or not you're singing the words. As you play, you'll notice that you're hearing the lines you're not singing in your head. Eventually, that will also happen for your children. When they can hear the music in their head without singing it out loud, they're one step closer to being able to pull any tune out of the air without accompaniment.

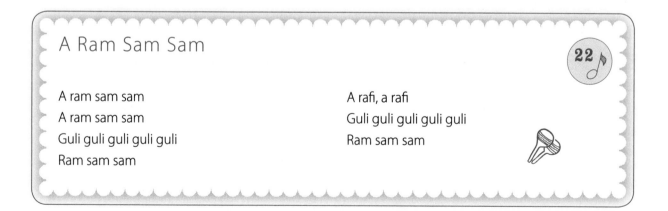

### A Ram Sam Sam

**22**

A ram sam sam
A ram sam sam
Guli guli guli guli guli
Ram sam sam

A rafi, a rafi
Guli guli guli guli guli
Ram sam sam

Here's a description of the hand movements to make while singing this song:

Start by sitting. On "ram," lift your hands with the palms facing down, and then on "sam sam," pat your legs twice (once for each "sam").

On the "guli guli" line, hold your arms at about chest height and roll your hands over each other.

Lift your hands again, palms down, on "ram," and pat your legs on "sam sam," as before.

On "A rafi," lift your hands above your head, wiggling your fingers. You can bring your hands down between each repetition so that you're raising your hands twice for this line.

Follow the previous instructions for the final "guli guli" and "ram sam sam" lines.

Once you have the hand movements down, you can leave out portions of the singing and do the motions in place of the words. The trick is to stay on rhythm so that a roomful of people—or at least you and your child—know when to come back in together. This happens through audiation. You will hear the words in your head as you raise your hands above your head and wiggle your fingers. You will eventually be able to come back in together on "guli guli." It's possible to do the entire song without words. Our favorite way to play this game is to sing only the "a rafi" line.

Be sure to laugh when you make mistakes, as you undoubtedly will (it's half the fun).

# GAMES TO PLAY WITH ANY SONG

Some games emanate from the song itself, while others work with any song at all. Let whatever music you love most be the backdrop for the games in this section. Invoke your family musical canon and choose your favorites.

## Parade

A musical parade is the perfect cure for a rainy day, when your kids are starting to climb the walls. Parades are also great when play dates need a little direction—a parade can break up almost any disagreement between toddlers.

This game is kind of self-explanatory: gather your kids, some instruments, and some props, and hold a grand musical parade through your house. You can either sing a song as you march or come

*The Musical Family*

up with a fun chant, such as "Go away, rain!" or "Let's all make a parade, a parade!"

Small instruments that are easy for little ones to play while they walk are perfect for a parade. Here's where you can use that basket of small instruments that we wrote about in chapter 2. (See page 28, and chapter 9 for ideas for homemade instruments.) Other important props for a great parade are funny hats, scarves to use as capes or flags, and ribbons attached to a stick or a cloth handle.

## Name That Tune

Name That Tune is a great game for car rides. The only important component is to make sure you're using music your child knows. You probably have a stack of CDs that are on repeat in your car or your home. Choose songs from that collection. You can play this game by singing the first word or words, increasing the number of words until it becomes clear to your child which ditty you're trying to convey. Alternatively, you can hum the whole song and let your child audiate the words.

For a variation on this game, tap out the rhythm to the song—this is an especially interesting way to communicate music to a kinetic learner. You can literally tap the music on your child's back. This is sometimes fun at bedtime or in the morning before you're ready to get out of bed. For this variation, the music has to have an iconic beat; "Jingle Bells" is always an easy one with which to start. It's much harder to guess a song from a tapped-out rhythm than from a hummed melody, but it's no less enjoyable.

Lila likes to make us guess what song she's playing by bowing its rhythm on the E string of her violin. William's favorite way of playing Name That Tune is to pucker out his lips and vibrate them as he wiggles his finger over his lips and hums a song. (He always prefers games where spit is involved.)

## Katryna

I was out to dinner with my son a few weeks ago. It was just the two of us, and we were in the café of our local grocery store. He'd had a long day at school, and I'd had a long day of teaching. We should have been at home, but we needed groceries.

William has recently become a serious Beatles fan, taking to all things Beatles the way kids his age often take to dinosaurs, cars, trains, or Star Wars. I'm actually not quite sure how it happened, but he listens to them, uke in hand, for large portions of each day. So I decided at dinner that we could play a little game of Name That Beatles Tune. I would sing the first word of a song, then the first two words, and so on, until he could guess what it was. Most of the time, he was able to get it after two words. I made sure to choose his favorites at first, but as time went on, I branched out. He then wanted to sing the first word to me. We had a wonderful time, and now I know it's a game we can come back to whenever we want. Traffic jams, long lines, and errands will never feel as tedious again.

## Alphabet Game

Look at your family's musical canon and try to think up songs that begin with each letter of the alphabet. Each member of the family gets a turn at each letter. There is no need to be rigid about what constitutes the name of a song. For example, your kids might use the first line of the song to indicate the title. In our family rules, "The Star-Spangled Banner" could be used for *T*, *S*, or even *O* (for "Oh, say can you see").

Your alphabet game might go like this:

A = Away in a Manger
B = La Bamba
C = Car, Car (for "Take Me for a Ride in Your Car Car")
D = Down by the Riverside
E = Eleanor Rigby

We sometimes do an all-Beatles version of this game. We have to skip a couple of letters, but because our family has studied the Beatles' canon extensively, it's a good place for us to start. Choose your family's favorite band and play the game with just that group's songs. Or try choosing only Christmas carols. Maybe your family is partial to musicals; you could try sticking to Broadway for this game. See how far you get.

We often revisit this game. It's always satisfying to finally think of a song that begins with *K* or *V* or *X*. (Actually, let us know if you come up with a Beatles song that starts with *X*.)

# EVERYDAY SONGS

WE GREW UP IN A FAMILY WHERE MUSIC seemed to come out of every room of every house and building we entered. Music was part of everyday life; we spontaneously broke into song, and we used music to get through everything from small tasks like brushing our teeth to large events and tragedies.

Music can be a great way for you and your child to get through difficult moments and tasks. It's an effective calming device, and the more you use it, the better it works. When you really need something to entertain your little ones, or when you really need something to help motivate your child to do chores or travel, you have music—even when your hands are occupied, you're out of energy, and you're standing in line or sitting at a restaurant table.

For example, when we were flying to Nova Scotia with Nerissa's two children to play a show, we found ourselves at the back of a crowded airplane with very tired kids and a long wait to disembark. As Katryna played with Lila, Nerissa calmed her crying one-year-old by singing "Babar the Elephant." It might have worked with any child, but it totally worked with Johnny because Nerissa had been singing it to him for months.

When your child is very little, you will need four essential song types in your bag of tricks: cheering-up songs, work songs, travel songs, and lullabies.

## CHEERING-UP SONGS

Just as each kid seems to gravitate toward a particular toy for comfort and entertainment, so they each favor a particular song. For our kids, "When the Saints Go Marching In" (see pages 70–71) was a perfect cheering-up song. If ever they were bored or grumpy and we needed them to stay awake for some reason, we just scooped them up and started marching and singing. One of the values of music—if you use it—is that it can be incredibly useful in getting through hard times, from bandaging skinned knees to losing a beloved pet. Every child and every family will probably find their own cheering-up songs. We knew a family who turned religiously to a Gilbert and Sullivan patter song for their infant. Somehow, "I am the very model of a modern major general" cured all ills. So don't limit yourself.

Use what works, if your kids are getting older and more discerning about lyrics and you're stumped, here are some suggestions: "Lean on Me," "I Can See Clearly Now," "If You Want to Sing Out, Sing Out," "Over the Rainbow," and "My Favorite Things" from *The Sound of Music*. The following is a song we wrote that we found helpful for cheering up our children.

## Whatever I'm Feeling Now Feels Just Fine

SOMETIMES IT HELPS TO REMEMBER THAT the moods our kids (and we) have will pass. This song helps us remember that telling a kid not to be angry is a fruitless task. It works much better, in our experience, to hunker down with a frustrated or tantrum-throwing child and let her know that we, as humans, have been there too. "It will change in time" is helpful even in the moment when it really doesn't seem like change is possible.

# Whatever I'm Feeling Now Feels Just Fine

  C     Em     Dm     G7     Am    F

   C        Em  Dm    G7
How do you know when I'm happy?
      C    Am   Dm G7
You'll know because I'll smile.
    F   G        Am
The smile I can't help smiling
       Dm      G7
Says I'll be happy for a while.
   F     G7     C Am
Please don't talk me out of it,
 Dm          G7
It will change in time,
        C  Em  Dm  G        C
Because whatever I'm feeling now feels just fine.

| | |
|---|---|
| How do you know when I'm angry? | How do you know when I'm lonely? |
| You'll know because I'll frown. | You'll know because I'll cry. |
| The frown I can't help frowning | The tears I can't help crying |
| Says I'll be angry when I'm down. | Say I'll be lonely by and by. |
| Please don't talk me out of it, | Please don't talk me out of it, |
| It will change in time, | It will change in time, |
| Because whatever I'm feeling now | Because whatever I'm feeling now feels |
|    feels just fine. |    just fine. |

*continued . . .*

How do you know when I'm frightened?
You'll know because I'll hide.
I feel much safer hiding
When I am on the frightened side.
Please don't talk me out of it,

It will change in time,
Because whatever I'm feeling now
        feels just fine.

[Repeat first verse.]

Bah - Bah

## WORK SONGS

Work songs, of course, have a long history about which many an eager young ethnomusicology doctoral candidate has written his dissertation; work songs go back to the days of Jason and his Argonauts, as well as slave songs like "Keep Your Hand on the Plow," and so on. It's well documented that everyone works more efficiently and pleasantly with a soundtrack or, better yet, a fight song to spur on the adrenaline. Why should family life be any different? A pleasant way to get your kids to do what you want is to sing them a song about what they're doing—brushing their teeth, taking a bath, cleaning up, running faster to keep up with your long legs.

Music Together teacher and folk singer Lui Collins sings a simple phrase—just a descending fifth sung to the syllables "ba-ba"—that indicates to children that it's time to put toys or instruments back in the bucket.

Children as young as a year or fourteen months understand what this means. We've taken her idea and often sing, "Thank you, Johnny," to the descending fifth when he puts his blocks back in their box or his Brio train tracks in their container.

The following songs take this notion of music as a cue to get things done.

# Time to Take a Bath

**N**ERISSA MADE UP THIS SONG WHEN LILA was between twelve and eighteen months and just beginning to resist some elements of bathtime, specifically the hair-washing and rinsing part. The song worked like a charm. We decided to put it in a HooteNanny curriculum and soon heard from other parents that their kids insisted on it as a provision for being shampooed. Try it if you're having bathtime struggles.

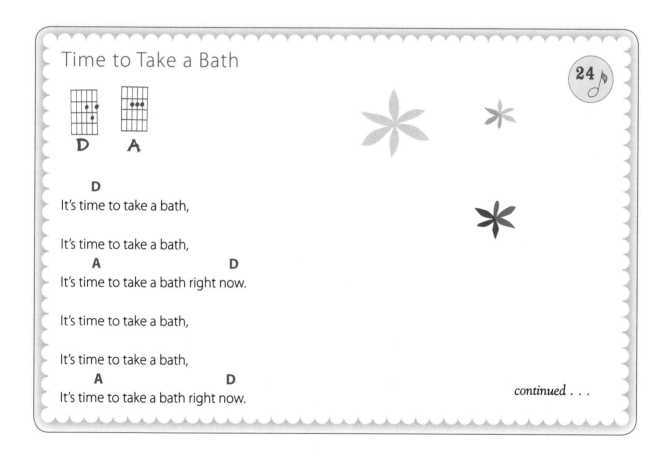

## Time to Take a Bath

**24**

D A

    **D**
It's time to take a bath,

It's time to take a bath,
    **A**              **D**
It's time to take a bath right now.

It's time to take a bath,

It's time to take a bath,
    **A**              **D**
It's time to take a bath right now.

*continued . . .*

**D**          **D**
Yea, a little bit of water in the tub,
**A**
Water in the tub,
      **D**
Water in the tub.
                    **D**
Yea, a little bit of water in the tub,
**A**                         **D**
Let's put some water in the tub.


It's time to wash our hair,                It's time to rinse it out,
It's time to wash our hair,                It's time to rinse it out,
It's time to wash our hair right now.      It's time to rinse it out right now.
It's time to wash our hair,                It's time to rinse it out,
It's time to wash our hair,                It's time to rinse it out,
It's time to wash our hair right now.      It's time to rinse it out right now.


Yea, a little bit of soap in your hair,    Yea, a little bit of soap out of your hair,
soap in your hair,                         Soap out of your hair,
soap in your hair.                         Soap out of your hair.
Yea, a little bit of soap in your hair,    Yea, a little bit of soap out of your hair,
Let's put some soap in your hair.          Let's get the soap out of your hair.


Continue by adding your own verses. Here are some extras that we sometimes tack on:

It's time to splash around . . .
Yea, a little bit of water out of the tub . . .
Not too much water out of the tub.

It's time to towel off . . .
Yea, my towel is so soft and warm . . .
Find me a towel soft and warm (please).
It's time to brush our teeth . . .
Yea, a little bit of toothpaste on the brush . . .
Let's put some toothpaste on the brush.

We also sing this song when we're at the dinner table or at circle time, and we pantomime the actions or "bathe" a doll or stuffed animal. Doing this continues to help Lila prepare for bathtime.

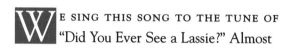

## This Is How We Clean Our Toys Up

WE SING THIS SONG TO THE TUNE OF "Did You Ever See a Lassie?" Almost everything goes more smoothly with a tune to sing along.

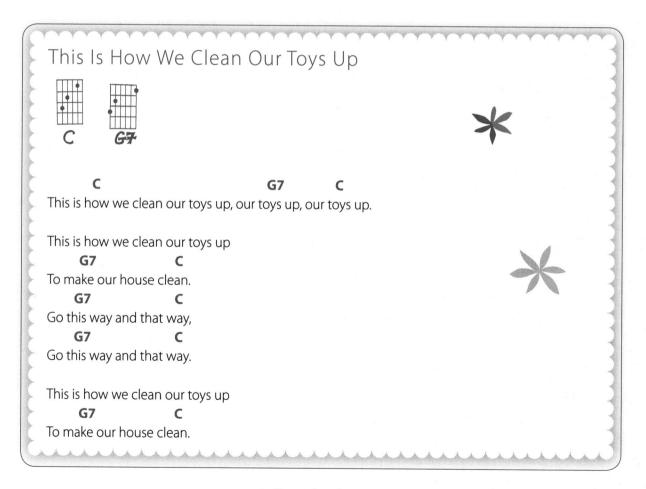

### This Is How We Clean Our Toys Up

C — G7

      C                           G7       C
This is how we clean our toys up, our toys up, our toys up.

This is how we clean our toys up
     G7            C
To make our house clean.
     G7            C
Go this way and that way,
     G7            C
Go this way and that way.

This is how we clean our toys up
     G7            C
To make our house clean.

As we sing, we pantomime (or actually do) what we're singing about.

We also make up words to whatever we happen to be doing:

This is how we do the laundry.
This is how we do the dishes.

This is how we sweep the floor.
This is how we brush our teeth . . . to make our mouths sweet.
This is how we bake our cookies . . . to make our mouths glad.

## TRAVEL SONGS

Travel songs are a staple for singers and troubadours everywhere, perhaps because musicians through the centuries have traditionally been an itinerant lot. "On the Road Again," Simon and Garfunkel's "America," "The Long and Winding Road," "Carolina in My Mind," Joni Mitchell's "This Flight Tonight," and of course, "City of New Orleans" are some of our favorites. For children, especially a couple of small boys we know, travel songs have the added benefit of incorporating vehicles, which seem central to life at a certain developmental stage. "Take Me for a Ride in Your Car Car" can be adapted so it involves nothing but different varieties of vehicles; for example "Take me for a ride in your backhoe," "Take me for a ride in your cherry picker," and so on.

Katryna's career as a songwriter began while driving a wailing baby Amelia around town and trying desperately to console her. She finally succeeded by making up songs about Amelia's stuffed animals. Nerissa frequently finds inspiration for

songs in things her kids say while observing the world from their car seats and booster seats. While Katryna wrote about Amelia's animals, Nerissa writes about motorcycles, trucks, and kitty-cat cars.

Her personal favorite comes from a *Sesame Street* episode from the early seventies: "Goin' for a Ride" by J. Raposo and J. Moss. She can't remember the words, so she makes them up:

Yes, we're going for a ride,
Gonna travel very far.
Yes, we're going for a ride,
Going riding in a car.
Gonna wave at all our friends.
Gonna count the birds we see.
Yes, we're going for a ride,
Johnny, Lila, and me.

Of course, substitute the names of your kids for ours.

A list of ideas for more travel songs can be found in Appendix 3.

*The Musical Family*

# LULLABIES

After a long day filled with work and travel songs, what better way to wind down than with a lullaby. Lullabies help your child feel safe and fall asleep— so you can fall asleep! While we have written a great deal about our father and how central his singing, guitar playing, and "song leading" were to our musical development, when we think of nighttime and cuddling, we think of our mother. Although we're sure our father sang us down on occasion, it's our mother's voice that comes to mind when we hear the word *lullaby*.

Our mother has the perfect lullaby voice: gentle, sweet, soft, and low. Her voice is intricately woven in our minds with memories of being soothed, feeling safe and loved and held. We can't recall specific songs, just the general tone of her voice, its closeness to our ear, the love she poured out in singing to us. As children, we thought she had the most beautiful voice in the world. As adults, we're always surprised at how quiet it is. It was plenty loud and effective when it was an inch from our baby ears.

## How to Choose a Lullaby

Anything that soothes you and your baby is a lullaby. If you sing low in your voice, your chest will vibrate a little more, which is an added benefit in trying to lull a baby to sleep. So think of the lullaby as being more about delivery than content. Sing in a low voice, choose a simple song, and sing the same song every night. Because it's important to introduce consistency to your child, choose your lullaby carefully. Check out Appendix 3 for a list of lullabies. Maybe they will jog your memory or lead you to your favorite power ballad from your youth. Here are some guidelines to keep in mind when picking a lullaby.

Rule one is that there are no rules. You don't have to sing a traditional lullaby. It doesn't have to have the word *rock* in the title. It doesn't even have to have the word *baby* in the lyrics. It just has to appeal to you and your child.

Rule two is find something that relaxes both of you. A Coldplay song sung soothingly could work as well as a Broadway hit from the 1940s. Don't worry about the lyrics. They don't have to be about bedtime. But keep in mind that you might be singing this to your children for a long time. So if you don't want an awkward conversation when your kid is four, you might want to avoid "I'm Too Sexy for My Shirt."

Rule three is to find something you don't mind singing over and over again. Not only will you probably end up singing the same song every night, but you may find yourself singing it dozens of times every night. For a time, Tom had to carry Lila all around her room, singing "Sweet Rosyanne." The chorus of "Bye-bye, Mama, / Bye-bye, Dada" expanded to include a "bye-bye" to every single member of our family pictured on her walls (which was everyone), to all her stuffed animals, and to some of her dresses and shoes.

## Katryna

When I finally remembered the utility of a good lullaby, I was sitting in our green rocking chair trying to calm my baby down. I had such a romanticized notion that rocking in a chair and singing anything to her would mean peace and tranquillity for both of us. That's how it was in *Little House on the Prairie,* right? So I chose a song I had loved since childhood, "Night Rider's Lament" by Michael Burton. I rocked and sang, and still Amelia was grumpy and sad. I was getting blearier, and she wasn't calming down. I realized pretty quickly that she already had an opinion about the songs I could sing to her. She wanted something else from Mama jukebox. So I went to the song my parents had sung to me, "Hush, Little Baby." It's probably the song I can sing with the least amount of effort. Having heard it repeatedly as a sleepy child, nothing came to my lips more easily as a sleepy adult.

As I sang and rocked and walked, I could feel my baby's body relax into me. I felt her giving in to the sleepiness and melting into my shoulder. Those moments were hard at the time. I was exhausted, sleep deprived, and anxious. I felt like she would never give in. It was like meditation. Like focusing on the breath, I was focusing on the song and its soporific power. Now I treasure those memories of my children falling asleep on me.

We get a lot of say in what we sing to our children, but that doesn't mean our first choice is going to be their first choice.

## Judicious Use of Your Boom Box (or iPod) as a Virtual Lullaby Singer

When all else fails, when you're too tired to sing the seventy-eighth round of "Hush, Little Baby," there's no shame in finding a delightful CD and letting it play on repeat in your child's boom box. We had the distinct advantage of having many recordings of our own voices, so this trick worked especially well on our kids, but it will work on yours as well.

When Amelia was a baby, Katryna traveled everywhere with a boom box and a copy of our then-new CD, *Love and China.* This would soothe Amelia in strange hotel rooms, in moving vehicles, and backstage at rock clubs. By the time

Nerissa's kids came along, we had made a CD to order; one of the two *Rock All Day/Rock All Night* CDs is all lullabies.

Our kids love their little boom boxes. Each one has a (disorganized) stack of CDs next to it, and they go through phases where they have a particular favorite that they listen to while dozing off or have playing in their rooms during quiet time. But truth be told, nothing beats a real lullaby, complete with cuddles and the closeness of a parent's voice to the child's ear.

# Hush, Little Baby

H ERE IS A VERSION OF "HUSH, LITTLE Baby" that Nerissa adapted, in case the materialistic and paternalistic aspects of the original bother you. Lila calls it "The Firefly Song."

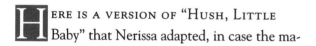

**Nerissa**

We used to believe that any song would do as a lullaby. Tom was very successful in getting Lila down with "Take Me Out to the Ball Game," but Johnny won't have it. Johnny wants "Hush, Little Baby," "All the Pretty Horses," or the Beatles' "Good Night." When Tom and I are out for dinner, the babysitters report that four-year-old Lila often has success getting him down with her version of "Tender Shepherd" from *Peter Pan*.

# Hush, Little Baby

C           G7

**C**              **G7**
Hush, little baby, don't you cry.

                        **C**
Mama's gonna catch you a firefly.

          **G7**
And if that firefly won't light,

                        **C**
Mama's gonna show you a moonlit night.

And if that moonlit night is dark,
Mama's gonna take you for a walk in the park.
And if that walk in the park is too short,
Mama's gonna build you a cozy fort.
And if that fort's not cozy and warm,
Mama's gonna hold you like a shelter in the
    storm.

And when that shelter in the storm holds
    tight,
Mama's gonna give you a kiss good night.
A kiss good night and a lullaby,
Hush, little baby, don't you cry.
A lullaby and a story to tell,
My little baby, may you sleep well.

# HOMEMADE INSTRUMENTS

P ART OF OUR MISSION IS TO SHOW YOU that your home is filled with musical instruments, many of which are already available. Don't throw out that yogurt container. Turn it upside down, grab a pencil, and you have a drum. Fill glasses with different amounts of water, tap them with a chopstick, and you have a makeshift xylophone. Grab a tennis racket and you've got a guitar. Turn a hairbrush bristle side out and you've got a microphone. Maybe you're even more adventurous than this. Perhaps you're a little crafty. This chapter will show you how to make drums, percussion instruments, and even guitars out of ordinary items.

## HOMEMADE PERCUSSION

There are drums all over your kitchen. Any pot, pan, Tupperware bowl, or oatmeal container is a drum. Give your child a wooden spoon, and you can actually make dinner while she bangs away on your flour container. Most people we know have at least one cabinet they haven't baby-proofed. It's filled with baby-safe kitchen items that inevitably turn into an orchestra. Our friend Val keeps an old hatbox and a set of drum brushes on her coffee table at all times, just in case a sing-along breaks out and someone wants to join in.

Here are some easy ways to add more percussion instruments to your home.

### Shakers

Shakers can be made out of old film canisters and rice. If the term *film canister* means nothing to you in this digital age, you can fill any small plastic container—Rubbermaid or Tupperware—a quarter full with rice; you have a shaker.

For older kids who want a craft project, take old toilet paper rolls and fill them with rice or beans. Tape off the ends, and decorate your creations with anything from paint to tissue paper stuck on in layers with a little Mod Podge. Just be careful with children under age three; these shakers can be pried open, and the rice or beans can be a choking hazard.

## Woodblocks

Woodblocks are especially fun when covered in sandpaper. Then you have two sounds: one from bonking them together and a scratchier one from rubbing them together. Two pieces of scrap wood about 3" × 4" × 1" can make perfect woodblocks. Sand them down so they won't splinter, then cover them with sandpaper, and you have some cool, scratchy woodblocks.

## Portable Drum Kit

This small drum kit can be worn around your child's neck—perfect for a family parade! Gather items from your recycle bin: a small, sturdy box; a yogurt container; a big tomato can; an old planter. Test the items out and see how they sound.

Tape your drums together with duct tape. Start by taping the containers to each other, then wrap tape around the whole kit. You can also make a minicymbal by taping a pencil or chopstick to one edge of your drum kit and attaching an old pie tin to the end of it.

The final touch is to get an old, thick ribbon or a piece of material and make a strap so your child can wear the drum kit while marching in a parade. Pencils or chopsticks make great drumsticks for this kind of kit.

## Hand Drum

If you want to take a little more time and make a slightly bigger mess, try making this drum. The finished product looks surprisingly realistic and sounds pretty good too. It's fun to make a bunch of these at a time. If you start with different-sized cans, you'll have an array of sounds when you're done.

### What You Need

An old tin can, the bigger the better (You could even go to the school cafeteria and ask for one of their industrial-sized tomato cans.)
A paper grocery bag
Glue, water, and a flat container for mixing them together
Scissors
String
Colorful tape

Decorate your can with the colorful tape. Making stripes around the can in alternating colors can look excellent.

To create the drum head, place your can on the paper bag and trace a circle that's about 2" bigger than your can. Cut out your paper circle, then crinkle it up as much as possible, being careful not to rip it. The crinkling makes the paper resemble a drum skin, and also softens it so the glue can get into the creases. Mix the glue and water together, and place the circle in the glue mixture. Make sure it's coated all over, then squeeze it out. Place the gluey, gooey paper over the top of the can, and tie a piece of string around the paper to hold it in place.

Allow the drum to dry overnight. You'll have a cool hand drum in the morning. The paper looks and feels like the skin of a real drum.

## HOMEMADE GUITARS

There are lots of great ways to make your first axe. Our first homemade guitar was a Halloween-inspired creation. John Lennon just wouldn't be John Lennon without a guitar, right? Once we got started, we couldn't stop.

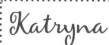

William was just starting his mandatory gun fascination phase. We are not a big gun-toting family, and I come from a land of all sisters. I tried my best not to shame him when he picked up a stick and said, "Bang, bang." Even the sons of the most pacifist parents will pick up a carrot and pretend it's a weapon. I noticed that when he became enraptured with guitars, his whole reality switched. Rather then every stick becoming a gun or a sword, everything became a guitar.

## Cardboard Guitar

Cardboard guitars are our family favorite. Remember, even if you don't know how to play a real guitar, you can certainly mimic Eddie Van Halen on a cardboard one, your tennis racquet, or a big ladle. These are fabulous first instruments.

William prefers cardboard guitar to air guitar. He has about seven guitars made from color photocopies of famous Beatles guitars and card-board. His favorite birthday present this year was a nonworking microphone on a stand with a nonworking cord coming out of it. When he asked where to plug it in, Katryna put it through the handle of a kitchen drawer, and he was happy as a teenage girl at a Beatles concert in 1964. If music weren't a part of their lives, she couldn't offer that form of entertainment to her kids. As we've said, the more music is a part of their lives, the more it interests them.

# How To Make A Cardboard Guitar

You will need:

cardboard box

Scissors * or Box Cutter *

* KEEP AWAY FROM KIDS!

Guitar

DUCT TAPE OR PACKING TAPE

Picture of your dream guitar →

Ribbon about 2ft long

STEP 1:
DRAW DREAM GUITAR ON BOX

STEP 2:
CUT IT OUT USING EITHER SCISSORS OR BOX CUTTER

STEP 3:
USING DUCT TAPE, ATTACH RIBBON TO THE BACK OF THE GUITAR →

HAPPINESS!

## What You Need

A sheet of posterboard or an old box, cut to about
   6" × 18"

Ribbon or string for a strap

First, gather your cardboard. The thicker the cardboard, the sturdier the instrument, but also the harder it is to cut. It's great if you can cut the whole guitar from one piece of cardboard, but if you need to cut a separate piece for the neck, you can use tape and some kind of reinforcement to hold it on. Our guitar is about 6" at its widest point and about 18" long.

Here are drawings of an electric guitar and an acoustic guitar. Use them as a guide to draw your child-sized guitar on the cardboard, then cut it out.

To finish your guitar, draw the strings, pickups, nuts, tuning pegs, fretboard, and so on, just as you see on page 232 in Appendix 2. Let your child decorate his guitar however he likes.

To turn your cardboard guitar into a *deluxe* cardboard guitar, take a photo of your favorite guitar to your local copy store. (Myriad online sites have photographs of guitars.) Have the store make two color photocopies—one of the neck and tuning pegs, one of the body of the guitar—and blow them up to the appropriate size for your child's guitar. Glue the photocopies onto your cardboard, and you'll have a very authentic-looking instrument.

Finally, you'll need to find a strap of some sort. Katryna always uses ribbon—thick ribbon from a holiday package works great—and attaches it to the guitar with duct tape, as shown in the drawing.

## Katryna

While most of his classmates were busily identifying velociraptors and *T. rex,* William was obsessed with guitars. He poured over books with pictures of them and stared at CD covers, learning which guitars were played by which of his favorite musicians. William had the good fortune of attending a Reggio-Emilio–inspired preschool. Much of the educational philosophy was reflected in the teachers' emphasis on discovering and exploring their students' passions. For my son, this meant that the teachers followed him on his guitar adventures.

First, he would bring in the guitars we made together at home. Then he would ask us to stay in the classroom to

*continued . . .*

help him make a guitar. Sometimes that was possible, but not always. One thing that I learn over and over as a parent is that just when I think that I'm letting my child down, I'm actually opening a door for him to figure out how to take care of himself. So William started making guitars by himself. First, he would ask the teachers for help, but all they could do was wield the scissors when it was too tough for his fingers. They didn't know how many pickups went on a Fender Strat. They didn't know whether the tuning pegs went on one side of the neck or both (for a Strat, it's one side). They didn't even know what a fret was.

But William did. He taught himself, the teachers, and eventually all the other students how to make a guitar, how to hold a guitar, and, of course, how to rock out. He's in a mixed-age classroom, and he's one of the oldest because his birthday falls in November. One afternoon when I went to pick him up, one of the teachers showed me a drawing by one of the youngest members of his class. A kid who was barely three and not at all drawn to the art table had done his first drawing at school. It was of a guitar. I bet William could have told me whether it was a Strat or a Tele.

## Shoebox Guitar

This guitar is great for a "pluckier" experience. The shoebox serves as the body of your guitar, and a piece of cardboard forms the neck. Ultimately, your child will be happy to have something to strum, but if authenticity is important to you, then use four strings (rubber bands) for a ukulele and six for a guitar. The number of strings may also be determined by the size of your shoebox.

## What You Need

A shoebox

3 pieces of cardboard, one cut to about 12" × 3" and two cut to 4" × 4" each

Duct tape

4 to 6 large rubber bands (Have a few extra on hand, as they sometimes break.)

A large marker, paint, construction paper, glue, and colorful tape for decoration

Ribbon or string for a strap

Cut a round hole in the middle of the top of the shoebox. This will serve as your sound hole. Roll up the two small pieces of cardboard tightly, and affix them to the shoebox on either side of the sound hole as shown. This will raise the rubber bands slightly above the box top, which makes them easier to strum.

Place the rubber bands on the top of the shoebox over the sound hole, and attach them with duct tape. Now place the top back on the shoebox and tape it shut.

Next, cut the tuning pegs out of the top of the cardboard. Draw frets on the neck with a large marker. Affix the cardboard neck to the shoebox with duct tape.

You can decorate your guitar now with paint, construction paper, or colorful tape. Don't forget to attach the string or ribbon to it to act as a strap.

Voilà! A pluckable guitar. Nothing is more satisfying than playing your homemade axe standing up.

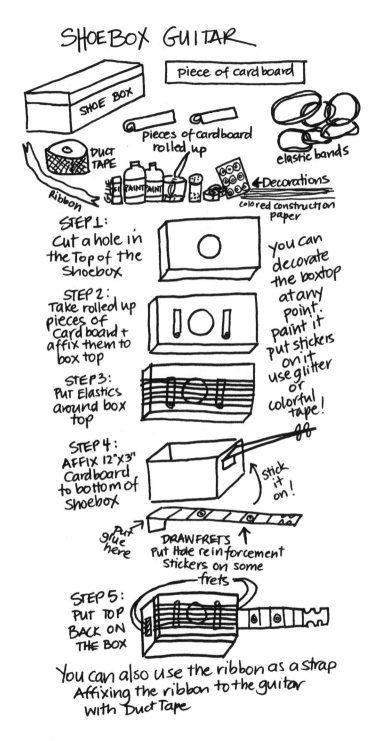

# How to Make A 12-String Guitar
## OR
## The Scrapwood Novelty Guitar

Find a piece of wood.

ours was about 8" x 24" x 1"

12 elastics/ rubber bands

24 Thumb Tacks

2 small eye hooks

twine or string for a strap

← you might need these too!

① Cut rubber bands to make them straight pieces of elastic

② Attach rubber bands to the board with thumb tacks

magnified look at the thumb tacks

③ Finally, attach eye hooks to each end and tie twine to hooks

## Twelve-String Guitar

William needed a twelve-string, so we made this version with a piece of scrap wood. He was completely convinced that he had a twelve-string Rickenbacker electric guitar.

### What You Need

A rectangular piece of wood. Ours was about
8" × 24" × 1" (Any size will do; be creative with what you have in your garage.)
12 elastic bands
24 thumbtacks
2 small eye hooks
Twine or string for a strap

A single piece of wood can serve as both the guitar body and the neck. Simply cut the elastic bands and use the thumbtacks to attach the ends of each to the top and bottom of the front of the plank of wood. Attach the small eye hooks to each end of the back of your wood plank, then tie a piece of twine to the hooks and used the twine as a strap.

### Katryna

The "frying pan" was the first electric guitar ever made and was so called because it was shaped like a frying pan—a small circle at the end of a long fretboard. It was invented by George Beauchamp in 1931, and although it bore a resemblance to its acoustic predecessor, it was really a novel-looking instrument. Once guitars were amplified electronically instead of by the sound of a hollow body of wood, there were no more rules about their shape.

There's a long history of guitars with novelty shapes. On the cover of Live Aid's album, there is a guitar shaped like Africa. Jimi Hendrix played the Flying V, a guitar whose body was shaped like the letter *V*. There are guitars shaped like hearts, stars, circles, and squares. They can be any shape you can imagine. My son decided at some point that he absolutely needed to have a twelve-string guitar. George Harrison plays a Rickenbacker twelve-string electric guitar on "A Hard Day's Night" and many of William's other favorite Beatles songs. To follow my son's lead, we asked him how to make the guitar he so desired, and he came up with the twelve-string version we describe here.

Despite its unusual shape, William was thrilled with his "Rickenbacker guitar." I have a feeling that's because his own vision was realized.

# SONGWRITING

As WE PROGRESS IN ANY ACTIVITY, ART form, or practice, there is a natural inclination to move from the role of practitioner to that of creator. So it is with songwriting. As we enjoy music, singing, and the particular form and structure of a song, we're inevitably drawn to writing songs of our own. For Nerissa, this happened early; by the age of six or seven, she was intentionally composing songs. She now considers songwriting to be her primary vocation. For Katryna, this interest and talent grew during young adulthood and flowered once she became a mother, and she terms it more an avocation. No matter where you find yourself on the spectrum of potential songwriting, we're here to encourage you to explore this wonderful, unique art form with your children. You have nothing to lose, and many fun and memorable songs to gain.

The earlier you start any endeavor, the less emphasis there is on perfection. Songwriting seems to be a completely organic and natural developmental stage. Many kids we see come through HooteNanny begin making up songs as soon as they can vocalize. Just as all children love to draw, and we can see the beauty and creativity in their work, all children are musical and will—given a good opportunity—compose songs. This should be encouraged with an open mind as to what constitutes a song. When your children first put fingers to paint or colored pencil to paper and present you with the results, you don't say, "That's not really a painting," or "That's not really a drawing." You say, "Wow! I love your painting!" We suggest that you do the same for the nascent bits of music your children produce and recognize them for what they are—songs.

The simple act of rhyming, the creation of two lines in which the last words of each sound alike, is beneficial to children's little growing synapses. Rhyming is a way of linking sound and sight, finding musicality in the utterances they hear around them. By age three or so, most kids will be able to identify rhymes. Lila is always delighted when she recognizes one and brings it to her mother's attention: "Mama! *Boat* rhymes with *float!*"

You don't need to rhyme or make sense or have a tune that resolves in order to make a satisfying song. However, all of these elements do help

in a particular way: they make the song easier to remember. One of the main positive attributes of a song is its memorability, and this quality is enhanced greatly by rhyming, meter, a coherent and consistent story, and certainly a tune that sticks in your head after only one or two listens.

But songwriting can be daunting at first. It can seem impossible to create anything new out of those same twelve tones, those same twenty-six letters. Yet you'll amaze yourself at how easy it is

## Nerissa

For me as a parent, nothing has been more fun than writing songs with my kids. Granted, I'm a professional songwriter. I'm sure that nothing was more fun for my mother than playing tennis with us. If you're a cook, you probably love baking muffins with your kids. Even so, I have a sneaking suspicion that the fun my family has writing songs has very little to do with our level

of skill. My husband, Tom, who would call himself a non-musician, has written many fabulous family songs.

My children write songs all the time. Johnny has an ongoing ballad called "Scooters and Busses and Trucks," and Lila regularly narrates her day to whatever tune happens to visit her head. For example, she wrote this after breakfast one day:

I am a milk container,
I do not laugh.
I am a milk container,
I do not laugh.

"Nice song," I told her as she danced and skipped around the kitchen, and I wrote down her lyrics lest I forget them. While I'm unsure about the efficacy (or wisdom) in praising my child for every little creative act, I did want to point out to her that what she was doing was writing a song: she was singing a tune she'd made up to words that occurred to her. She was narrating her experience, as surely as Chaucer.

*The Musical Family*

to become a songwriter if you let go of your own high standards and explore the medium with the innocence of a child. And have fun.

In this chapter, we demonstrate how you can teach yourself to be a songsmith by reworking the songs of others to make them your own. We start with one we grew up with and sang each spring at the Spring Revels: "The Muffin Man." To make it fresh, we added some characters. Later, we take on simple rhyming with "A Hunting We Will Go," and finally, we tackle meter with "Hal An Tow." Before long, you'll be composing original tunes of your own. If not you, certainly your children.

## ADDING LYRICS TO EXISTING SONGS

As art, songs easily lend themselves to reinterpretation. This can take the form of simply modifying or changing the order of lyrics to any given song.

For example, Amelia and William change the animals in "Organic Farm" every time they sing it; last spring, we had a mosquito on the farm, and yesterday it was a cherry picker. Reinterpretation can also mean writing additional lyrics to a favorite song. No matter how extensively you rework a song, modifying an existing one is a perfectly respectable way to introduce kids to the art of songwriting.

To start, pick a song your kids know, such as "Jingle Bells," "Row, Row, Row Your Boat," or even a current pop song if it's not too complicated. Then make up new words to describe something you're doing—taking a bath, making dinner, baking cookies. Your new lyrics don't need to rhyme, especially if you're using a traditional melody like the two we've suggested. A general rule of songwriting is that if the melody has a strong structure, rhyming is not as important. Leave space in the song for your children to add their own lyrics.

## The Muffin Man

WE DECIDED THAT OUR OLD FRIEND THE Muffin Man needed a family. There are no rhymes in our additional verses, but we did use the song's original alliteration—when two adjacent words have the same first letter or sound the same—to keep things interesting. Thus, the Muffin Man might be married to the Waffle Woman,

father of the Grapefruit Girl and Breakfast Boy, and sired by Granola Gramps (who was suggested by a parent in one of our HooteNanny classes).

To play in the same key as the recording, place the capo on the second fret and use the chord fingerings below.

# The Muffin Man

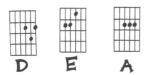

## 26

**D E A**

**D**
Do you know the Muffin Man,
    **E**        **A**
The Muffin Man, the Muffin Man?
**D**
Do you know the Muffin Man
    **E**    **A**    **D**
Who lives on Drury Lane?

Yes, I know the Muffin Man,       Yes, I know the Muffin Man
The Muffin Man, the Muffin Man.   Who lives on Drury Lane.

Our additional lyrics involve the Muffin Man's family:

Do you know the Waffle Woman?
Do you know the Grapefruit Girl?
Do you know the Breakfast Boy?
Do you know Granola Gramps?

*The Musical Family*

**T**HIS IS A GREAT SONG WITH WHICH TO practice songwriting. You only have to come up with one rhyme! The rest of the song is written for you. (In addition, the tune is the same as for "Noble Duke of York.")

## A Hunting We Will Go

**27**

E   B7   A

      **E**
Oh, a hunting we will go,
  **B7**
A hunting we will go,
     **E**
We'll catch a fox
     **A**
And put it in a box
     **E**    **B7**   **E**
And then we'll let him go.

Write more verses by making up your own rhymes:

We'll catch a kangaroo and put it in an igloo.
We'll catch a mouse and put it in a house.

We'll catch a dog and go for a jog.

Our all-time favorite rhyme was made up by a mom in our HooteNanny class named Lisa Papademetriou:

From here, think of other ways you can change this song. Perhaps you want to branch out to think of different verbs: "Oh, a sailing we will go," "Oh, a shopping we will go," or "Oh, a strolling we will go." You can narrate your entire day along with your three-year-old using this song.

## REWRITING EXISTING SONGS

There is an art to writing new song lyrics to pre-existing tunes. You can't just take a line and make it rhyme with another. A crucial element of song lyrics is internal meter. We know many wonderful poets who, when they try to turn their craft to songwriting, end up with long, rambling sentences that rhyme but don't scan; that is to say, the beat that naturally occurs by the inflection of the words is all off. Consider the following examples:

Hal an tow, jolly rumble-o,
We were up long before the day-o
To welcome in the summer,
To welcome in the May-o,
For summer is a-coming in and winter's gone
    away-o.

If you say these words out loud, there's a natural inclination to emphasize *Hal, tow, jo,* and *o* in the first line and *we, up, long,* and *day* in the second. This means there are four iambs per line, as common a meter for songs as five iambs is for poetry.

You could make a chorus that rhymes but doesn't scan (meaning the spots where you stress the syllables are all uneven and not pleasing to the ear); the iambs, or "feet," will be off:

Hal an tow,
I wish I were a golf pro.
Then my friends would
All be full of envy and woe.

Yuck! The lines technically rhyme, but the meter is all off. Where are the beats? Where is the emphasis in that silly third line? Do you emphasize the *All* or the *be* in the fourth? Let's try this:

Hal an tow,
Would I were a golf pro,
For then my golfing friends would be
Full of bitter envy-o.

See how this is better? Can you hear the internal rhythm?

A song has an inherent meter provided by the melody and rhythm of the music. This is why it's so helpful to start out with preexisting songs, replacing the lyrics with your own. To do this properly, rely on your newfound understanding of audiation (see page 109). As you get good at this, you can move on to your own melodies.

## Nerissa

You can think of *meter* as I use it as "the rhythm of the lyrics apart from the tune." It is defined for any poem or song by the number of "feet" in a line. The most famous kind of poetic meter—the one used by Shakespeare—is iambic pentameter, in which the sequence of the syllable types go "da DA, da DA, da DA, da DA, da DA" for each line. Lyricists want this kind of inherent rhythm. (It's easier than you think. Once you establish the meter in your mind, as with audiation, your brain seems to take over to maintain it. Try it for yourself!)

## Hal an Tow

**H**ERE'S HOW WE REWROTE THE LYRICS TO "Hal an Tow." This song was written to celebrate May Day and probably derived from "haul and tow," reflecting the agricultural work to be done during late spring and early summer. The original verses referenced legendary characters like Robin Hood, Little John, and Saint George, the patron saint of England. But we adapted this song for our music class, adding crocuses and dance steps so that it would feel like the coming of spring for our twenty-first-century kids.

While you're at it, dance along with the suggestions in the lyrics!

## Hal an Tow

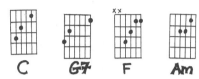

C    G7    C          G7
Hal an tow, jolly rumble-o,
C    G7    C                  G7
We were up long before the day-o
            C              F
To welcome in the summer,
                    G7
To welcome in the May-o,
        C          Am          G7          C
For summer is a-coming in and winter's gone away-o.

    C          Am
Take a step off to the left
        F              G7
And take one to the right-o.
    C              Am
Turn around and touch your toes
        G7          C
For winter's gone away-o.


Jump up in the air so high            Pretend to be a crocus
And crouch upon the ground-o.         Who shoots up from the ground-o
Wave your hands like willow trees     And makes a charming flower
For winter's gone away-o.             So we should feel so glad-o.

## OLD TUNE, NEW LYRICS

By the time we were adults, the tradition was well established in our family that whenever there was any kind of occasion—birthday, wedding, or graduation—someone, usually my father, would write a song for the event. He would take as his starting point a well-loved song known to our family members, usually "Torra Ly-ay" or "Harry Pollitt" or "The Unicorn Song"—songs with strong choruses that would lure listeners to sing along. He would then write many verses, telling a story and usually lauding the individual with a lot of praise and just a bit of teasing. He wrote the lyrics out on yellow legal paper with a simple dash above the syllable where the singer needed to put emphasis (as we discussed under meter earlier). Then he'd recruit his wife and daughters to stand up with him, hold his lyrics, and add harmonies to his song. All three of us daughters learned to write these kinds of songs, and to this day, an occasion isn't "real" if someone hasn't written a song to mark it as such.

Using a famous song, write your own lyrics to praise your birthday child, graduate, or bride/groom. Make the chorus something simple and memorable so your listeners can join you.

## OLD LYRICS, NEW TUNE

Once you've mastered the art and craft of rewriting previously existing songs, begin to make up your own tunes. At first, you can do this in the way we've already discussed—taking a preexisting song and writing a new tune.

When we were kids and our parents were driving us somewhere far away, we would do what most kids do and ask the world's most annoying question: "Are we there yet?" Once, when the answer came back "We're almost there," Nerissa promptly began singing this phrase to the tune of "Nanny Nanny Boo Boo" (which is the same tune as that for "Ring Around the Rosie," "Rain, Rain, Go Away," and the more prosaic "You're gonna get it!") Katryna joined in, and for the next ten minutes, our poor parents had to hear this "song" over and over. Finally, several car trips later, our mother said, "I don't like that song. Sing a different tune." So Nerissa wrote a lovely, melodious version—same annoying words but a lilting tune that no one could find fault with (proving that boredom plus a little parental nudging is the mother of invention).

Choose a song whose words you like but whose tune you don't—or at least something that can be improved on. Then experiment. You can go about tunesmithing in two different ways: intellectually or intuitively. If you have no musical experience per se, you'll probably want to just rely on your intuition and ear; see what comes out of your mouth as you play with your own notes and the words that are already written for you. See if one word wants more than one note (this is called a *melisma*):

Or just climb the scale:

If you have some training or once played an instrument, you can be a bit more academic. Find a chord progression that you know will work by sticking within a given key. Once you've established this, branch out. Add some unusual chords, or if you want, make up some chords by adding notes that don't normally "go" in that key. Sit at the piano and play your melody. Can you improve it by experimenting and substituting other notes?

If you can write music, all the better. Jot down what you've just composed. But if you can't write music, no need to worry. Most of the great pop songwriters of the twentieth century were musically illiterate (think John Lennon, Paul McCartney, Bob Dylan, and Billy Joel) Hint: if you do know simple chords, start and end on the tonic. (More about this in Appendix 2.)

*The Musical Family*

# Nerissa

Elizabeth, our father's sister, is a potter. She and her husband, Roy, and their son, John, lived out in the countryside west of Oneonta, New York. Roy was a painter, and John was one of those babies everyone knew would one day be a musician. At the age of six months, he sat on his mother's lap and listened intently to our Aunt Jenifer play the Bach Concerto in G on the piano with a focus and interest far more intense than you usually find in infants. As a small boy, John started playing piano using the Suzuki method. By the time he was in his late teens, he had taught himself the guitar as well, though he continued to play piano and organ at his church. He possesses an easy, natural musicality and is now a student at the Berklee School of Music.

In January 2003, I got a call that was not unexpected. "Roy is dying," my father told me. He had been partially paralyzed as the result of a car accident ten years earlier. He was almost eighty-two and had been failing for the past few months. He was in tremendous pain, and Elizabeth had been caring for him almost single-handedly, with the help of John, who was then nineteen.

We all drove out to the country to be with the family and help with funeral arrangements. At one point, Elizabeth said, "Nerissa, I want you to write a song for the funeral."

I hesitated. This was not a situation where we could throw some funny lyrics onto "Torra Lei Ay."

We had a gig in the Midwest between Roy's death and the funeral, and in a hotel room, I wrote a song called "This Is the Work That We Do." I can't overstate how satisfying it was to take that song back to Elizabeth and John, full of images of their life and of Roy, and to sing it for their friends and our family at his funeral. In that moment, standing in church and singing a song for my beloved uncle, every single choice I'd made in my life as an artist, writer, performer, and musician made perfect sense. Music does what nothing else can do. It's like water to clay: it softens, binds, holds the atoms of our experience together, and more than that, it holds us together. By the end of the song, the whole room was singing along on the chorus.

This wasn't the first time we'd performed an original song at a family member's funeral. Toward the end of my grandmother's life, as she was suffering from Alzheimer's, we wrote a song that we recorded for our first major-label album, *Gotta Get Over Greta*. The song, "All My Pretty Horses," was from the point of view of my silent grandmother, remembering back to her younger days. We recorded the song four months before she died, and Katryna and I sang it at her funeral. I was twenty-seven at the time, and I remember feeling that the act of singing an original song in front of my family elevated me from the role of child to that of adult coparticipant more than anything had so far in my life, including graduating from college or getting married.

## WRITING ORIGINAL SONGS

Songs come unbidden sometimes. As in any creative effort, there is a balance between seeking inspiration and just waiting for it to find you. (Picasso said, "Inspiration exists, but it has to find us working.") As you begin to write songs, turn your attention to the world as if you were a documentary filmmaker. Notice all the funny things your child says, and see if you can catch them on paper. Do the same with your own thoughts and responses to situations. Keep a little notebook or even just scraps of paper and a pen with you for this purpose, or type texts and send them to yourself on your cell phone. Nerissa often calls her home phone from her cell phone to sing little bits of tunes into the voicemail recorder.

Set a time for songwriting; perhaps a Saturday afternoon when the kids are napping, or if you want to write songs with your kids, try after they've woken up and had a snack. Listen to your recorded bits; sift through your notes. See what you find. Give yourself permission to write a terrible song—or several. All songwriters, especially the famous ones, wrote zillions of terrible songs before they ever wrote a good one. You might surprise yourself with your own learning curve.

If you play an instrument, take it out and strum or strike the chords you know. Let your eyes go blank; you want relaxed attention, not focused attention. You want to engage the part of your brain that comes up with images. Let your hands go where they will on the instrument. Try your lyrics over various chords until you find something you like. Let your kids help. Take a phrase and see who can come up with the most interesting tune.

Refer to your notebook of ideas. Noodle around until you've come up with something you like, then record it right away. Don't trust that you'll remember it. Nerissa has lost many, many bits of songs this way.

Eventually, you'll have your own family canon of original songs. Document this in any of the wonderful new ways technology has given us.

Create your own CD with basic recording software or make a video. Soon you'll have a library of original family tunes, some of which may be passed down for generations. We never know, on any particular day, when one of our creations will take on a life of its own.

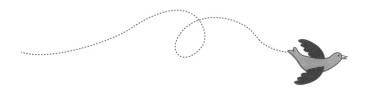

Part Three

# DEEPENING YOUR RELATIONSHIP WITH MUSIC

# 11

# MUSIC EDUCATION

**T**HERE'S REALLY NO NEED FOR YOU TO have any formal music education in order to love and appreciate your chosen favorites, be they the Clash, Brandi Carlile, Thelonious Monk, or Schubert. But if you and your child are curious about this art form, there is much to be gained by investigating the various wonderful music education systems artists and educators have developed over the years. This chapter is not intended as a final word on what music school or method is best (we actually have no idea or opinion about this); it's more an overview of the methods from which you may choose.

The real reason to take a music class is that it's fun to learn about music in a group setting, just as it's infinitely more interesting to be a part of Little League than to toss a ball back and forth in the yard. There is also, of course, the possibility of making friends with other music-loving families.

At some point, your child might want to deepen his relationship with singing and join a choir, take music theory to learn to compose, or learn to play an instrument. We get asked all the time if we would be willing to give someone's child singing lessons. Usually what the parents are looking for is an outlet for their child's singing. Our advice is to wait until your children have their adult voices—boys' voices change obviously and dramatically, but girls' voices change as well—to seek formal vocal training. If you have a child who wants to sing more, try to find her a spot in a chorus or in one of the wonderful group classes described here. Philosophies and schools abound; our advice is to see which individual teacher seems excited and experienced. There are many roads to Rome.

## FAMILY MUSIC CLASSES

Early childhood music programs, which are generally intended for children from birth to age five, tend to have similar philosophies. Anyone taking the time to teach music to babies and toddlers believes there is value and benefit to their work. A quick survey of their websites will give you lots of the same language: "Children are naturally/inherently/born musical beings." There are subtle differences and emphases in the different classes. If you're trying to choose, the most important thing to consider is the individual instructor. Does your child respond to the teacher? Do you?

The other essential thing is to compare the music. If you don't enjoy listening to or singing the music, you won't play the CD. The more exposure your child gets to the music, the greater the benefit to your whole family. Having said that, here are descriptions of the most popular early childhood music classes that may be available in your area.

### Music Together

This program has been around since 1987. It is a well-researched and carefully assembled series of forty-five-minute classes that run for ten weeks. Classes are multiage (birth to five), and adult involvement is the cornerstone of the program's philosophy. The belief is that the program is most effective when the whole family is invested in it. The goal is to teach children to become "musi-cally competent," which is defined as "the ability to sing in tune and move with accurate rhythm." To aid in that goal, tonal and rhythmic exercises are included on all CDs and during class.

The music is a mixture of traditional songs and original compositions written by Music Together founders Ken Guilmartin and Lili Levinowitz and it has a sweet, folkie vibe. Curricula always aim for a balance of time signatures and tonal modalities. There are songs from other languages and cultures so children can benefit from hearing as much musical variety as possible.

In most Music Together classes, children and adults are asked to participate at whatever level they desire. Even if a child is roaming around the room, it is understood that he's still soaking in the music that's being taught. You can find Music Together classes all over the world. Of course, as in everything, classes are a reflection of the instructor. Katryna took these classes with her kids and had a wonderful instructor named Lui Collins.

### Kindermusik

This program has been around for more than thirty years. The main difference on paper between Kindermusik and Music Together is that Kindermusik divides its classes by age. Some people prefer this approach because they don't want their quiet

nine-month-old to be in the same classroom as a noisy, bouncy five-year-old. Kindermusik is a little more focused on the benefits of music as it relates to other types of learning and not just for its own sake. They have four different levels of classes: birth to eighteen months, eighteen months to three years, three to five years, and five to seven years. The selections for Kindermusik will probably be what you think of as "kids' music" ("The Farmer in the Dell" and "Wheels on the Bus," for example). In the classes for older kids, children are taught using glockenspiels—small, metal xylophones. Kindermusik is found in the United States, Australia, New Zealand, the United Kingdom, Canada, and the Phillipines.

## Music for Aardvarks

Music for Aardvarks is a relatively new program that originated in New York City. Created by David Weinstone in 1997, it emphasizes the urban landscape—think taxis and skyscrapers. This program is hugely popular in New York and has spread to many other cities around the United States. It seeks to celebrate and explore the experience of growing up in a city. The music comes from a musician who was a former rock-and-roll musician who decided the children's music education scene needed a program that reflected the musical tastes of young urban parents. So if folk music and show tunes are hard for you to take, this course might be for you.

## HooteNanny

HooteNanny is the program we developed, so naturally, we're partial to its philosophy. For now, it is only available in our area, Western Massachusetts. There is no question that we hope the kids and parents in our classes become musically richer for the experience. We strive to create curricula that reflect a wide variety of musical and cultural experiences. We choose different time signatures, different modalities—minor, major, and so on. We include songs from different languages in every session. We try to reflect the current season, as well as the history of folk music. But our goal is to give HooteNanny families the language of music to help them forge connections. We want to give them music in the form of CDs, songbooks, and (most of all) songs that they will sing with and to each other. We want to give each family and also our community a platform where they can connect and dance and play. For us, the most important component of HooteNanny is to choose and compose music that everyone will enjoy.

We choose only music that we enjoy singing. We engage in the musical play with as much joy as the families do. If we find that we dread singing a given song, we'll cut it from the curriculum and replace it with something we love. HooteNanny families have been instrumental in helping us create our curricula. We firmly believe in the folk process. Some of our favorite songs have come from parents in our classes, including songs they learned from their grandparents. HooteNanny is about drawing all communities—generational, geographical, and cultural—together.

# EARLY MUSIC EDUCATION

As your child approaches school age—kids start Suzuki at age three, and other methods at around four to five—these are the "big four" in early music education. All except Suzuki are group classes, though Suzuki does employ group work as a crucial adjunct to individual lessons.

## Dalcroze Method

*I look forward to a system of music education in which the body itself shall play the role of intermediary between sound and thought, becoming in time the direct medium of our feelings.*

—Émile Jaques-Dalcroze

Émile Jaques-Dalcroze was a Swiss musician and educator who developed his method in the early 1900s. He believed that music was the fundamental human language and could best be learned kinesthetically—through the body itself. This program is widely known as a movement-based methodology, which means your child will do a lot of skipping around. Dalcroze classes also employ solfège (using the syllables *do, re, mi, fa, sol, la, ti,* and *do* to denote the notes of the C major scale) and improvisation, focusing on listening, learning

about intervals, phrasing, and form. The emphasis in a Dalcroze class is more on listening than literacy. Nerissa took a Dalcroze class when she was between the ages of four and six, and she loved it.

## Kodály Method

*Singing connected with movements and action is a much more ancient and, at the same time, more complex phenomenon than is a simple song.*

—Zoltan Kodály

The Kodály method (pronounced "Koh-die") was developed by Hungarian composer Zoltan Kodály in the middle of the twentieth century. Classes are primarily about singing, but children also come to understand what they are singing. Both through solfège and its related hand movements and through reading musical notation, children learn their way around the musical scales well enough to improvise and write their own music. There is an emphasis on studying the music of your own linguistic and musical heritage, which was more intrinsic to the philosophy in Hungary where Kodály taught than it is in American classrooms. Since the Kodály method is an amalgam of music education philosophies, teachers vary greatly. Every Kodály instructor has gone through rigorous training and brings that to the class, but different teachers are bound to emphasize different aspects. The core of the program is for kids to sing as easily as they speak their mother tongue.

## Orff Schulwerk

*Since the beginning of time, children have not liked to study. They would much rather play, and if you have their interests at heart, you will let them learn while they play; they will find that what they have mastered is child's play.*

—CARL ORFF

You probably already know Carl Orff from his masterpiece *Carmina Burana* (whose most famous cantata, "O Fortuna," has been heard in such movies as *Excaliber*, *Hunt for Red October*, and *The Doors*). Orff classes are known for their focus on engaging kids through their natural sense of play. We had an Orff teacher at the lower school we attended, and what we remember most is sitting on the floor, playing small xylophones and glockenspiels. Our experience involved learning rhythm patterns and music notation while playing coherent musical pieces together with our classmates. This was achieved in part by taking away bars of the glockenspiels so we were left with only notes that sounded beautiful together (rather like the Japanese Garden game, which uses only the black keys on the piano; see page 43). We felt like we were playing, but we were learning about quarter notes, syncopation, rests, and countless other musical ideas.

## Suzuki Method

*Musical ability is not an inborn talent but an ability that can be developed. Any child who is properly trained can develop musical ability, just as all children develop the ability to speak their mother tongue. The potential of every child is unlimited.*

—SHINICHI SUZUKI

Shinichi Suzuki developed his world-famous method in postwar Japan. He believed playing music was a way for children to build character traits and make their souls more beautiful. He saw clearly that music was a language, and as such, it could and should be learned at a very young age, preferably when the child was still preliterate. So Suzuki kids learn by ear, usually directly from their parents who attend the lesson with them. There is lots of praise and repetition in this method; the focus is on creating "a beautiful tone" and on daily practice (Dr. Suzuki says, "Knowledge plus ten thousand times" produces ability), but it is not for the parent who wants to drop her child off for a half hour or get the dishes done while her child practices. Parents learn right along with their children. There is a triangular relationship between the student, parent, and teacher, with the parent acting as the "at-home teacher." You don't need to know any more than your child does about music. Unlike the other three methods, Suzuki involves both a group class (where kids play for and with each other) and individual lessons. Both aspects are crucial to the method.

# LEARNING INSTRUMENTS: WHEN TO START AND WHAT TO START WITH

While yogurt containers and coffee tins make excellent drums and are an inexpensive way to introduce the concept of instruments, here are our recommendations should you want to add more instrumentation to your family's music making. (Also see chapter 9 on how to make your own instruments to form an orchestra or rock band.)

## Percussion Instruments

In chapter 3, we discussed the benefits of small percussion instruments. If your child is ready for something more, we think the piano is the best instrument for a child—we see it as the mother of all Western instruments. Underneath that gorgeous wood, ebony, and ivory are metal strings that reverberate when struck and make that lovely sound. This makes the piano not only a stringed instrument—with a wide range of notes for an experimenting player to discover—but also a percussion instrument, which means it takes only a small amount of pressure to sound a note (unlike a stringed instrument, which requires a little more dexterity, or a wind instrument, which requires a level of physicality that small children

don't yet have). But one of the best things about a piano is that it sits in the house inviting people to play it; it doesn't get put away in a case. Once it is introduced as a noise maker, most children have a hard time keeping their hands off it. It calls to them every time they walk past it.

More than that, when musicians talk to each other, they come back to the keyboard to translate the language of one instrument to another— the piano acts as a sort of musical baseline from which all other instruments and voices can meet. It is visual, aural, and kinesthetic; a piano has it all. It's hard to make a truly awful sound come from a piano. If you're looking for one instrument to choose for your child, piano has our vote. Having said that, we wouldn't force a child who was passionate about violin or guitar or drums to take piano first. There's nothing like passion, and we should never ignore that in our children.

## Stringed Instruments

There is a plethora of toy acoustic guitars out there. Most of them can't be tuned and are therefore nothing but props. Wouldn't it be wonderful if there were a small, guitarlike instrument that could act first as a prop and later as the real thing? Something your child could use as an air guitar, but which either you or your child (or both of you) could learn to play at some point? Something with fewer strings than a real guitar? Such an instrument does exist!

Behold the humble yet delightful ukulele; it's

even easier than the guitar and more portable to boot. Since it has just four strings, you can learn to play those three chords—and therefore, about a billion songs—in a very short time. The other benefit to having only four strings is that it's a little easier developmentally for a young person's brain and fingers. It tends to have nylon strings, which are less painful for a beginner or casual player than the steel strings on many adult guitars. Ukes are lightweight and cute, and they make great air guitars for small children. We highly recommend ukes and harmonicas as first instruments for kids up to age eight. You can get a standard uke for small children from birth to five years; it's just the right size for their bodies. As a child gets older, you can opt for a tenor ukulele, which is a little larger—about the size of a child-sized guitar.

Perhaps because of the popularity of the Suzuki method, which was founded by a violin player, tiny violins abound in the marketplace. Violin is a terrific first instrument for a child if you can afford the rental fee and the cost of lessons. Violin isn't as intuitive as piano—without some guidance, it's difficult to know where to finger the notes, how to tune it, and even how to care for the bow—but there are reasons it is such a beloved instrument for the preschool set. When a violin fits its small player, the child can easily maintain it, and the lessons she learns in playing and caring for her instrument are huge. Plus, it's just plain cute to see a little person mastering such a complex and gorgeous instrument. Tiny cellos are also available

for little ones, so if you can stand the sound of an occasionally screechy bowed instrument and have several children, you can soon have the beginnings of your own string quartet.

## Instruments You Play with Your Hands and Mouth

For the most part, instruments you play with your mouth require too much control for really young musicians. A child is generally not ready to take on a brass or woodwind until fourth or fifth grade. The strength and control needed to get a pleasing sound is a skill that comes only in later childhood. It can be discouraging for a child to have a wind instrument as his first musical experience. Unlike playing a piano or ukulele, it can take hours of practice time before he can consistently make a satisfying sound on a clarinet or trumpet.

There are a few notable exceptions to this rule. The recorder can be attempted at a younger age. In our elementary school, every third grader was given a recorder and weekly lessons. Though the recorder can screech if blown too hard, most children that age can modulate their breath to make a mellifluous sound. Recorders are inexpensive and small enough for an eight-year-old's fingers to reach all the sound holes. They're often used in elementary schools to teach children how to read music. We were given several recorders when our children were four and under. They were dubbed "closed-door" instruments until lessons were available. The temptation to try to make them sound like trumpets was too great in our household to allow them to be played in the kitchen while dinner was being made.

The most accessible wind instrument is definitely the harmonica. A four-year-old, given the right key, can play along to any song in that key. No note she plays will be wrong. That's pretty satisfying for a young player, and even better, it's pleasing to adult ears. Harmonicas are also wonderful instruments for adults who love a sing-along but are self-conscious about singing. The most common harmonicas are dedicated to one key or another. If you get yourself a C, a D, and a G harmonica, you'll be able to join in on most songs at your next potluck sing-along. Simply ask the guitarist or pianist what key the song is in and choose that harmonica.

Of course, there is an instrument that might be considered even easier than the harmonica— the kazoo. Some music snobs scoff at the kazoo even being called an instrument, since its "music" comes merely from the humming of the practitioner and not from any manual dexterity. Who cares? We have yet to meet a child who isn't amused and satisfied by making the cool humming sound that only a kazoo can achieve. Speaking of cool sounds extending from one's voice, try taking a drum, turning it upside down, and singing into it. You will hear a marvelous echo that turns your drum into a kind of crazy microphone.

## Katryna

My daughter started taking piano lessons when she was in first grade. My basic rule of thumb about when to start lessons was to wait until the child can repeat a rhythm accurately and can sing on pitch. This theory derives from the notion that you want the child to know when she's making a mistake. If your child is playing a simple melody and can't tell that she's playing a wrong note, it will be hard if not impossible to teach her.

At six, my daughter's pitch was still inconsistent. One day, she came home from school and played a familiar tune on the piano. I was stunned. When I asked her where she'd learned it, she said that her class had sung the song in music that day. I realized her inconsistency of pitch when singing was due to physiological development and not her ear. She could hear and match pitch, but her ability to control her voice box was just a little slower. My standards might have been a little high too.

*Deepening Your Relationship with Music*

## Instruments You Play with Your Body

Don't forget your voice, clapping hands, snapping fingers, and stomping feet! Our friend, the musician Chris Smither, has made his foot stomps so essential to his sound that he carries a board with him and sets up a mic for it at concerts so the rhythms his feet tap out along with his guitar playing are amplified.

### Nerissa

The beloved classic *Peter and the Wolf* is certainly one of the favorite parts of Katryna's and my family musical canons, and it's a great way to introduce kids to the instruments that make up an orchestra. This piece was written by Russian composer Sergei Prokofiev, who was commissioned by the new Soviet Union to write it to encourage and educate children about music and the various functions of the instruments in an orchestra. Legend has it that Prokofiev composed the piece in four days, and it was first performed on May Day 1936. The characters in the story are represented by particular instruments: Peter is the violin, Grandfather is the bassoon, the hapless duck is the oboe, and the bird is the flute. The hunters are represented by both booming kettle drums and a delightfully Russian harmonic-minor melody that marches them into the scene.

Lila was enchanted with this piece from the moment she first heard it and announced shortly afterward that she was going to learn to play the flute, the violin, and the French horn. She was, at three, fearless about such things, just as Peter is fearless about wolves. During this time, we came across Lila banging on her father's conga drums with a wooden rolling pin, her arms rising grandly high above her head. "I'm playing the kettle drums," she announced. "I'm the hunters."

"Peda Woof" is Johnny's bedtime music these days. We sit on the bed listening together. We stare into each others' eyes, reacting at the dramatic moments and speculating about what's going on in the musical story. When we're having a hard time getting him to go to bed, we play this recording on his little boom box and let it play on repeat. We often have to

*continued . . .*

## CHOOSING ONE INSTRUMENT OR MANY

So which instrument is the right one for you or your child? How do you choose? How is poor Lila going to decide between the French horn, the flute, and the violin? How is Amelia going to decide between the piano, the guitar, or the bass?

We don't know. We come back to our usual theme, which is that we care much more about kids and parents gleaning joy from the family practice than we do about creating little maestros (if we did care about maestros, we might be uptight about encouraging our kids to choose early so they can collect ten thousand hours of practice all on one instrument). We know a teenager who diligently practices seven different instruments, and knowing how a familiar one works does help her understand how a new one might, just as knowing a foreign language can help a student learn even more about his native tongue.

Go with your gut if you're choosing an instrument for yourself. What appeals to you? Instruments can be sensual and irrational and personal. You'll be developing a relationship with your instrument that is every bit as real and complex as the relationship with a friend. As for your child, go with her passion, her rage to master. If you want her to play the guitar but she's obsessed with the upright bass, no amount of cajoling will change her mind, and she won't practice the instrument you're pushing on her.

*Deepening Your Relationship with Music*

(Feel free, however, to institute a rule that she can only play instruments she can pick up and carry herself.)

Remember, instruments can and should be rented from your local music store. Don't buy until you're sure your child wants to pursue the practice and has stopped growing. Meanwhile, shop around. Rent different instruments. Give each one a minimum of six months with regular practice (several times a week).

If your child really can't decide, and time or money or both are obstacles, you'll need to help him make a decision. As we keep saying, the tie goes to the better teacher. Even if you hate the sound of a poorly played stringed instrument, if there's a fantastic cello teacher and only a mediocre piano teacher in your area and your child is enthusiastic about both, we suggest opting for the cello.

Once you or your child has selected his instrument, find a good teacher. If there isn't one, find a good book and a musical friend to help direct you. You'll be amazed at how quickly your child will learn. Music is a language, and like all languages, kids' brains master them at light speed. And if the instrument is chordal (uke, guitar, piano, or accordion), it takes only three chords to make something that truly sounds like music.

## FINDING A GOOD TEACHER

Don't worry as much about the methodology of the teacher (Suzuki, Orff, Dalcroze, solfège, or just your neighborhood piano guru) as the quality of the teaching. Since we're probably annoying you by now in our exhortations to find that good teacher, we'll just offer some concrete tips on how to do it:

• Listen to word of mouth! When you notice that a friend's child loves her lessons, ask the parent who the teacher is.

• Ask a local musician. Musicians often moonlight (or daylight) as music teachers, and they tend to know each other, the local music scene, and who's good.

• Ask your school's music teacher for recommendations (unless you have reason not to agree with him, in which case, ask and do the opposite).

• Ask at your local instrument shop/music store. The folks who work there see all those tiny violins coming and going. They'll have a good idea about who the good teachers are.

• Remember, every teacher is different, and every kid is different. One style might work beautifully with your older child, while a different teacher with a different style might work better with your youngest.

• Does the teacher have a long wait list? Get on it now, even if your baby is three years away from starting his first iteration of "Hot Cross Buns." You can always get off the list if your child exhibits more interest in kicking a soccer ball (or his

brother) than that gigantic black box (piano) in the living room. You have nothing to lose. And maybe if you're so interested, you're the one who should sign up for lessons.

• Does your child look forward to and enjoy her lessons? Does she grab her flute and race to the door when you tell her it's time to go? This is more important than her future at Julliard. If she's not enthusiastic, we'd certainly opt for trying a different teacher before abandoning lessons.

## BUYING INSTRUMENTS

Parents often ask us how much to spend on an instrument for their child. "I don't want to buy a Stradivarius, in case she ends up not playing it," they say. "But if the instrument isn't good quality, she might not want to practice." All true. There are no hard-and-fast rules here. John Lennon learned to play guitar on his mother's old, out-of-tune banjo. Small children might prefer a turned-over yogurt container to the tongue drum you spent $80 on at the church auction.

Any instrument you think of getting new, you can get used for less. As with furniture, instruments appreciate with age; like the Velveteen Rabbit, they don't become "real" until they've been well played. A ten-year-old guitar will sound richer and more sonorous than a six-month-old instrument. It might be easier to find the exact model you're looking for in a big store, but in this age of the Internet, even that shouldn't be a stumbling block, although you might have to take the musical qualities of the instrument on faith.

On the other hand, when you go to a music store to "test-drive" instruments, you have the advantage of being able to hold and hear them, which is an argument in favor of the new. But if you're patient, it's always better to buy used. It's cheaper, you'll get a better instrument, you won't be contributing to the erosion of the planet, and in most cases, you'll be putting some extra money directly into the pocket of the broke musician who's hocking his instrument.

Moreover, bargains abound. In our estimation, $800 is a good price for a new guitar for a professional, whereas $400 is a good price for a decent guitar that doesn't need to be played onstage. Go lower than that and the workmanship may be

questionable. A good-quality used guitar can be found for considerably less, and a well-loved guitar is probably a better instrument than a new one costing four times as much. For your child, you need a guitar that is tunable and easy to play. There's a big difference between a toy and a playable instrument. Listen to a note as it's played on fret one and then fret thirteen. It should sound like a clean octave. If it doesn't, don't buy it.

If you're looking for a piano, understand that there are scads of people looking to unload theirs. For the cost of having it moved, you might be able to get a very good one.

## A WORD ABOUT PRACTICING

One of the best reasons to take up an instrument or accept the challenge of calling ourselves musicians is to come face-to-face with the notion of practicing. No other art form requires its practitioners to, well, practice in a more obvious way.

In his wonderful book, *Outliers: The Story of Success*, Malcolm Gladwell writes that if we want to master anything, we need to spend ten thousand hours doing it. One of the first examples he uses is about concert violinists and pianists. In the study he cites, researchers "couldn't find any 'naturals,' musicians who floated effortlessly to the top while practicing a fraction of the time their peers did, Nor could they find any 'grinds,' people who worked harder than everyone else, yet just didn't have what it takes to break into the top ranks. Their research suggests that once

## Nerissa

My father refused to teach me to play guitar, let alone buy me one, until I was eleven. His reasoning was that my hands weren't big enough to fit around the neck and that I would hurt them by trying. Looking back, I'm glad he made me wait. I think I wanted a guitar from the age of six or seven, and having to wait those five years made my desire grow and intensified my determination to play. When I did receive that first guitar for my birthday, I learned to play it immediately. (With the guitar I received an index card from my father with the words "Good for five guitar lessons" in his neat handwriting. As wonderful as the guitar was—I named it Michelle after the Beatles song, and it was my most prized possession—the lessons were even better.)

The guitar he bought me probably cost about $80. It wasn't a fine instrument, and I no longer have it. But I did love it when it was my only guitar, and I played it constantly. When I graduated from high school, my father bought me a fine, handmade classical guitar. Its quality told me that he believed I would continue to play guitar for the rest of my life. I'm not sure I would have appreciated that guitar as a beginner, but as a teenager, I felt very proud; it was like an affirmation that my father had faith in my long-term relationship with music.

Years later, when I was within two days of giving birth to my daughter, I got it into my head that our family needed a piano. So I went on Freecycle.com and posted: "Wanted: piano." I got back dozens of responses and offers, mostly for pianos that needed a bit of work. Basically, I could have had twelve free pianos if I had been willing to pay for their removal from the owners' houses. I ended up paying $200 for an incredibly nice antique upright with ivory keys. Now my kids bang away at it whenever they pass by. Someday soon, I hope, we'll be hearing "Twinkle, Twinkle, Little Star." Maybe in ten years, that will turn to "Für Elise" and in twenty, to "The Moonlight Sonata." A mother can dream.

# Katryna

As we were approaching my daughter Amelia's ninth birthday, it was clear to us that she wanted her own guitar. She was able to reach her hand around her dad's electric guitars and basses, but the acoustic guitars were too big to fit on her lap. She was beyond the toy (untunable) guitars that we had.

My husband remembered having a small acoustic guitar as a child. It kept its tune; his fingers could fit around the neck to form chords; and it had nylon strings, which are gentler on little fingers. We proceeded to search for just such a guitar. I considered buying one off the Internet, but my husband was nervous about purchasing an instrument without playing it. I trolled Craigslist and eBay for used kids' guitars in our area; they were harder to find than I would have imagined. In the end, we went to our local music store. We had the choice of a Martin with steel strings for $300 or a Yamaha with nylon strings for $180. The Martin's neck was a little smaller, and more important, it was fun to play. We ended up spending the extra money because its sound quality was satisfying, and we figured that if Amelia rejected the guitar, we would want to play it ourselves. I've never regretted the decision.

Nerissa gave Amelia an easy guitar Beatles book on the same birthday that we gave her the Martin. She can spend hours now in her room, figuring out new chords from the charts in the book and singing the whole Beatles catalog. I love to play her guitar, but I rarely get my hands on it. It also fits easily into our small car when we go on family trips. I still think I would have bought a used child-sized guitar if I'd found one. But since they're so scarce, maybe it will be easy to get our $300 back when Amelia outgrows the Martin.

a musician has enough ability to get into a top music school, the thing that distinguishes one performer from another is how hard he or she works. That's it."[1]

Over the course of writing this book, we have heard or overheard versions of the following statistics from several different sources: "It takes twenty tries to get it right. If you want to do something well, you have to repeat the movements fifty times." Twenty, fifty, ten thousand—the number isn't the point. The point is that spending time doing anything with focused attention will increase your skill. And most of us prefer performing activities that utilize our skills.

What we like about this is the suggestion that there is no such thing as talent: just motivation plus elbow grease. We also like the idea that repetition presents our children with a powerful life lesson in how to move incrementally and humbly along, taking small steps toward a goal.

For the purpose of encouraging families to make music a rich and essential part of their lives, we think it's ideal for young children to approach music as play. If your family is already playing together and your child sees music as fun, rather than as another chore that he gets punished for neglecting, then the whole experience of music becomes an extension of a beloved family pastime and not an academic or extracurricular exercise.

Nevertheless, while your child may have the desire to learn an instrument, the reality is that it can be a real struggle to practice—for children

and often for us. Somerset Maugham said, "I despise Resistance. I will not let it faze me; I will sit down and do my work." This attitude is a useful one for parents to adopt when it comes to "getting" a kid to practice. Worry about carving time out of a day and not how your child is "progressing." Reward him for showing up. And above all, model this kind of behavior yourself, if not on an instrument, then in some other way. If you're a runner, stay loyal to your training schedule. If you're a scrapbooker, lovingly maintain those books. And if you play an instrument, play it regularly and with joy.

Our father never seemed to practice his guitar, but every single evening, as he waited in the bathroom for the tub to fill, we could hear him strumming away and singing whatever new song he was teaching himself. It was by learning new songs rather than practicing scales that his skills improved. His bathtime singing was certainly not for our benefit, but it did much to convince us that practicing our instruments would make a wonderful difference in our lives.

Finally, we've written a lot about the joys of simply being a music appreciator and listener, but making music can be hard work. There are moments of frustration if you choose to pick up an instrument or go deeply into your singing. There will certainly be moments of disharmony, bad notes, and annoying mistakes. But this is part of life. If you don't plunge into your musical practice, you can certainly rest in the music others have made, and this is perfectly fine. But if you (or your children) do want to master an instrument or singing, you have to learn to get comfortable with frustration, disharmony, bad notes, bad days, and plateaus where you don't see improvement for a while. If you can model acceptance of these imperfections to your children, you will give them an unparalleled gift.

## Nerissa

As a kid, I took piano lessons. I showed up for the teacher, played my little Bach minuets from the *Anna Magdalena Notebook* painfully and badly, and resisted practicing as much as I could. When I was thirteen, after months of nagging me to keep my fingernails trimmed, my piano teacher frustratedly told me, "Listen, Nerissa. You're going to have to decide. Are you a girl who plays the piano, or are you a girl with long fingernails?"

I decided I was a girl with long fingernails and thus ended my career as a pianist. But fortunately, I had still managed to learn something. I knew my way around a piano keyboard, and I could read music.

I'm grateful that I know what I know about the piano. I'm grateful for the years of lessons. I didn't always enjoy them, but that didn't stop me from loving music. Sometimes I wish that teacher hadn't given me the fingernail ultimatum. My abilities grew during the phases of my life when I wanted to experience what I felt when I saw others playing and singing. Sitting

around the campfire in the Adirondacks, watching the older people sing their songs, I wanted to be one of them. I wanted to make people feel the way the singers and players were making me feel. This desire propelled me toward a more faithful practice when I started playing guitar (right after abandoning piano), and my skills increased.

I notice that my one-year-old son bangs on the piano every third time he circles the playroom. My daughter pulls two unmatching sticks out of the box where we keep all of our percussion instruments and beats on one of the many small drums we own. I know this because I catch her at it and because I find the sticks in random places around the house. When I tidy up at the end of the day, I almost always find myself putting those unmatching sticks away. Of course, I don't tell her to practice her drumming any more than I tell her to practice playing with her dollhouse or making puzzles. To her, it's all play.

Lila's little ukulele (she calls it a "yoko-lele," which is somehow the perfect descriptor for the timbre of that instrument) is constantly in her hands. She doesn't know any chords, but she loves to hold and strum it. Johnny, at sixteen months, was plucking individual strings and attempting to turn the tuning pegs. The jury is out, of course, on whether a fond-

ness and affection for an instrument will translate to good musicianship later in life. Frankly, I care much more about them maintaining that fondness for music than becoming skilled players. Music is too important. If they have the rage to master, I trust they will find their way to a more intense practice than their mother's attempt at piano.

## Katryna

Amelia's piano teacher is very clear about her expectations for her students' practice. The first year, Amelia was given five tasks that she was to do twice a week. They were always a

mixture of boring (such as learning scales) and fun (improvising and getting comfortable with the instrument).

Amelia is a pretty driven kid; I rarely have to remind her to do her homework. Still, for those first couple of years, I had to pester her to practice. Practice was about ten to twenty minutes twice a

week—completely doable for a six-year-old. Any more might have made her resentful. I could look at the week's calendar and know that there were busy days and less-busy days. I needed to remember to help her get practice sessions in on her less-busy days.

By year three, something happened. I noticed that

when I told her to practice, she would stay at the piano longer. She would check off all the tasks her teacher had given her and then play what she wanted. Soon, she couldn't walk past the piano without playing a few notes. We heard that famous Bach Minuet more times than I can count. It had taken two years for her to feel like the piano was her instrument.

Holly Near, the wonderful folk singer and activist, once said, "The only way to creativity is through boredom." I tell my kids that all the time. I know they need space, time, and boredom to discover what really makes them come alive. After third grade, Amelia went to music camp for five days at the start of the summer. She played a half dozen instruments and learned to compose songs, write charts, and perform. She hung out with girls who also wanted to make music. Then she came home and had empty days for about a month. I rarely heard the perennial, "Mommy, I'm bored." She knew that if she was bored, she could just go and make music. She'd sit at the piano playing Cyndi Lauper or Bach. She'd pick up her guitar and try to master barre chords. She'd sing herself to sleep every night, usually to a tune she had made up herself. Music belongs to her now, and the days of bugging her to play the piano are long gone. I still need to ask her if she has practiced what her teacher asked her to, but that's usually all it takes: "Stop playing Bach for a minute and make sure you've done all of your exercises!" It reminds me of when she was little and I had to tell her to stop eating her peas and take a bite of chicken. They were both good foods, but she needed balance and variety.

# TIPS TO GET YOUR CHILD TO PRACTICE

The idea behind the Suzuki method is that learning an instrument is much like learning to speak; if a child hears language spoken at a certain age (from birth to age two), he will learn it effortlessly. The same can be true for an instrument. The child learns the instrument kinetically, aurally, and naturally. Just as he learns to talk long before he learns to read or write, so a young violinist learns to play his instrument before he learns to read or write music.

Parents are crucial to the Suzuki method. One parent is designated the home teacher and is responsible for creating a practice space and being mentally (as well as physically) present for the whole experience of practicing. Parents are encouraged to create a half-hour practice time *every day*, but fortunately for Nerissa and Lila, their teacher says to just do a couple of tasks every day. In the beginning, it ended up being five to ten minutes most days, and that was feasible. Later, their enthusiasm grew naturally along with Lila's increased skill, so that a half-hour practice seemed delightful and essential.

Here are some wonderful practice ideas that are inspired by the wisdom of the Suzuki method:

- Have your child practice in pajamas.
- Pretend the practice session is a concert.
- Don't dwell on one part of the lesson too long.
- Practice when your child isn't tired.
- Have your child teach you how to play.
- Applaud your child's efforts!
- Hug your child a lot.
- If your partner can't be at the lesson, tell him or her how well your child is doing.
- Show how excited you are when your child achieves his goals.
- Be respectful of your child's abilities and frustrations.
- Invent games to make practicing fun at all times.
- Sing a part before you play it.
- Listen to the radio for rhythms you use in practice.
- Find something good in every attempt.

- Periodically practice with another student and parent.
- Color in a practice chart as you complete daily practice sessions. Or use lots of stickers for your practice chart, and extra stickers for the violin case.
- Play for your child's stuffed animal or doll.
- Give your child a small plant (preferably one that grows quickly). Water this plant each time she practices (a half-full Dixie cup works well without drowning the plant), and see how it grows.
- Make up your own song and play it for your teacher!

## HOW NOT TO LOSE YOUR MIND WHEN YOUR CHILD PRACTICES

So you've achieved your goal. She's found the perfect instrument, and it's no problem at all to get her to practice. In fact, she can't stop playing it and doesn't want to do anything else. Maybe it's the viola or the trumpet. Most instruments don't necessarily sound sonorous and sublime when a child first puts bow to string or lips to mouthpiece. How do you support your child's enthusiasm while protecting her from the barbs of her older brother or even her other parent, who might not be as enthusiastic as you and she are?

On the one hand, budding musicians can be very sensitive. If we had a dime for every person who has come up to us over the years to tell us how he was shamed out of singing by some mean kids in choir or teased about the chalk-on-blackboard effect of her violin playing, we'd be rich. On the other hand, if you were to interview every rock-and-roll drummer whose band broke the top one hundred, the percentage of them who were told to "Keep it down!" would probably hover around 98 percent.

When your child picks up an instrument for the first time, you can explain about practice time versus quiet or family time. Just as you help to create the container of space and time for your child to practice in, you also need to create containers of space and time for quiet. All of us, including musicians, need to learn that we're not the center of the universe. We live in community with others, and you can explain that even Yo Yo Ma might irritate his family if he were to practice in the middle of the kitchen while supper was being prepared. Even Sarah McLachlan has a private piano room where she practices. At Katryna's house, there is a policy for both closed-door instruments and closed-door toys. When either of these is too loud for the rest of the family, the player needs to find a room with the door closed. To everything its place and time.

## When Your Eight-Year-Old Decides She's a Drummer

We have many fears about what our kids' choices might be as they grow and become autonomous. Will they do drugs? Get tattoos? Have terrible taste in music? These are Nerissa's fears. Katryna's top three were that either of her kids would want to be a ballerina, a smoker, or a drummer.

She's still scared of the smoking, but the other two have come true, and she actually thinks it's wonderful. Owing to the fact that her husband, Dave, is a music producer, they have always had a drum kit of some sort in their house. The studio is separated from the rest of the house, so the kids don't always have access to it, but for Amelia's ninth birthday party, they moved the kit into the house.

This made Katryna think about how to survive life with a budding drummer:

**1.** Start with something other than real drums. Katryna bought a set of three hatboxes at IKEA. For about ten bucks, she had something that satisfied William's yen for a rock-and-roll drum kit. You can use an old cardboard box for a kick drum, and the three different-sized hatboxes served us well for the toms and snare. William found that the snare drum really came to life when he put a shaker egg inside it.

**2.** Don't use real drumsticks. No need for that volume unless you're on a big stage or in a studio. We happen to have drum brushes around our house, but if you don't, chopsticks work well. For an even lighter sound, cut the pointy tips off of some shish kebab skewers and use those.

**3.** Put the drum kit outside. This will require a weatherproof kit. Katryna made one out of those big buckets people use for gardening. Our local supermarket was getting rid of them for a dollar apiece. Old plastic flowerpots work well too.

**4.** For a more advanced player, there are electronic drum kits. You just need to be careful of the volume in the headphones if you go this route; check it often. We only get one set of ears, and children don't always know what a safe limit is.

**5.** Watch any YouTube video of the Beatles' *Let It Be* movie. Note that Ringo covers his drum with blankets. Many children will be so impressed with this that they will want to follow suit.

**6.** Get a detached garage and several layers of insulation to soundproof it.

*Deepening Your Relationship with Music*

# FAMILY TRADITIONS

W E HOPE WE'VE DEMONSTRATED HOW to begin to discover and nurture your musical family by bringing music into the everyday, by demystifying music and claiming it as your birthright. This chapter is all about how, once you've established a musical foundation, you can begin to use music to deepen family bonds by bringing it into special times. Music can take us through the hard times, the scary times, the mundane times, and the joyful times. It can be the glue for family traditions that last a lifetime and outlive you, even if your chosen seasonal traditions are off the beaten path. We've learned that music can be the element that connects us to our loved ones throughout our lives, from before birth to death.

We are hardwired to encode memory while still in the womb, and we can hear music through the amniotic fluid. In *Mindsight: The New Science of Personal Transformation*, psychiatrist and neuroplasticity expert Daniel Siegel writes about how

he would sing the wonderful Russian song we learned from Pete Seeger, "May There Always Be Sunshine," when his wife was pregnant: "I knew the auditory system was wired up enough to register sound coming through the amniotic fluid. Then in the first week after each child was born, I invited a colleague over for a 'research study.' (I know, it wasn't controlled, but it was fun.) Without revealing the prenatal song, I sang three different songs in turn. No doubt about it— when babies heard the familiar song, their eyes opened wider and they became more alert, so that my colleague could easily identify the change in their attention level. A perceptual memory had been encoded."[1]

Perceptual memories are not necessarily conscious ones; rather, they form a kind of mood backdrop to our experiences, which can be pleasant, unpleasant, or neutral. Obviously, as parents, we want to create as many pleasant experiences as we can, and music is a sweet and efficient way to do this.

As we get older, music continues to play a vital role in connecting us to our family. An article in the *Los Angeles Times* titled "Brain Booster" states, "Five months after we are conceived, music begins to capture our attention and wire our brains for a lifetime of aural experience. At the other end of life, musical memories can be imprinted on the brain so indelibly that they can be retrieved, perfectly intact, from the depths of a mind ravaged by Alzheimer's disease."[2] Both of our grandmothers suffered from Alzheimer's at the end of their lives, and in both cases, the music their children and grandchildren made reached them in a way nothing else could. Our paternal grandmother—the one who believed herself tone-deaf—danced, beaming and holding hands with the rest of us, while our father lead the family in "Lord of the Dance" one year at Christmastime. It brought her to life during a visit when she had previously seemed irretrievably far away from the rest of us.

Our maternal grandmother lived to be 103. She too suffered from dementia for the last decade of her life. Grandmummy was not the kind who played with kids in the typical way. We didn't bake cookies with her or cuddle up and read "Lyle, Lyle Crocodile," but she did take us to museums, theater productions, Paris, Kenya, and Greece. She taught us yoga, encouraged us to try acupuncture, and massaged our heads when we had headaches.

She loved to watch us sing and perform. We don't believe she recognized us for the better part of her last decade, but she was happy when we visited. She loved to see her great-grandchildren. When we went to visit, we would hug her and kiss her and hold her hand. Katryna sometimes played piano, and we all sang to her, sometimes together, surrounding her with our voices the way we do with babies. Grandmummy had been a performer herself—an actress and a dancer—but never considered herself particularly musical, believing that she lacked the talent her two daughters clearly evinced. Ironically, as her critical faculties failed her, she seemed to be left with the ability to simply enjoy music, perhaps the way she had as a child.

## MUSIC IN HARD TIMES: THE VALUE OF SAD SONGS

One summer when we were kids, we were on vacation in Maine. It was bedtime, but it was still light outside, and we lay in our little beds in our great-aunt Barbara's guestroom. We could hear the grown-ups singing downstairs, and although we didn't think about it at the time, our parents must have been engaged in exactly the kind of music making we're encouraging you to do in this book. Aunt Barbara had probably asked them to sing for her friends. At any rate, we could hear the sound of our father's voice singing "Banks of the Ohio," and our mother's voice joined his. It's a really sad

# Nerissa

I recently learned that the definition of *nostalgia* is literally "pain for home"; *nosta* meaning "home" and *algia* meaning "pain." Nothing brings me home faster or more surely then the sound of one of my parents' voices.

When I was seventeen, I rediscovered the folk trio Peter, Paul and Mary. My parents took us to a concert at Wolf Trap, an outdoor music venue near where we grew up in northern Virginia. Their music resonated with me instantly, and I knew that I had heard them before, specifically on a children's LP titled *Peter, Paul & Mommy*. We had worn the grooves out on this record back in the seventies. But more than that, when I heard them singing in front of me, their music reverberated off my bones. I wanted to get up and dance, sing along at the top of my lungs, celebrate a kind of musical homecoming. They felt like family. It was easy for me to sing along, even when I didn't know all the words.

I went home and dug up all my parents' old Peter, Paul and Mary LPs and played through them one by one. There was a certain song on one of them called "For Baby (for Bobby)," on which Mary sang lead. The moment I heard it, I was overwhelmed with that feeling of nostalgia—a deep, sweet ache in my chest, tightness at the back of my throat. Tears formed in my eyes. I picked up the album cover and ran into my parents' bedroom, pointing at the title of the song on the back cover and asked, "Have you heard this song?" I sang a bit of it and choked up, the tears silencing me.

They looked at each other in astonishment. "You burst into tears just like that when you were three and we played you this album. You must remember it from before you were born."

As it turns out, my parents had bought that album when it came out in 1966. All through my mother's pregnancy, they played it on their little turntable in their apartment in Philadelphia. They especially loved "For Baby (for Bobby)," a beautiful song written to a baby or a small child that perfectly describes the wonder at the power of love young parents have for their new arrivals.

## Katryna

I know how memory works, that if I could have conjured up a song from my grandmother's childhood, it would have meant more to her than singing her "Country Roads" or "Goodbye Yellow Brick Road." Snuggled up in an accessible part of her brain resided the songs she learned as a three-year-old or an experimenting teen. But whenever I was with her, all I could remember were songs from my childhood. Not quite the same thing.

On my last visit, I had an epiphany. I thought to sing Gershwin and Cole Porter. I sat next to her on the couch, with her head on my shoulder, and sang, "There's a somebody I'm longing to see, / I hope that he / Turns out to be / Someone to watch over me."

She pulled away from me, opened her eyes, and stared into mine. She took my face in her hands and pulled me toward her and kissed my face repeatedly. I felt for the first time in a decade that she knew me. She recognized my voice, the song, or the combination. It's so hard to know how to relate to someone suffering from dementia. For me, music is the easiest path.

It turned out that I wouldn't get to visit my grandmother again. A couple of months after that visit, at the age of 103, she passed away in her apartment with her daughters at her bedside. For six hours, they held her hand and sang to her. After she passed, my mother and aunt called me up. Aunt Sarah took the phone into Grandmummy's bedroom and asked me to sing the Gershwin song that I had sung when we were last together. So I sang for my grandmother, for my aunt, for myself, and for the cherished memory of that last visit.

song about a jealous lover who kills his beloved because she refuses to marry him, but we didn't know that then.

Nerissa remembers hearing the muffled sounds of our parents' voices in the living room below and understanding for the first time that they wouldn't live forever; that this moment was infinitely precious, and that one day we wouldn't be able to hear them sing anymore. This might have been connected to the theme of death in the song itself, or it might have been just the developmental stage she was in. Or maybe she just wished she were downstairs cuddling on our mother's lap while our father played the guitar and all the grown-ups got to be part of the music. But for whatever reason, she leaned into the sound at that moment, taking it in so she would remember it forever. Then she buried her face in the pillow and sobbed. The thought of losing our father's voice and our mother's lap was so powerful that, to this day, she feels a pain in her chest when she puts herself back in that strange bed. We're convinced that the reason she still remembers this moment is that music sealed the emotion in her mind, in her memory, and in her body; as we've said, there is a profound connection for a child in those first, most-beloved voices he hears.

These days, many parents and educators shy away from exposing their children to difficult, painful topics. While we aren't suggesting that

you subject your kids to Eric Clapton's "Tears in Heaven," at some point, they'll be ready for "Puff the Magic Dragon" ("A dragon lives forever / But not so little boys") or "Deep Blue Sea" ("It was Willy / What got drownded / In the deep blue sea"). Sometime around age four, children begin to be curious about death. Songs and music speak to this reality more profoundly than any other medium, even fairy tales. A song can be a powerful way for a child to work through her feelings, because in addition to the words, the music can so effectively mirror an emotion. (We have kids in HooteNanny who burst into tears when we play certain songs that are slow and/or in a minor key.) Though we don't want to make our children miserable, sad songs can give them a full palette with which to explore emotions and experiences.

Musician Dan Zanes talks about the value of sad songs: "If we throw out these songs, we throw the baby out with the bathwater, because these

## Nerissa

I can remember hearing "Puff the Magic Dragon" and taking in the sadness of the lyrics for the first time. We were at the beach with some other families, and my father was playing the guitar. I ran away and sobbed. My mother came after me and sat with me, and we talked about my feelings. I don't remember the content, just that it was so comforting to have her listen to my fears and hold me and reassure me. Each subsequent listening was a bit easier, combining the sadness of the song with the remembered sweetness of my mother's comfort.

songs really need to be told. They really mean something to people for a reason, and we have to have a sense of our histories and our traditions and our cultures. If we don't have these songs, then we can't tell our stories to people from another culture. The minute we lose that stuff, we can't build the bridges we need to build to be able to connect with each other."[3]

To us, this is the real reason to sing sad songs. Without them, we lose valuable—priceless—opportunities to connect. And if we don't connect with our kids (and our partners, neighbors, and friends across the seas), how are we going to connect with our enemies? It is through sharing our brokenness, our pain, that we create empathy and a space for others to understand why we're the way we are and why they're the way they are.

## USING MUSIC TO HEAL

Just as songs can help us to express all our emotions, including the hard ones, songs can heal us too. How many of us broken-hearted lovers have sung along with gusto to songs like "It's a Heartache," "I Will Survive," or "Love Has No Pride" in the aftermath of breakup? Or, more happily, to "Reunited" when we were ready to give our fallen beloved another chance.

When our little country church burned down in the winter of 2010, the minister called Nerissa and asked her to come to a meeting at the parish house later that afternoon. "Bring your guitar," he said. "We're going to need music." Indeed, the music she and the church's music director brought to the congregation lifted people's spirits and filled them with the knowledge that we could rebuild the church. It would be hard, but we would have each other. And we would have music as a bond to keep us together when the going got tough.

Since the time of King David and his harp, or Orpheus and his lyre, music has been known for its power to heal. We have one particular family story that fits this topic. One warm afternoon in May, Katryna roller-skated home from a tennis lesson at the neighborhood court. It was a warm spring day, and she had just gotten the skates for her eleventh birthday. She was getting good on them; she jumped nimbly down five long, wide cement steps and then up a five-inch rise to the front door of the house. Suddenly she lost control of her speed, and to break her fall, she raised her right arm in front of her face as she went crashing through the glass door. The sheets of glass fell fast and cut the main artery in her right arm. Our neighbor ran over while our mother held Katryna, intending to pick her up and drive her to the nearest hospital. Fortunately, our neighbor knew it would be faster and safer to call an ambulance. In less than five minutes, there were three paramedics on our lawn, and to our mother's surprise, instead of tossing Katryna in the back right away, they applied tourniquets to her legs. "We'll move her when there's enough blood getting to her heart," they explained.

On the drive to the hospital, a paramedic asked Katryna what her name was, how old she was, what she had eaten last. Thinking somehow she could help if she provided the right answers, our mother replied for her. The paramedic said, "It's important to keep her engaged by asking her these questions. We don't want her to lose consciousness."

The ambulance pulled up to the bay, and Katryna disappeared on a gurney, leaving our mother standing in the opening. She wasn't allowed in the operating room, so she sat on a bench in the waiting room. At one point, a nurse came out. Our mother put her fear into words: "Is my daughter going to live?"

"We don't let anyone die here," the nurse said, looking her in the eye.

Our mother tried to reach our father, who was in court. The judge called our father up and said softly, "Your daughter's had an accident, and we're going to postpone proceedings. My clerk will drive you to Arlington Hospital."

Our father walked into the room where Katryna was recovering to find our mother singing, "There Is a Balm in Gilead," a hymn our church had just sung on Maundy Thursday the month before. It had a particularly strong message for our family that year: our long-time pastor was dying of Hodgkin's lymphoma, and our father's father—the grandfather who loved music so much—was sick with throat cancer that would end his life the following January (appropriately, on Mozart's birthday). But on that day in Arlington Hospital, the song was our mother's way of communicating as purely as she could to her daughter, letting her

know both the seriousness of the situation as well as her absolute faith in the nurse's assurance.

"I was fearing things I wasn't putting words to," our mother said recently when we asked her about this story. "I just remember Katryna wasn't able to hold my hand, so I held hers. I took her hand and started singing. The nurse had told me, 'Don't disturb her, but you can be with her.'"

The operation was supposed to take two hours. It took four. The doctors were able to save her life, but not the nerve or the artery.

Whether the prayerful song helped Katryna survive we will never know, but we do know that she will never forget it and neither will our parents. This shared experience, bound with music, drew us closer together.

## USING MUSIC TO CONNECT

Of all the reasons to build and maintain a musical foundation with your family, the one that speaks the loudest to us is the hope that music can be a bridge to your teenagers during those notoriously difficult years. Those years are hard enough as it is. Young people often struggle with experimenting and finding their own boundaries, and they set some up that are intended (or so it may appear) simply to shock and alienate their parents. The music they choose can be a way for them to make those walls come across as impenetrable.

Every generation seems to create some kind of music that older folks find hideous and younger ones find irresistibly delightful. Even though we ourselves dread these years and fear having to eat our own words, we'll say them anyway: if you can find a way to embrace your child's taste in music, if you can cultivate some curiosity and try to see what she loves about something that you find as lovable as a bag of dry cement, you will let her know that even though you appear to be far away, you are and always will be right on the other side of the wall, waiting for any opportunity to make a window. She might not thank you this year, but she will someday.

In our family, we three sisters all liked many of the same things our parents liked, at least for our first thirteen years. We were all Democrats; good students; tennis players and hikers; ecologists (or at least passionate antilitterers); and fans of the same foods—pesto, crusty French bread, smoked fish, and sesame noodles. We attended church, and while we might have had somewhat different theologies, there was ultimately way more on which to agree than to disagree.

 We formed a sort of tribe. Opinions were sharp, and it was important to have and articulate them well, but mostly we shared these too.

We even converged on music to a great degree, although it didn't always feel that way at the time. Looking back, there was little our parents loved that we didn't, though they adored country and we liked classic rock. We all loved folk music and the same eras of classical music (pre-nineteenth century). But at the time, it seemed as though the Rubicon that divided us could never be crossed. Nerissa kept her door shut when she played her sixties rock and wore earphones to savor the panned stereo of the Rolling Stones' "Paint It Black" during the long country and western–infused family car trips. And as we mentioned earlier, our parents were not fans of the Beatles. Try as we might, we couldn't convince them that the Fab Four were the greatest musicians of our time. When we first told them about our newfound enthusiasm (we were nine and seven), they scrunched up their faces and imitated Ringo shaking his head while playing the drums and made dismissive gestures. Later, when we took Beatles songs to our father to try to get him to teach us how to play them on the guitar, he was game but vague.

Then Nerissa graduated from high school. It was 1985, and our family took a trip to Great Britain to celebrate. We older girls were not impressed; Abigail, at eleven, was completely cheerful and made up for our sullenness by enthusiastically going along with the program. We, on the other hand, felt dragged around, forced into activities that seemed to be from an earlier era— climbing mountains (even when it was raining, which it always was in Ireland), singing folk songs to Irish people, and eating foods we didn't like.

So we were surly teens who didn't communi-

186          *Deepening Your Relationship with Music*

cate well with our parents, who in their turn must have felt that we were squandering our opportunity for family harmony on our one and only European vacation.

At the beginning of week two, we boarded a ferry from Dublin to Wales, and while on the boat, we spotted a map. Our next destination was Scotland, and we saw clearly that our route was to take us through Liverpool. We momentarily lost our crankiness along with our minds and exploded with giddiness and joy. It even occurred to us that our parents were planning on surprising us by taking us to this Beatles mecca. Surely they had consulted a map in planning their trip! Surely they were going to let us stop at the city that had produced our greatest heroes! Why, that must have been the entire purpose of this wet, Irish vacation all along!

Surely not. When we ran up to them on the deck, almost incoherent with delight, they shrugged and said, "No. Liverpool is really just a dirty industrial city. It would depress you. We're going to drive around it to get to Scotland."

Three hours out of the way to drive around it.

To our minds, this was one of their poorer parenting moves, though as parents now, we understand it better. We too get wedded to an itinerary and don't want to stray from our ordered program, and going to Liverpool that day would have created exactly the chaos parents try to avoid. In this case, our parents simply didn't know how completely Beatlemania had taken over Liverpool by 1985; in the early sixties when they had last been

to Europe, Liverpool *had* been just a dirty industrial city. It turned out their kids knew something they didn't, which is a situation in which we often find ourselves as parents.

Nevertheless, our parents came to regret their misstep. Maybe not right away, though we punished our dad every time he sang one of his favorite songs, "The Leaving of Liverpool" by altering it thus: "It's not the leaving of Liverpool that grieves me / *But the fact that we never went there in the first place!*"

Over time, our parents changed, particularly in the way they related to our inclinations about music. They became more curious. They learned from what we now refer to as their One Parenting Mistake. All parents are imperfect, even great ones. The idea is to grow from our mistakes. By the time Abigail was a teenager, they had found ways to actively support her love of popular music.

This leads us to the most famous concert story to date in our family. As we noted earlier, Abigail may be the world's biggest Bruce Springsteen fan. When she was between the ages of ten and eighteen, her bedroom walls didn't see the light of day for the posters of the Boss. So when she won tickets to his *Tunnel of Love* tour in 1989 from a local radio station, she lobbied hard and successfully convinced our mother to drive her to the concert.

On the day of the show, Abigail came home early from school with the stomach flu—the kind that leaves most people beating a path from their bed to the bathroom. When our mother got home from work, she took one look at her sick daughter, clearly incapable of any activity, and said, "We're going, right?" To this day, Abigail insists that this was our mother's shining hour of parental glory.

Our mother took two plastic bags with her. Abigail threw up in one in the parking lot as they were in line to have their bags checked. (The security guard must have been pleased to search through the contents of that particular bag.) Abigail made use of the second bag at intermission. But she and our mother made it through the entire show, and this remains one of Abigail's most cherished memories, even though she says today that it was actually her least favorite Bruce show (as Bruce shows go), because of the material he played and how lousy she felt. The connection she had with our mother that night is what she remembers and cherishes.

As we grew up, our parents became our most ardent supporters, from the time we got our start as a not-entirely-folk band when they showed up at grimy rock clubs all over the country, to the present when they fly as far as Canada to babysit grandchildren while we perform at folk festivals. Most important, they listen to us today. They listen to our music, they engage with it, and they listen to our fears and excitement, encouraging us to stay the course in a musical life that doesn't always seem practical.

We have grown too. Today, we actually like country music (at least the country of the 1970s); it's a common reference we share with our parents and sister. There's a whole slew of artists, like Willie Nelson and Dolly Parton, at whom we turned up our noses when we were teens but who are now included on our own iPod mixes. Even the awful stuff has a soft spot in our hearts; we may not have loved "You Can Eat Crackers in My Bed Anytime," but we love that we can sing all the words to its chorus years later. We love that everyone in the car agreed that when "Take This Job and Shove It" came on the radio, whoever was driving would turn it off. In short, we have always loved sharing music with our family, even music we didn't like. Beyond that, we pay attention to what our parents love now too. We listen to the new songs our father has discovered and do what we've always done: make up harmonies, learn the words, and sing along.

One final thought. When we started working together as sisters in a band, we made up a song with great usefulness (almost as great as "We're Almost There"; see page 149). Ironically, we stole the tune to the vilified "Old Macdonald Had a Farm." Whenever one of us wanted to apologize to the other (not that we wanted to, but there was often a need), we sang,

You are right, and I am wrong.
Ee-i-ee-i-o
You are right, and I am wrong.
Ee-i-ee-i-o
You're always right, I'm always wrong.
You're always right, I'm always wrong.
You are right, and I am wrong.
Ee-i-ee-i-o

It's extremely satisfying to have your sister sing that to you. Try it with your teenager and see what happens. With preschoolers, we've found it wise to modify it:

I'm sometimes right, I'm sometimes wrong. You're sometimes right, you're sometimes wrong.

## Nerissa

The other morning I jogged over to Staples to buy an adapter for my phone.

The clerk looked at the total and said, "$19.84."

Without looking up, I handed him my credit card.

"A good year," he continued, "for those of us who were alive then. And a really good Van Halen album."

This got my attention. I hadn't thought about Van Halen in years, and suddenly there was the image from a 1984 video—the one where David Lee Roth is flying through the air like a long-haired trapeze artist.

I replied, "That is a good CD."

The clerk, who was about my age, and I went on to expound about David Lee's many virtues, and to agree that, while Sammy Hagar was fine, the golden era of the band was certainly that of Roth.

I made it a practice, from the age of about thirteen, to study rock and roll, which for me included devouring *Creem* magazine, *Rolling Stone, Musician,* and anything by Jon Pareles from the *New York Times.* I wanted to be in the know. It was important to be able to speak intelligently with my peers who were interested in rock music, but most especially, I wanted a common topic for speaking to the opposite sex. To this day, I'm not sure exactly why; I might've chosen football or baseball—that would have served equally well, but sports weren't my thing. Music was. And it was effective: being a girl who knew the names of every Rolling Stones member (including all three non–Keith Richards lead guitarists and both bass players) and every Who album; why the Kinks'"All Day and All of the Night" was far superior to the Doors' "Hello, I Love You" (the latter being a complete rip-off of the former); and what the nuances between new age and punk, reggae and ska, rap and hip-hop were all about. These bits of knowledge gave me purchase at my rare social interactions with boys (Katryna and I went to an all-girls high school).

Usually, a kind of Venn diagram would occur: the guy I was trying to impress and I converged, often on the Stones, Van Halen, or Bob Dylan, but didn't completely overlap. While I'm amused by AC/DC, I just don't get Metallica or Rush, and the guy usually didn't appreciate Joni Mitchell, let alone Pete Seeger.

Clearly, it mattered to me to connect. I had a huge motivation, besides the obvious evolutionary one: I gained instant respect by being so knowledgeable. Besides, it was easy and pleasurable to find common ground, to learn about the bands I didn't like as well as the bands I did.

So if I was once willing to grit my teeth through a Rush show, why is it so hard for me (and so many parents I know) to open my ears to the music my children love, the music that is shaping them, perhaps more profoundly than any other influence? Already I'm dreading my future car trips, shivering in advance at the possibilities that might emanate from the bedrooms down the hall. But surely the love I have for my children is stronger and more passionate than what I felt for some teenage guy at a dance. I'm hoping that when the time comes, I can rise to the occasion; give myself the challenge of learning the ins and outs of whatever bands, genres, or artistic proclivities my children choose to love; and show my respect to them (and to the teenager within) by evincing an interest in their musical choices. I might just have a lot of fun while I'm at it, uncovering my obscured teenage passion for some band I've yet to discover.

## SEASONAL CELEBRATIONS

As we were writing this book, countless friends confided to us that the only time they sing with their families is at Christmas. In fact, a friend of Nerissa's admitted that the only song she could think of when trying to comfort her fussy infant was "Jingle Bells," so that was his lullaby. This got us thinking about the important role music plays at Christmastime, when carols and seasonal ditties (and the monotone of the Salvation Army bell) are the literal soundtrack for shoppers everywhere.

## Katryna

When Amelia was a little more than two years old, Nerissa and I were playing a show with the wonderful singer/songwriter Dar Williams. We were in a theater on Long Island, where only a tiny corner of the stage sufficed as the backstage area—not enough room for an adventurous toddler. So I found myself in the lobby between sets, watching her run around among the legs of the grown-ups. I thought about how people referred to this era of childhood as "the first adolescence." Amelia was a great lover of the word *no,* and as she was demonstrating, she enjoyed exploring the world without holding my hand.

As I was musing about how much I dreaded her next adolescence, I noticed a man with his teenage daughter. The man was a typical, preppy Long Islander. His pink corduroys were embroidered with little blue whales. He wore a kelly green jacket and horn-rimmed glasses. The daughter, meanwhile, had purple hair and a pierced nose. They were standing together somewhat awkwardly. I thought their relationship was probably mostly monosyllabic. But that night they had found common ground; they had decided to go to a concert together. They might be getting different inspiration from the music; maybe the girl was moved by the message of empowerment. Maybe it was just thrilling for her to see women up onstage singing about life. Maybe her father was taken back to his college days when he would see Joan Baez on the New Haven Green. It didn't matter why they both loved this music; it just mattered that, for one night, music was a small bridge they could cross to find a connection at a time when those connections were probably hard to come by.

Some love carols and some hate them, but the one aspect we can agree on is that they become ohrwurms. And it's this sharing of ohrwurms that binds us together in powerful ways. Just as those of us who live in the same area can always come back to the topic of the weather in a given season, within a given cultural tradition, we can find a common dialogue in the music we share.

We take first the paradigm of Christmas carols, because they are arguably the most iconic example of the phenomenon of seasonal music. At their best, carols tie us to our earliest happy memories of family, love, mystery, and presents, not to mention the sacred and the holy. The last two, if you trace them etymologically, mean "set apart" (*sacred*) and "whole," or "coming together" (*holy*). This paradoxical juxtaposition sums up this kind of seasonal celebration. The parts become one, as the individual family members come together again. Yet the event—Christmas or any other holiday we imbue with a sense of specialness—also has that unique sense of "once a year." Particular traditions are associated with holidays, in part to emphasize their sacredness, or "set apartness."

If Christmas is not a holiday you celebrate, you can experience this combination of holy and sacred elsewhere. Do some digging, and you'll soon find all sorts of wonderful holiday songs. Learn them, share them with your children and friends, and see what favorites emerge. Some may catch on; others won't. No amount of convincing could get us to adopt "You're a Grand Old Flag," but we sing "America the Beautiful" every Fourth of July, and we make sure to include that luminous and humble second verse:

> O beautiful for pilgrim feet
> Whose stern impassioned stress
> A thoroughfare of freedom beat
> Across the wilderness!
> America! America!
> God mend thine every flaw,
> Confirm thy soul in self-control,
> Thy liberty in law!

---

## Nerissa

At one point, I attempted to write a song for every minor holiday in the calendar, and once we did a show using just those songs. It was at a small club in Bethlehem, Pennsylvania, called Godfrey Daniels. I believe we sang "Ash Wednesday," "Glow in the Dark Plastic Angel," "Planting an Even Row," "Living It Up in the Garden," "Harvest Table," "Just Like Christopher Columbus" (for Columbus Day), "Merry Christmas, Mr. Jones," and "Christmas Carol." I started to write a New Year's song, complete with a black-eyed peas reference, but it never got finished.

The calendar in pre-Christian England was based on a circle. At north and south are the solstices (December 21 and June 21), and at east and west are the equinoxes (March 21 and September 21). Halfway between each of these are special celebrations that, over time, were often merged with Christian holidays. Halfway between the fall equinox and the winter solstice is Samhain on October 31 (or November 1), which became Halloween; Imbolc on February 1 or 2 became Groundhog Day. Halfway between the summer solstice and the fall equinox is Lughnasa, which falls on July 31 or August 1. And halfway between the spring equinox and the summer solstice is the first of May, which was—and remains—May Day, or Beltane. Of course, you will add your own special days: anniversaries, birthdays, remembrance days. Maybe you'll want to create a whole ritual and song circle about the first or last day of school.

## Imbolc/Groundhog Day

No month has more holidays than the shortest one—February. Yet all these holidays seem somewhat strange and strained. How do you actually celebrate Groundhog Day? And apart from Christmas (for those who celebrate it), is there any more vilified holiday for single people than Valentine's Day? What about Presidents' Day? Can we even keep track of which presidents we're celebrating? Washington, Lincoln, all of them? What about Black History Month? Mardi Gras? Leap year?

We propose turning the whole month into one big musical celebration. Take as your themes the bleak midwinter; the slow, gradual brightening of the daytime sky and the shrinking of the dark winter nights; our African-American heritage marked by the legacy of emancipation (Lincoln) and the great musical gifts: the blues, rock and roll, and Cajun music from Louisiana, which we associate with Mardi Gras.

Rather than singing many holiday or season-related songs this time of year, we prefer to get down to the business of songwriting for February Album Writing Month (FAWM), which is an Internet phenomenon. Participants vow to write fourteen songs during the month of February, as fourteen is the standard number that constitutes an album. Nerissa took the challenge in 2008 and was so hooked into the process that she now does it every year, bringing Lila and Johnny into the act. One year, Lila helped write this call-and-response song:

> I want you to appreciate the Boo. (Boo!)
> I want you to appreciate the Boo. (Boo!)
> I want you to appreciate the Boo. (Boo!)
> And while you're at it, appreciate the view.

Try it for yourself! We've found it a wonderful way to get through the bleak midwinter. Or you could try singing the eponymous song ("In the Bleak Midwinter"):

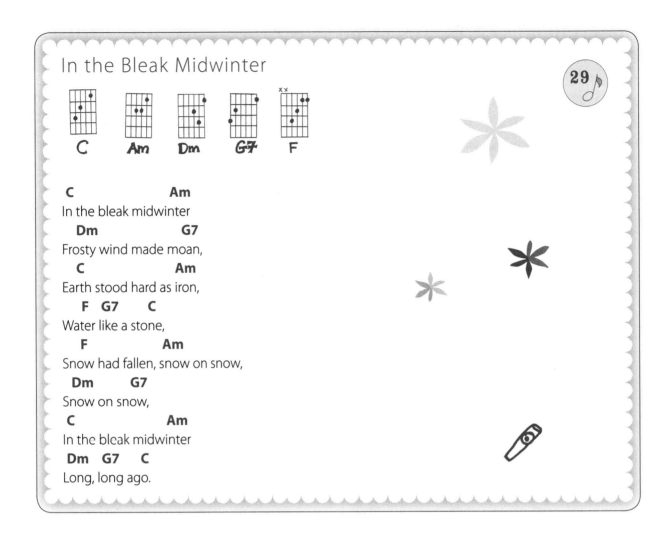

In the Bleak Midwinter

## 29

C — Am — Dm — G7 — F

```
  C                 Am
In the bleak midwinter
   Dm                G7
Frosty wind made moan,
    C                 Am
Earth stood hard as iron,
    F  G7      C
Water like a stone,
    F                 Am
Snow had fallen, snow on snow,
   Dm        G7
Snow on snow,
    C                 Am
In the bleak midwinter
  Dm  G7     C
Long, long ago.
```

## May Day

One of the many musical traditions that enhanced our childhood was the annual celebration of May Day. The plantings might be in the ground by the spring equinox, but the first of May is when we start to see the hints that there will be fresh new crops. The coming of spring is magical for everyone who lives in a climate with distinct seasons.

The days get longer, the world becomes colorful again, and delicious fresh foods start to be available.

Growing up, our school had a huge May Day celebration, complete with a teacher dressed up as a 'Obby 'Oss (wearing a gigantic hoop skirt around a kind of hobby horse), a Muffin Man, and a maypole whose many colorful ribbons we children braided together in a maypole morris dance. Parents even came to this event, marking its importance in the yearly cycle.

Many amazing songs have been written in celebration of May Day, but "Wild Mountain Thyme" is the most meaningful for us. We sing this song with our father on our CD *Rock All Day/ Rock All Night*, and both of us had our guests and family members sing this at our weddings. What a miracle that summer comes every year!

## Wild Mountain Thyme

**30**

C    F    Am    Dm

    **C**
Oh, the summertime is comin'
    **F**          **C**
And the trees are sweetly bloomin'
    **F**        **Am**
And the wild mountain thyme
    **Dm**         **F**
Grows around the purple heather.
    **C**  **F**  **C**
Will you go? Lassie, go?

     **F**     **C**
And we'll all go together
     **F**     **Am**
To pull wild mountain thyme
    **Dm**         **F**
All around the bloomin' heather.
    **C**  **F**  **C**
Will you go? Lassie, go?

*continued . . .*

I will build my love a bower
By yon clear and crystal fountain,
And on it I will pile
All the flowers of the mountain.
Will you go? Lassie, go?

And we'll all go together
To pull wild mountain thyme
All around the bloomin' heather.
Will you go? Lassie, go?

If my true love she were gone,
I would surely find no other

To pull wild mountain thyme
All around the bloomin' heather.
Will you go? Lassie, go?

And we'll all go together
To pull wild mountain thyme
All around the bloomin' heather.
Will you go?
Will you go?
Lassie, will you go?

## Halloween

Halloween is hands-down our kids' favorite holiday, mostly because of the candy. But in this day of increased interest in feeding our kids organic, local foods with somewhat less sugar, we propose that you add a few songs to your trick-or-treat bag.

Growing up, three students at our school dressed up as witches and recited "Double, double, toil and trouble" from Shakespeare's *Macbeth* on Halloween morning. We were taught several wonderful Halloween songs, and our favorite was a round that went like this:

Have you seen the ghost of John?
Long white bones with the skin all gone!

Wouldn't it be chilly with no skin on?

And another, with a simple minor tune:

Stirring and stirring and stirring our brew,
Ooooh-ooooh, ooooh-ooooh!

Stirring and stirring and stirring our brew,
Ooooh-ooooh, ooooh-ooooh!

Stirring and stirring and stirring our brew,
Ooooh-ooooh, ooooh-ooooh!

Tiptoe, tiptoe, tiptoe

Boo!

Scary and you get to shout at the end. What could be better? We sometimes amend this by adding as many disgusting things to our "brew" as possible:

> I think I'll throw in a stinky old shoe,
> Ew, ew, ew, ew!
> I think I'll throw in some bread that's turned blue,
> Ew, ew, ew, ew!

## Winter Solstice and Revels

Our family has participated in Revels since the 1970s, not long after its founding by Jack Langstaff. In the early eighties, when he brought Revels to Washington D.C., our sister Abigail was in the first children's troupe, and our father joined the chorus. He sang with them for eighteen years, and in the middle of those, Nerissa sang with them for two years after college as well. Katryna sang in a teenage troupe for French Revels while in high school. Revels has spread all over the country; to date, there are ten companies in Massachusetts; New Hampshire; New York; Washington, D.C.; Texas; Oregon; California; Washington State, and Colorado.

We know many families who build their holiday traditions around attending or participating in a Revels performance. Though the themes are unapologetically Christian in tradition, they're not religious per se, and many who perform in Revels are strong members of non-Christian backgrounds. The emphasis is on the solstice and the season we all share—the dying of the daylight, the peace of darkness. With song and silliness, the oldest story—that of the Earth dying and renewing herself, which so many cultures celebrate on the shortest day of the year—is retold.

The performance includes the master of ceremonies singing "Lord of the Dance" at the end of the first act, and the troupe dances off the stage to grab hands with the audience members and form a line that snakes its way out into the hall or lobby. The end of the second act includes leading the audience in some three-part singing of "Dona Nobis Pacem" and the "Sussex Mummers Carol."

If the idea of celebrating the season in this kind of focused, communal way appeals to you, check out Revels.org and see what they might be doing in your area. If you're ambitious, you can start your own.

## Christmas Carols

We know we're not alone in loving Christmas carols. Even people who are secular in every other way may have a fondness for these ancient songs.

They're sung at the same time each year, either in a church setting, at home on a well-worn CD or LP, or as was the case in our family, around a piano every Christmas Eve. Carols are the quintessential example of family music and what it can do; no matter how crazy family dynamics can be around the holidays, music can be the bridge to calming down and settling into the goodness and simplicity, the "being togetherness" that we all crave at this time.

Growing up, we always celebrated Christmas at our father's family's house, though my mother's mother and sister (our Aunt Sarah) always came too. Our father had three sisters, two of whom considered themselves nonsingers and one of whom was a concert-level pianist and classically trained soprano. Our Aunt Jenifer would take her seat at the piano bench right after Christmas dinner, and one of the younger kids, usually Nerissa or Katryna, would hand out the caroling books—simple paperbacks that had the tunes and lyrics to many standard carols. We weren't particularly adventuresome in those days; we sang the basics like "Away in a Manger," Deck the Halls," and our grandmother's favorite, "It Came Upon a Midnight Clear." We always sang "Good King

Wenceslas," dividing the parts by gender and chuckling at the line "Mark my footsteps, my good page," because our Aunt Laura had married a man named Mark Page. We usually ended with "Silent Night."

As children, we looked forward to carols and loved this part of Christmas even more than the presents or the food. The carols were predictable, beautiful, and mysterious, and they locked us in a tradition that felt ancient and personal all at the same time.

Today, we sing carols a few days before Christmas when our Aunt Elizabeth comes through town with her son, John, the fine musician mentioned earlier who plays both piano and guitar. Our father plays his favorite Revels songs on the guitar, and the three of us often sing an a cappella version of "The First Nowell." Last year, Lila and William and Amelia added their incredibly focused and intense drum orchestra to "Deck the Halls" and "Jingle Bells," three little heads peering over the coffee table, eyes like lasers on the song leader or guitar player to get the beat right. When we get around to the classics—"O Come, All Ye Faithful," "Joy to the World," and the like—we drop our books. We all know all the words.

*Deepening Your Relationship with Music*

# Katryna

There are always two things that deter me from the heavenly fantasy of wandering from house to house through gently falling snow, caroling and bringing joy wherever I go. One is that some people are really irritated by being interrupted by strangers singing on their doorstep. The other is that it can be freezing outside in December in Massachusetts. Even if I'm warmed by the experience, my kids might be grumpy and cold.

When I was working with a group of families as their choral leader, we decided we wanted to go caroling. Many of them had young children and were daunted by the idea of going out in twenty-five-degree weather. Another member of the chorus had a mother who was living in a nursing home. She suggested that we carol there. I remember feeling completely overwhelmed by everything that December serves up. I was so busy and felt angry at myself for agreeing to lead the caroling that night.

I walked into the nursing home with my guitar in hand, thinking, *I'll be here for half an hour, and then I'll do some errands on the way home and be done in time to put the kids to bed.* I was all frenzy and no feeling. Then I saw these families gathered together to sing. We had learned about five carols with parts and knew the words and chords to a few others. I had thought that we would be singing in the dining room during dinner to a small crowd of residents. But when we got there, we were told that dinner was over and they would prefer that we go hallway to hallway.

Many people could not leave their floors or even their beds. We set off, singing our way through the halls of the facility. We ended up singing the five songs over and over. Our presence was appreciated in a way that wouldn't have happened in a big neighborhood. The smiles on the faces of the residents were genuine and appreciative. On some halls, the residents would sing along with us. I think the part that moved me the most was the interaction between the young children in our group and the older patients to whom we were singing. As we noted in the previous chapter, the older brain holds on to long-term memories even when short-term recall is inconsistent. These Christmas carols were ancient memories for all the people we were singing to; they were familiar and tied to good memories.

As it turned out, nothing could have made me feel more uplifted. I was so grateful that I'd had to show up for that caroling. It fed me more than anything I have ever done during the Christmas season. It is now a tradition for me, albeit a slightly off-season one. Nursing homes and hospitals are often inundated with requests from carolers during December. Last Christmas, Nerissa tried to arrange for our families to carol at the hospital in town. She was told she needed to get on a waiting list. So the chorus at our elementary school always makes a date to go to the local nursing home in January when all the carolers have gone home for the season.

For more seasonal song ideas, please see Appendix 3.

*Deepening Your Relationship with Music*

# COMMUNITY CELEBRATIONS

W HEN WE THINK BACK ON OUR CHILD-hood, one of the most indelible images is that of our father carrying his old, nylon-string guitar into the homes and backyards of our friends to share music with them. We can remember the rich cigar-store smell of the interior of that guitar case; the broken capos in the yellow, plush-lined accessory compartment; the old sheet music stashed above and below the guitar; the way he tuned the pegs. We remember the faces of his friends who had never heard him sing before, and more important, the way those faces lit up as they recognized an old tune and joined in the chorus. We remember how our mom sang her harmony with our dad and how they both encouraged us girls to sing along. We remember the way the other grown-ups thanked our parents at the end of the evening. We came to regard the guitar as a kind of goodwill ambassador.

That guitar traveled many a mile with our

family and was certainly a passenger in our station wagon on our long drives up to Maine and the Adirondacks in August. We'd sit out on the rock shore of Bar Harbor singing to the Blue Nose ferry as the sun went down, or we'd sit around a campfire in the High Peaks, sharing songs with friends with whom we vacationed every year. The guitar went to church where our parents led something called Junior Worship for the kids, which usually included a Bible story, a brief explanation and discussion, and then a song. The guitar went with us to Ireland, where we hoped to learn some Irish songs and instead mostly ended up singing our own songs to our bed-and-breakfast hosts around their kitchen tables. The guitar went to every wedding, birthday party, and funeral at which our father (or later, one of us) marked the occasion with a song, usually one he'd written to a preexisting tune. That guitar was like a member of our family.

Once you've established your own musical traditions, or even while you're establishing them, you can take your show on the road in many different ways. Music is welcome almost anywhere. When our family first moved from New York City to northern Virginia in the midseventies, we slowly began to make friends. One of the first families we connected with was one with three small girls just like us. The parents, like ours, loved to sing and adored folk music. When they invited us over, they specifically included the guitar in the invitation. We have many memories of sitting on the floor of their living room or in their backyard, thumbing through songbooks and singing into the night until way past our bedtimes.

For this kind of family singing, you don't need any talent at all to contribute to the Song Basket. The only thing you need is enthusiasm and an idea for a song to share. And you don't need all the lyrics of the song. A two-year-old can shout, "La Bamba!" and as long as one person knows some piece of the song, you're off to the races. Of course, it's more satisfying when the lyrics are in someone's head or a handy book, and we highly recommend taking songbooks with easy guitar chords with you to musical get-togethers. We're big fans of Peter Blood and Annie Patterson's fabulous *Rise Up Singing*, a collection of all sorts of beloved songs. We have many tattered copies stowed away in each family member's house, so it's always available whenever a sing-along is brewing.

At times, I have felt like the hapless Amelia Bedelia from the children's book series by the same title. Amelia Bedelia was a completely incompetent maid who never got anything right. But at the end of every story, she managed to make a lemon meringue pie for her bosses, and all was forgiven because the pie was so good.

When I was a young adult, I had a job as an administrator at a school. I seemed to fail at every task assigned to me except one: whenever I pulled out my guitar, sang to the students, and got them to sing along, all my bosses and the highers-up praised me and seemed to forgive all my other transgressions. I came to see my guitar as a kind of magic wand—I waved it, and suddenly everyone was in a forgiving mood. People really like to sing. It turns crankiness to cheerfulness.

## PERFORMANCES BIG AND SMALL

Most young children love to perform. Often, we just have to give them the opportunity, and they're off creating their own dance routines, plays, or songs to share in front of an audience. Whether at home, in a community group, or in school, allowing children to be the stars of their own production is an empowering opportunity.

At the Falcon Ridge Folk Festival, we always do a show or two at the kid's tent. A week after our nephew Trenor was born, our parents drove out to the festival with Trenor's siblings, Emmett and Reese, who were aged six at the time. Katryna handed each of them one of William's cardboard guitars, also giving one to Lila and one to William. We got the kids up-front and center with mics at their level, dubbed their quartet the Guitarchestra, and cued them to our first song—"Going to Boston." All four kids took their performance very seriously, singing into their mics, "strumming" their cardboard guitars, and graciously receiving the tumultuous applause that followed. The skill of performing is challenging for even the most well-rehearsed, advanced practitioner, so we think it's helpful to get kids up onstage in front of their peers and elders as much as possible. Nothing beats stage fright like experience. Plus, sharing the stage with our family was the most fun we ever had at Falcon Ridge.

Kids don't need much to put on a show.

Recently, after a family dinner, our four kids decided to perform a circus for us. William played cardboard guitar; Lila did clown kicks; and Amelia did cartwheels and round-offs. Johnny smiled and put his hands over his eyes. But the essential element—the kids' announcement that the parents must assemble to witness their performance—was in place. There was a moment of unspoken agreement, and the fourth wall was constructed. We parents stood mindfully and respectfully in the doorway to the living room while our children performed in the middle of the area rug. At the end, we clapped.

And that's show business.

## MUSIC IN YOUR CHILD'S SCHOOL

At the Potomac School, where we attended elementary and middle school, we had weekly assemblies that were filled with music, poetry, performance, and communal singing. We both loved these all-school meetings so much and felt we got so much benefit from them that we have each made it a priority to pass down what we've been given to the schools our own children attend—and to schools everywhere, whenever possible.

All-school meetings were the result of every kid in the school having already spent a significant amount of time standing up in front of their individual classrooms, singing, reciting poetry, performing in a play, or reporting on a subject they had studied. As with most schools, there was a firmly established social hierarchy by junior high, but we believe its effects were tempered by the added experience each kid had as a performer. Even the shyest, most socially awkward kid felt comfortable standing up in front of the whole school and reciting a John Donne poem, singing a folk song, or being a witch in Macbeth. We would guess that most of the kids who went to our school grew up to be perfectly comfortable speaking in public.

There are three huge benefits to all-school assemblies. The first is that actually gathering the entire school community together teaches the children that they're part of something bigger than their classroom. The second is that they have an opportunity to learn some music and to share the experience of singing in a large group. Finally, they get over that notorious fear of speaking or performing.

These days, schools are under a lot of pressure to raise their test scores and meet certain benchmarks. Though that pursuit may be valid, they need to cover more than just academics. The students need to learn about social structures and how to build community. The mother of one exceptionally bright child in Amelia's class told Katryna that although she wanted her son to be intellectually challenged at school, she also wanted him to learn the value of going to his neighbor's house to help raise a barn.

All-school meetings have the potential to make the school community feel like a family.

Teachers get to know the younger kids long before they enter their classrooms, and teachers continue to watch former students blossom as they move from grade to grade. The younger kids get to see the older kids as mentors. They get to look forward to the skills they'll acquire when they're older, while the older kids experience that incomparable feeling of impressing the younger kids.

Music is an obvious activity for these all-school meetings. Most schools today, try as they might, are not giving our children anywhere near enough music. We think this is a mistake for many reasons, but a big one is this: no one has any real idea what the world will be like in twenty or thirty years when our children are part of the workforce. As educator Ken Robinson says, the greatest tool we can give our youth is creativity. In fact, creativity is the only thing we know for certain they can use, no matter what the future holds.[1] Music seems an obvious path to creativity, self-expression, and self-confidence.

A variation on the all-school gathering is something our friend Penny organizes at the Hilltown Charter School, which she cofounded fifteen years ago in Haydenville, Massachusetts. Four times a year, the students put on a production called *Il Teatre* (Italian for "the theater"). Up to twenty or so students, or student groups, volunteer—or in some circumstances, are volunteered—to perform a song. There is great variety in the numbers in a given "show." At the production we saw, a teacher tap-danced while a student played the guitar; three kindergarteners performed and sang a fairly orthodox "London Bridge" while a first grader played it on the piano; a fourth grader danced a Scottish sword dance while her older brother played bagpipes; a second-grade boy stomped and clapped and led the school in "We Will Rock You"; several seventh graders played Mozart on the violin; and several eighth graders sang original songs while accompanying themselves on guitar. A group of sixth graders who called themselves the Oranges performed a skit titled "Fashion Show," which consisted of a number of toga-clad models sashaying down the makeshift aisle while onlookers made wry comments.

There were no lights for this production, no props or sets, no makeup, and no stage—just a space in the center of the biggest room in the school, with a piano off to one side and a mic in a stand that was only occasionally used. The kids from the school comprised most of the seated audience, and they sat on the floor. There were a limited number of chairs for adults, but the major-ity of parents and visitors stood up or leaned against the walls. It seemed as though the parents of every child had interrupted their work morning to come to this performance. Four kids of different ages acted as masters of ceremonies, with Penny at the ready to help out with last-minute stage-managing, such as turning pages or helping to move the mic. When performers finished their numbers, the students went wild with applause and yelling. Performers exited the "stage" by simply walking back to their seats on the floor among their classmates, all of whom lifted their palms to high-five the performers.

One eighth-grader introduced her song, "Over the Rainbow," by telling the audience that she had sung it eight years earlier as a kindergartener. There weren't a lot of dry eyes among the parents during this hour-and-a-half show. The kids who had performed practically levitated as they returned to their classrooms.

## Katryna

When my daughter started kindergarten at our local public school, I was hanging out on the playground with some other parents after school as the children played. I said to another mom that I wished our school gathered all the students together more often. She concurred, and the two of us started a conversation about how to create all-school meetings. We were lucky in that the kindergarten teacher had been lobbying for more all-school events.

Eventually, I went to the principal and told her the other mother and I were interested in volunteering in the classrooms to teach music that would later be sung at an all-school meeting. She was very receptive. We were careful and respectful as we approached the teachers, all of whom were also receptive. I think it was essential that we recognized they were giving up class time, both for the music lessons and for the morning of the assembly.

Our first all-school meeting was a musical May Day celebration. Together with another mom, we wrote a local cultural council grant to help pay for an outside artist who was trained in creating such celebrations. After learning from her how to do it, we have since been able to repeat the event each year without her.

The all-school meetings have evolved and culminated the first year in an all-Beatles, all-school sing-along, with a band made up of students' parents. In creating these all-school sing-alongs, we choose songs with the kids' input. We listen to their musical inclinations, and they feel they're a part of the creative process

The students were overjoyed to be singing songs that felt like part of them and not an academic exercise. Parents have told me again and again that the all-school Beatles sings have turned their kids on to music in a whole new way. An added benefit to the assemblies is that the town feels like a community—the parents playing their instruments, the kids singing the songs, and the faculty staff and audience all enjoying the moment.

## How to Start an All-School Meeting with Music

Here's a quick guide for putting together an all-school sing-along for your child's school. While it takes some effort and planning, all you really need is a willing principal and faculty and some other parents, songs, someone to accompany the singers on a piano or guitar, and a tiny bit of courage.

1. Contact the principal and say that you would be interested in helping to teach and lead a sing-along at the school. Start by offering a one-time event. Later, you can convince the principal and teachers that it should happen more often. Katryna's goal is to have weekly all-school meetings, but she has started with monthly events.

2. Find other parents who are musically inclined and see if they want to help bring more music into the school.

3. Choose music carefully for your first assembly. This is always one of Katryna's favorite parts of creating an all-school sing-along, but it's also the scariest part. What if the kids hate the songs? What if the teachers hate the songs? What if the songs she chooses are too easy or too hard? To get you started, we've included a few of the songs we've used successfully in Appendix 3.

There is an endless supply of great music to pass down to the next generation. Try to remember which songs you sang in school. Which ones do you still remember? Which ones do you feel every child should know?

4. Ask teachers for their input. Sometimes they're already using music in the classroom to illustrate subjects they're teaching. They may want to tie your music into their curriculum. If a class is learning about the geography of the United States, teach them the "Fifty Nifty United States." If they're learning about world geography, you could do They Might Be Giants' "Alphabet of Nations." Every January when the kids are learning about Martin Luther King Jr., we sing songs from the civil rights movement: "Ain't Gonna Let Nobody Turn Me Around," "If You Miss Me from the Back of the Bus," and "Sister Rosa Parks" by the Neville Brothers.

5. Ask the students for input. Though Katryna has yet to fulfill some kids' wish that we do an Eminem song, the Beatles, They Might be Giants, Johnny Cash, Bob Marley, and even Journey have made their way into our grammar school repertoire. The more invested the kids feel in the process, the more they enjoy it.

6. Find a time to teach the music in the classrooms. Most all-school meetings require about two twenty-minute sessions with each class to prepare. Katryna's children go to a very small school. At a larger school, there are more classrooms to get to. If you have enough parent volunteers, that's not a problem, but if it seems daunting to get to every class, ask the music teacher for help. Rotate which classes you go to. You can teach the verses to one class and just have the rest of the school learn the chorus. With a simple or familiar song, you can often use the all-school meeting itself to teach the chorus.

7. Schedule the actual meeting time. Be flexible and let the teachers dictate what time of day and what day of the week work best for their schedules. Allow five minutes per song on average. If you are given twenty minutes for an assembly, you might prepare four songs.

8. Finally, don't expect perfection. The easier, simpler, and less stressful the event is, the more likely that everyone will want to repeat it.

All-school sing-alongs are not rehearsed, perfect performances. There are other times for those types of events. This is an opportunity for the students to feel like they're just casually sharing music they've learned with each other. This should be fun and low stress. It should feel like you're in a giant living room or around campfire, not at Lincoln Center.

## STONE SOUP SINGING: THE BENEFIT OF MUSICAL GATHERINGS

One of our favorite authors is Jon Muth, who writes and illustrates children's books. He has written a Chinese Buddhist version of the famous European folktale known as *Stone Soup*, a story about a cold, hardened town where no one wants to share with anyone else. In Muth's version, Zen monks come to the town and set up a small pot in the middle of the courtyard, light a fire, and place water with three stones in the pot. Eventually, a curious girl comes by and offers her mother's larger pot. A scholar brings salt and pepper. A farmer's wife brings carrots, and someone else brings onions. Soon everyone wants to get into the act, bringing dumplings, bean curd, mushrooms, and the like. By the end, there is more soup than anyone can imagine, and the townspeople have a giant banquet, with much joy, merriment, and—of course—music. From inedible stones, the ancient miracle of heating water, and the latent generosity of a wounded community comes a pot overflowing with food and festivity.

In our opinion, the absolute apex of communal music is an informal gathering where magic happens spontaneously. The musical memories we remember most are not our moments of onstage glory and applause, playing to tens of thousands, nor are they our moments in the recording studio. The best moments came when something unplanned, unrehearsed, and amazing happened. No one recorded it, we weren't onstage per se; instead, we were sitting around at a party, after dinner, at a campfire in the Adirondacks, or on a top bunk at summer camp, and something came together. Someone sang a harmony that seemed obvious, but we'd never thought of it before. Someone shared a lost verse of an old, beloved song. A new instrument part appeared to perfectly fill a space that had existed. These moments were often filled with more than just the focus on the music; they combined some element of nature (the gloaming of midsummer; the crackling fires of midwinter, the sound of a rushing brook, or late summer crickets) and fellowship (us in our mom's lap, our children in ours, good friends wanting to hear what new tunes we might know, or our wanting to hear theirs). These are the reasons we practice. These are the reasons, in fact, to be a musician: to add our voices to the stone soup of the musical get-together.

# THE COMPLEXITY CHOIR

In his book *Mindsight: The New Science of Personal Transformation*, Daniel Siegel writes of an exercise called Complexity Choir, which he often gives to groups of therapists when he lectures to them on techniques for understanding mental health. He teaches that what we understand as "the mind" is really something that's always working in concert with both our physical brain and the minds and brains of other people; we need to understand the concepts of health and happiness in the context of our relationships with others.

Before he begins, though, he asks for volunteers to lead some group singing. For the first part of the exercise, everyone is told to sing one note. Soon all the participants are humming along on key or close to it. Everyone shares the pitch, but nothing more happens. It's kind of boring after a while, as conformity can be.

Next, he tells everyone to sing their favorite song at top volume. The room is soon filled with the cacophony of all the chosen tunes of different genres sung in different keys, rhythms, and meters. It sounds like a bazaar: interesting but chaotic, and ultimately not very soothing.

Finally, Siegel asks for a suggestion for a song everyone may know. Often, someone chooses "Amazing Grace," which is well known and has a simple but elegant chord structure, predictable changes, and familiar harmonies. At first, most people sing the melody, but as the tune warms up, singers find different parts that suit their vocal range and inclinations, and by the last verse, the room is filled with harmony—or perhaps more accurately, a mellifluous unity. When harmony is achieved, the result sounds like the proverbial whole that is greater than the sum of its parts. "Once the melody is established," Siegel writes. "Individual voices begin to emerge, weaving their harmonies above and below, playing off one another, moving intuitively toward a crescendo before the final notes. Faces light up in choir and audience alike; we are all swept into the flow of the singers' energy and aliveness. At these times, people have said—and I've experienced this as well—there is a palpable sense of vitality that fills the room."[2]

It's not surprising that those who participate in the Complexity Choir are frequently moved by the experience, which aurally demonstrates the differences between rigidity (singing one note) and chaos (the bazaar effect). There are times and places for both. For example, in a yoga class, the group chants the word AUM together, and the meaning of this one tone and its three distinct letters bring the group through a beautiful shared experience.[3] Here, the rigidity serves the group well for the purpose of bringing everyone into a collective awareness of the sacredness of that particular practice and bringing the practitioners into their own bodies as they center themselves.

Likewise, there are times for singing our own song loud and strong. We all need to express our unique voices and ideas. There is certainly a time and place for joyful cacophony, and it's useful:

think of the moment when all the members of the orchestra are tuning their individual instruments. It might not sound lovely, but it's extremely important to establish individual pitches before joining together as a whole.

What's different about harmony is that it achieves balance by finding unity in diversity through the skillful action of each individual; we take our unique talents and make the most of our differences to create a stronger, more interesting, richer experience. It is when we find our own best voice—what our voice can do particularly well—that we thrive in a group setting. Singing is a wonderful way to explore this kind of integration. And singing harmony, which by definition means we participate in a group, provides us with a perfect opportunity to practice being part of a whole, seeing how our small part makes the whole stronger, just as family life does.

## THE CAMPFIRE

Our family spent at least a week every August in the High Peaks region of the Adirondacks mountains in upstate New York. The High Peaks are thus named because there are forty-six mountains, all over four thousand feet, within a 300,000-acre area, and for the past century and a half or so, many people have endeavored to climb them all. Mountain climbing was a great sport on our father's side of the family, and we allegedly went to the Adirondacks to hike. Although we did love to hike, eventually even climbing all forty-six

peaks, the real allure for both of us was what happened after dinner in a cabin with walls that were attached by hinges at the edges of the roof; they could be propped up and out, lifting from the top, to invite in the sounds of the summer woods and the stream at the base of Giant Mountain. This cabin was named "The Stoop," and campers gathered there for dessert, coffee, and mingling; they often pulled out guitars and banjos and gathered around the homemade tables or the fire pit outside the cabin to sing.

The camp director, John Case, played banjo and twelve-string guitar, and he had a number of wonderful songs the staff all knew, like Bill Staines's "Waltzing with Bears" and "River." Whenever Kathy Wiegand came to stay, she and John would sing Stan Rogers's "The Mary Ellen Carter" and Leonard Cohen's "Suzanne." Cal Johnson always sang Lefty Frizzell's song about Saginaw, Michigan. I'm sure it wasn't the only song he knew, but it's the only song I ever heard him sing, and it came to be known at Putnam Camp as "Cal's Song."

Our father had his own songs: "Night Rider's Lament," Odetta's Freedom Trilogy, "Oh Mary, Don't You Weep, Don't You Mourn," and "Four Green Fields." He too had grown up at Putnam Camp, and he remembered the oldsters singing their trademark songs (usually without guitars), such as Doodle Page's "Me Father's a Bonnie Wee Man," complete with pig snorts, squeaks, and whistles. As the years went by, we girls would sing along to those songs we knew as part of our family canon, Katryna matching our dad's pitch an octave higher, while Nerissa—an alto—adapted by making up harmony parts in a more comfortable place for her range.

For those of us who struggle with an instrument, who labor all year to master certain chord progressions or guitar riffs, or who work to sing with a group or on our own—this is why we practice. We do it so that in that one moment, in a shared musical environment around a campfire, we can contribute our part to the whole. In a kind of musical stone soup, a simple and humble three-chord tune can boil and bubble and become fragrant with Anne's harmony, Bill's guitar solo, Dan's banjo flailing, Joanie's drumming, Kathy's new idea for a fifth verse, Rachel's lovely soprano, and that gaggle of kids who suddenly pick up the chorus with gusto four verses in.

As we were finishing this book at the end of summer, our two families gathered together in the Adirondacks. Katryna's family arrived first, and Nerissa's family drove in a few days later. As the car approached the house, Johnny and Lila pointed to the small airfield in town that abuts the main road. "Look!" they shouted. A rescue helicopter was descending through the trees. We stopped to watch as it landed to pick up a ranger and then took off again, presumably to find a missing hiker.

While the grown-ups were enjoying dinner upstairs later that evening, the four kids ventured downstairs. The normal cacophony simmered down from shrieks to silence; curious, Nerissa snuck down to spy on them. The kids were hunkered down in the smallest room in the house. Amelia's back was to the door, and she was playing the small acoustic guitar she'd just received for her ninth birthday. William sat on the baby Adirondack chair, his cardboard bass guitar in his lap. Lila had her violin on her shoulder, bow at the ready, and Johnny was dancing. Amelia was leading the group in "Let It Be," but when William saw Nerissa, he said, "Listen to this! Listen to Amelia's song!"

Amelia then proceeded to sing a song she had just written called "We're Driving in a Race Car Made for Johnny." Johnny, initially dancing ecstatically, said, "No! He'copter through *trees*!" In his bordering-on-verbal way, he had just told his cousins about the rescue scene he'd just witnessed, and Amelia incorporated his vision into her song. It began to dawn on us that Amelia and Johnny (at twenty-four months) had just *cowritten* their first song, now changed to "We're Flying in a Helicopter Made for Johnny." Though we would be the first to insist that effort counts as much as output, we have to admit, we're proud. The song is really good.

After some cajoling, the kids agreed to put on a show for the grown-ups. We all went down to that small room. William acted as master of ceremonies, and each child performed a song. Amelia played another original called "Fairy Tale," William sang some rock and roll, Lila played "I'm a Little Monkey" on the E string of her violin, and Johnny danced to his eponymous song. The grown-ups clapped—a lot.

## Nerissa

The summer I was fourteen, while we were all singing around the campfire in the Adirondacks, someone handed me the guitar. I had been learning to play for the past three years, and that particular summer, I'd started writing my own songs and progressing at a faster clip, devouring the Beatles, Bob Dylan, and anything with three chords in the keys of C and G. I played Bob Dylan's "Mr. Tambourine Man," and as I played and sang all four verses, I felt the hairs on the back of my neck stand up with pleasure. I felt seen by the adults, people I admired and respected, for the first time in my life. When my song was over and greeted with applause and approbation, I felt a kind of warmth and love that I'd never felt before. I was hooked on performing.

## Katryna

One of my best musical memories is of singing "When the Saints Go Marching In" up in the Adirondacks. On one particular night, the Stoop was crammed full of people, and guitars were being passed around. Cal had sung "Saginaw, Michigan," our dad had sung "The Unicorn Song," and John Case had given us "River." But it wasn't until someone chose "When the Saints" (see pages 70–71) that the cabin filled up with voices. Everyone knew that song. Even if they didn't, by the second chorus they could sing along. Since the chorus is call and response, we didn't have to remember any words; we just had to wait for someone to sing them and repeat them back. I'm sure that if I'd been outside the building, I would have seen it sway with the sounds that were created that night.

# FAMILY CHORUSES

Many communities have choruses and choirs that you can join. If you belong to a church or synagogue, there may be choirs where you can learn challenging music on a weekly basis. But if you're yearning for an opportunity to sing together as a family, you might have to get creative.

Perhaps you've tried gathering your friends together for an evening of good food and singing, only to discover that no one is proficient enough at an instrument to lead you all in song. Or maybe you're frustrated by not having harmonies and no one is confident enough to make them up. One solution to this problem is to hire a local musician to help you out. If you're able to find six to twelve families who want to broaden their singing skills, you can probably afford to rent a space and a musician to help you create your own family chorus.

A few years ago, Katryna got a call from a local group that was hoping to start a family chorus. This group was made up of about eight families, with children ranging in age from one to nine. They were musical, but they needed some help building a repertoire and making up harmonies. They also knew that if they all paid a little money (about $15 to $20 per family per week), they would feel committed to singing together and would show up for each other each week. At one point, they thought the group might last for a few months, until they had their songbook. It ended up lasting for about three years. Some families moved away, while others' children became too busy with soccer or ballet to attend, but new families joined and filled in the gaps.

Katryna asked for song suggestions that the group wanted to learn and also took along a pile of material that became their songbook. Group members worked best when there was a songbook and a CD that they could study and return to each week for a period of ten to twelve weeks. They learned three- and four-part harmony and countless rounds, and they expanded their family canons.

Here are some tips on starting your own family chorus:

**1.** Find a space that is conducive to singing. A piano is a huge plus and possibly a necessity if the songleader is a pianist and not a guitarist. Having a separate room for kids who are having a hard time concentrating while the adults are learning harmonies can be helpful, but it's not essential. It is important to find a space that's pretty empty, so that parents of toddlers aren't spending the entire time policing their children. In the summer, you can find a park to sing in. Just be sure to have a backup location in case of rain.

**2.** Find a musician to lead you. Finding the right leader can be tricky. Make sure you're on the same track about whether you want the group to work toward a performance or just have the experience of singing along. You want someone who knows how to teach harmonies, who can play an instrument to accompany the group, and who has knowledge of the world of music you wish to draw from. Don't choose a jazz expert if you want to learn folk music. Don't choose a folk musician if you want to learn Handel's *Messiah*.

**3**. Get the word out to other families. You want enough people to keep the costs down, but not so many that the evenings feel chaotic.

**4**. Have fun. Keep your eyes and ears open for music you want to learn. Practice the music often so that it becomes part of you.

The chorus Katryna worked with eventually disbanded, but they still go camping together a couple of times a year. They now have what they set out to find: improved skills to make singing together even more fun. When they go camping, they can still remember all of their harmony parts to their favorite songs.

## GARAGE BAND OF OUR DREAMS

An alternative to the family chorus, of course, is the all-American garage band. Maybe that old guitar in the closet has made its way back into your hands as part of parenting and creating a musical family. Maybe you now remember all the chords and fingering to "Stairway to Heaven." Perhaps every time you get to that power chord section at the end, you miss John Paul Jones's bass and Jon Bonham's drums. You begin to yearn for a rhythm section of your own. You begin to toss

around the idea of starting a band with other parents at the soccer field on Saturday mornings. Parents have support groups of all kinds—book groups, play groups. Why not a rock band?

Our friend Peter is part of a band called The Dadz. Every year, they get together and sell out our local club, The Iron Horse. They donate all the funds to the Northampton public school system.

The creation of a band can do wonderful things for a community in completely unforeseen ways. Take our friend Gerry's reggae band. After spending much of his adult life writing and singing reggae music in the comfort of his living room, Gerry had a vision of the kind of band he wanted, and he started asking local musicians to join his band. Within a few months, they were booked into a local reggae festival and played several shows around the region at restaurants and clubs. The band is wonderful for what it does for its members. They're making music they love, and they're having a blast playing together. But the truly remarkable result is that the band brings the whole community together. Neighbors would gather at whatever venue the band chooses, and they spend time together; laugh together; dance together. By the end of that first summer, our community had come together more than it had in years.

So how do you build a band? There are two ways of going about it. The first is to imagine your dream band and then go out and try to find members to fulfill that dream. The second is to find people with whom you want to spend time and make music. Then create a band that reflects the strengths and capabilities of those people.

## POTLUCK SING-ALONGS

Our friends John and Andrea host parties four times a year on the "off" points of the solar calendar: Imbolc (Groundhog Day), Beltane (May Day), Lughnesa (midsummer, around July 31) and Samhein (Halloween). John used to be a member of a rock band called Big Bad Bollocks and a music director for a local radio station. Their parties have a sound system, a drum kit, and all sorts of instruments. Their guests take music making very seriously, and huge, wonderful, all-family jam sessions ensue. When we think of stone soup sing-alongs, theirs would be the gold standard.

Sometime at the end of the 1990s, when we were traveling 340 days a year, playing in rock clubs and folk coffeehouses and theaters and festivals all over the country, Katryna called Nerissa. "I want to have a sing-along," she said. "Patty [our manager] wants us to have a sing-along. She wants to hear us sing Nanci Griffith. I'm going to put together a music book and invite everyone over to my house. We'll sing great old songs like the ones we sang at Camp Greenway."

Katryna put together a book of photocopied lyric sheets, including copies of songs her husband, Dave, had been given by his first guitar teacher—the theme from *Welcome Back Kotter*, "Rocky Raccoon," and "Heart of Gold." We went online and found the words and chords to "Trouble in the Field" for Patty. We invited over all our friends—some of whom were professional musicians, and some of whom couldn't carry a tune—and tore through the songbook

Patty decided that she was allergic to sing-alongs (we heartily acknowledge that sing-alongs are not for everyone) and vowed never to return, but other than that, the party was a huge success. The songbooks made their way over to Nerissa's house. She didn't have a drum kit or sound system like John and Andrea, but for years, she attempted to hold a potluck sing-along on a monthly basis.

The rules were easy. Nerissa cooked two roast chickens with yams, and everyone brought a dish to share. After food, we gathered in the music room and brought out the songbooks. Our neighbor Pablo brought over his bongo drum, and his son, Isaac, played a coffee mug with a spoon. Sometimes our friend Margaret played the piano, unless Pete was around. Ben occasionally showed up and sweetened the meeting considerably with his uncanny ability to find a third note to whatever harmony was called for. Our friend Rick drove down from Maine now and then to play "Greensleeves" on the musical saw. After Obama was elected, we sang version after version of "People Get Ready." "Irene, Goodnight" marked the end of the evening, as it had when our father sang to us as small kids.

At our last potluck sing-along, William, then age five, strapped on his father's Hofner bass (three times as long as he is), while our friend Aidan, age three, joined him playing a toy guitar with a blown-up photo of John Lennon's famous Rickenbacker affixed to the face of it. Sixteen-month-old Johnny pulled Nerissa's Taylor down off the guitar stand and tried to play it. Later in the evening he climbed the stairs to his bedroom and came out carrying a purple Little Tykes toy piano, which he proceeded to hurl to the bottom of the stairs as if to say, "I want to play too!" (We had laid out our array of drums and small hand instruments, but Johnny clearly had his sights set on something bigger.) At one point in the evening, William sang, "I'm Down," perfectly, including the big rock-and-roll scream before the guitar solo. We interspersed "Organic Farm" and "Allee Allee O" with "It's the End of the World As We Know It," "Deportees," and "Eight Days a Week."

These evenings are rich with connection and meaning. In the space of about two hours, we felt reconnected to our heritage, our music, and our community; we were deeply entertained and amused, often moved, and sometimes in (happy) tears. It's fun to watch our community of friends grow closer over the years; many folks have been coming to our parties since the nineties and know each other (not to mention the last verse to the theme song of *Welcome Back Kotter*) through repeated exposure at these parties. In the winter, we light a fire. In the summer, we play outside until the mosquitoes drive us in. We can't think of a better way to spend a Saturday night. Here's how to get your own potluck sing-along started:

**1.** Make songbooks! We like three-ring binders so it's easy to add material as your repertoire grows over time, as it will, along with your community of friends. Ask newcomers to bring copies of their favorites on three-hole-punch paper.

It sounds uptight, but it's helpful to keep the books organized alphabetically. If you number the pages, it's obviously more challenging to add songs later. Once you're in the thick of the sing-along, you'll want to be able to call out titles and have your guests find them easily.

**2.** Get a copy (or several) of *Rise Up Singing,* the invaluable songbook put together by Peter Blood and Annie Patterson. It's chock-full of song lyrics and chords.

**3.** Find a friend who plays guitar or piano by ear or can read a songbook.

**4.** Gather in a friendly and supportive environment. Musicians can occasionally be insecure, competitive, and domineering. Keep the atmosphere light and playful, and make it about having fun rather than rehearsing or "learning."

**5.** Designate a song leader. In some cases, even with seasoned musicians, you'll encounter shyness or reticence. A song will get played, everyone will sing their hearts out, and then there'll be a strange silence as if no one feels worthy of choosing the next song. This is why the most important role at a hootenanny is played by the person who acts as de facto song leader. That person needn't be the one who's playing or leading the music, just the person who calls out the songs. Pick someone who has good taste in music and explain ahead of time what the job entails. Give the leader a songbook. When there is a postsong lull, it's the leader's job to call out the next song and where to find it in the songbook.

**6.** Remember, use food and drink judiciously to get people in the mood.

**7.** Don't forget the kids! Keep them interested, unless your goal is to shoo them all to the second floor or out of the house. Mix up your program with songs they'll know or ask them for requests.

**8.** Don't forget the parents (include songs for both). Sing at least one song you really want to sing. Make sure you have fun too. It's your party, and you can sing Sonny & Cher tunes if you want to.

**9.** If you're invited to a hootenanny, be sure to take your own guitar and add your own song. Don't be shy! Remember that even if your voice is only one of many, you're adding something crucial to the stone soup experience. If it's too scary to sing, you can bring a few harmonicas in common keys, such as C, D, and G.

# AFTERWORD

ALTHOUGH WE'VE BEEN ENCOURAGING you to listen to music often as a family, for the purpose of full disclosure, it wasn't until just the other day that Nerissa finally had her stereo receiver fixed so that static-free music could play from her system for the first time in five years. From the time she was pregnant with Lila until last week, she just couldn't find the time to dismantle the stereo, drag it to the electronics store, lug it back home, and then reattach the speakers. It was a seemingly small act but hugely helpful to her grand plan of infusing day-to-day routines with music; however, the silver lining of not having the stereo was that she was forced to sing and make up songs for her children herself for five years.

Discovering, creating, and maintaining a musical family is not necessarily easy. We were raised with so much family music, have made it our profession for the past twenty years, and run and teach a toddler music program, but even we have to work hard at this—and we certainly fall short of our own ideal on a regular basis. We have to remind ourselves why it's worth it to fix the stereo so we can better discover new family music, to step away from the computer when the kids want to sing, to fit in instrument practice when it might mean someone is late to school or work. We have to make time for creativity or it doesn't happen. We have to build small pockets of time into each day to let kids (and our own inner kids) explore the soundscape, discover the box of percussion instruments, make a homemade instrument out of found objects or something new. We have to build time into our weeks for HooteNanny classes, for piano and violin lessons, for dance, for songwriting. Most of all, we have to be willing to drop our own agenda to crouch down on the floor and pretend to be sheep or chickens or cows or iguanas as we make up new verses to "Organic Farm."

We also have to struggle with the idea that somehow we don't have what it takes to be a "real" musical family. So we want to end with this last exhortation, which may be obvious to you, but it bears stating nonetheless: you are not a failure of any kind if your kids don't go on to make a living at music. You are not a failure if they aren't Broadway material or if they don't make it into the high school musical. You are not a failure, in fact, if your kids can't sing on key.

We have no ambitions for our kids save happiness; yet we will encourage them to make music and to practice and treat their instruments with dignity and respect. The instruments might not be priceless, but the time our children spend practicing on and playing them is. Our hopes for our children are the same as our hopes for yours—that they will discover the music around them in all its forms; that they will discover the musician within themselves with all the magical and transformative powers musicians possess; and that they will discover the myriad ways music can connect them to their friends, family members, community, and planet. Put simply, we hope that the music they discover, share, and create will bring them great joy.

## Katryna

As I have worked on this book, I have also been experiencing just how music shapes my family life. I grew up in a house where music was a joyful hobby. It was part of my schooling, my churchgoing experience, my interactions with friends, and my family's interaction with friends. It was part of every season of the year from carols around the piano in December to folk songs around the campfire in August. Music was one of the languages in which my family was fluent.

I spent a semester of college in Nepal, during which I trekked, learned Nepali, and sang. I took my guitar, and it was my connection to so many of the people I met. I sang with the other college students who were studying with me; I sang for the teachers at the school who taught me their language; I sang for the children of the family with whom I lived.

During my final oral exam in Nepali, the teacher asked what my job would be when I was an adult. I asked him how to say *lawyer* in Nepali. He looked at me, confused, and said, "Won't you be a musician?" It wasn't until then that I realized I was allowed to choose music as my career. It didn't have to be a hobby.

As we mentioned earlier in the book, we plunged into the professional musician's lifestyle. We spent most of our time traversing the country in a fifteen-passenger Dodge Ram van with an attached trailer, sleeping in Motel 6 rooms and on our friends' floors. We played shows four to five nights a week, and I mostly loved it. Our father's only concern for us when we told him we were going to "go for it" with music was that something joyful might be lost when we tried to make a living from it.

To a certain extent, he was right. Music became my job. Until my children were born, I rarely sang anywhere but on the stage, in rehearsal, and in the studio. Taking music back and singing to my babies, playing guitar to my toddlers, and making up songs with my preschoolers was the greatest gift I could have gotten.

As a result, we have stressed the value of music to your family life. Perhaps we sometimes take for granted the fact that our hard work and focus has allowed us to make music our vocation.

Though we won't discount how wonderful it is, and has been, for us to have the honor of calling ourselves professional musicians and to passionately love our job, we have focused here on how to get as much joy and connection from music as possible in everyday life.

As my daughter approaches her tween years, I meet parents of budding teenage musicians. They are curious as to whether I'm hoping that my child will follow in her musician parents' footsteps. They wonder if I'm a proud, excited stage mother who has dreams of record contracts and stardom for my young maestros. The truth is I don't want them to have music so they can achieve some kind of fame. I want them to have music so that when they are despairing, bored, curious, confused, or lonely, they'll have music to

keep them company. They'll have the ability to write their way out of their sadness. It reminds me of when they were babies and every baby book told me to help them find a transitional object—a stuffed animal that would soothe them when their parents went to bed. Music, I now realize, is their security blanket.

Like everyone, I have read the studies that say that music will make my children better at math; raise their SAT scores; and make them smarter, better, kinder, and more interesting. Ultimately, none of that matters. The reasons that I want my kids to have music are twofold. First, the one thing I'm sure of is that being passionate about something—anything—can protect and enrich a person. As a result, I'm always on the lookout for what lights my kids up, what makes them excited and expressive. We have no idea what the world will hold for the next generation, but we do know that curiosity and creativity will serve them well no matter what. So I keep my eyes peeled for their curious moments. I pay attention to what interests them and try to encourage them to dig deeper.

Perhaps because we have a house full of instruments, because I sang to my kids, or because we lucked into having a wonderful piano teacher, both of my children have gravitated toward music.

The second reason I want my kids to have music is that I now have a way to connect with them. Even when we

have a big family ruckus and everyone loses dessert for poor behavior, we may be able to make up by sitting around the music room, Amelia on the violin, Dave on the guitar, William on the drums, and all of us singing "Twist and Shout" at the top of our lungs. "Well, shake it up, baby, now!"

## Nerissa

Before Johnny was born, when Lila was still pretty much a baby, Katryna painted me an irresistible picture as we were driving to a gig one afternoon. She said, "We're in the most amazing stage these

days. Every night after bathtime, Dave takes out his guitar, and the kids put on this crazy cowboy hat, which for some reason they call 'La Bamba hat.' Whenever the hat is on someone's head, Dave has to play that song. We all sing it and then segue into 'Twist and Shout' and then to something else. Pretty soon we're doing the kind of sing-

ing I remember us doing with Daddy when we were kids. It's happened. I got what I always wanted."

This vision of family singing and fun was tantalizing to me. I too have always hoped I could bring music to my family in the same way our dad brought it to us, yet I've simultaneously feared I wouldn't be up to the job, that my kids wouldn't love music, or that Tom wouldn't think a La Bamba hat situation would be that much fun. I had the very thought that we hope to disprove with this book: "We'll never have that because we're just not that musical."

Flash forward three years. Tom and Lila and Johnny and I were in the Adirondacks for a week of summer vacation. As I was working on drafts of this book, I was actually trying to do all the things we suggest, so I made a family Adirondack playlist for the trip and took along our iPod and its speakers. The mix had something for everyone: lots of Dan Zanes, They Might Be Giants, Elizabeth Mitchell, and HooteNanny songs for the kids; Van Morrison, Bruce Springsteen, and Nanci Griffith for Tom; the Beatles and James Taylor for me.

After a dinner of fresh local corn, salmon, and summer squash with peaches, I put on the mix while we cleaned up. Dan Zanes's version of "Waltzing Matilda" with special guest Deborah Harry (from Blondie) came on. I love that song, but it's not in our repertoire. I grabbed my guitar and strummed around until I found the key—C. Easy. I figured out the chords the way my father taught me so many years ago, and in short order, I was playing along. Lila immediately ran to get her violin. At that time, she knew exactly two notes, E and A. Not bad notes for the key of C. She played those two notes, using a rhythm she invented that worked wonderfully and naturally with the tune coming out of the speakers and out of my guitar and mouth. Tom handed Johnny, not quite

two, some upside-down bowls and a wooden spoon, then he grabbed the tongs from the corn pot and used them as makeshift castanets. He and Lila paraded around the kitchen island, while Johnny and I remained in our seats to play. Whenever we got to the end of the song, Johnny shouted, "Again 'Tilda," and we pressed the back button and played it again. Finally, Johnny let us listen to the next song, which was They Might Be Giants' "Roy G. Biv" from their *Here Comes Science* CD for kids. This one has some funkier chords, but I figured them out while the rest of my family danced like maniacs around the living room.

We repeated this fun the next night and the

next. One night there was no iPod; just me playing the guitar and the kids making up vehicles to insert into the template of "I'm a Little Airplane Now." (Johnny's was "I'm a blue motorcycle now," while Lila challenged us with "I'm a pink princess racing car shaped like Tinker Bell now.")

Driving home, Tom and I kept reflecting back on the experience. We still smile from it, and I feel that glow you get when you achieve a lifelong dream. We do have "that." We have what I feared we couldn't. It was there all the time, just waiting for us to discover it.

# ACKNOWLEDGMENTS

WE WERE INCREDIBLY LUCKY TO HAVE grown up in a house filled with music. We cannot imagine writing this book or even conceiving of this book without the musical inspiration of our family: John and Gail Nields, Abigail Nields, Elizabeth Nields, Laura Page, Jennifer Nields, Sarah Tenney, John Nields, Sr., Lila Nields, and Midge Tenney. We also couldn't have written this without the legacy of our amazing music teachers Jill Bixler, Mr. Henderson, Mr. and Mrs. Lentz, Nancy Taylor, Mary Roberts, Katherine Nevius, Marge Silvis, and, of course, Jack Langstaff and everyone at Revels who generously and passionately help to keep his work alive. And to family friends who added to our musical world: John Case and Putnam Camp, Camp Greenway, Immanuel Presbyterian Church, The Potomac School, The Madeira School, and TUIB. Thank you.

This book would not exist without the encouragement of Johnny Marciano and Jess Bacal. We thank our fabulous agent, James Levine, and our incredible editor, Jennifer Urban-Brown, and everyone at Shambhala. We also want to thank our manager, Patty Romanoff, our booking agent, Lori Peters, and our publicist, Michaela O'Brien.

Thanks to the music teachers we have discovered as adults: Lui Collins, Penny Schultz, Emily Greene, Maggie Schollenburger, Music Together, and Katryna's Family Folk Chorus. And all the amazing families who join us on this musical journey in our HooteNanny classes. We love you, HooteNiers! Thank you!

Thanks to our wonderful readers Heather Abel, Lisa Papademetriou, Becky Serlin, Kate Cebik, Matthew Harvey, and all the writers in the Big Yellow writing groups who have listened with such patience and kindness to draft after draft.

Thanks also to Donna Ngai, Shawn Charest (for Granola Gramps), Karen Jasper for "merrily/row" calculus, Mary Jane Cuneo for the dulcimer story, Mike Biegner for sharing family mixes on car trips, Prudy Marsh for the "Red Red Wine" story, and Shakira Alvarez for "Jingle Bells" as a lullaby. The Chalfants for their musical son.

So, so much love and gratitude to our amazing husbands, Dave Chalfant and Tom Nields-Duffy. We are the luckiest.

Most of all, we want to thank Amelia, William, Lila, and Johnny. You have been by far our best teachers.

# APPENDIX 1
## How to Tune Your Voice

THERE'S A PLACE WHERE IT IS EASIEST FOR your voice to sing—your key. You've probably heard professional musicians talking about their key. "Play it in B♭," Mama Rose calls to the piano player when her daughters are auditioning for vaudeville. You can find your own best key simply by singing where it feels most comfortable and then matching those pitches to a keyboard or guitar, if you know the notes. (If you don't, ask a friendly neighborhood musician for help!). Your range—the notes you sing most easily—may be only five notes. That's okay. That's plenty. More likely, you'll have an octave to play with. Nerissa's favorite octave goes from the G below middle C to the G above. On good days, she can even comfortably belt the B♭ above middle C. Katryna's range is more like A to C. Our dad's, of course, is much lower, probably low C to the E above middle C. That doesn't mean we can't sing notes higher or lower, but they are "stretches." The more you sing, the wider your range will be.

Once you know your range, you can see which keys work best for you. Usually, the key you love most is designated by the letter in the middle of your range. So a person with a G-to-G range like Nerissa's will like the keys of B♭ and C. (If you listen to our albums, you will notice a predominance of this.) Katryna might prefer the keys of C and D, but only if she is well rested. If she happens to be vacationing in Hawaii, where it's humid (voices love humidity), she might opt for the key of E.

Children's voices are immature; their vocal chords and voice boxes are smaller than those of adults, which might seem obvious, but we stress this point for a reason. When you're trying to sing along with your child, it's important to pitch the song in a comfortable place for both of you. This might take some compromise. In general, a child's voice is a good fifth above that of the parent's. So Nerissa's key is C, and Lila's is F. Just as it's helpful for you to know your own key, knowing your children's will enhance your musical experience with them.

Don't worry if your voice isn't on pitch. Tone deafness (*amusia* is the technical term) is quite rare; only 4 percent of the population has this defect.[1] It's about as common as color blindness. You can still learn to sing. And definitely don't worry if your child's voice isn't on pitch. Many kids who go on to become excellent singers don't learn to match pitch accurately until they're in their teens. Singing in tune is, in part, a physical issue; think of riding a bike or throwing a ball. Just as gross or fine motor skills vary developmentally from child to child, so do musical ones.

It's much more important to instill enthusiasm for singing in them than to attempt to get them to hit notes with any kind of accuracy (which will probably be in vain). Revel instead in your children's gorgeous, unique tones and funny diction. And when you're singing with them, stretch your own voice up a few notes so they're comfortable. (It will be good for your voice to stretch. Just be sure you're singing gently and not belting away in your chest voice.)

# APPENDIX 2
## Quick and Easy Music Theory

A DISCUSSION OF MUSIC THEORY REALLY merits an entire book by itself. What you'll find here is a quick summary of what we think you need to help you understand the most common song forms: the three-chord folk, pop, and rock-and-roll songs (three genres—same three chords). We'll discuss notes, triads, and how triads make chords, and we'll give you a quick and easy guitar lesson and a brief explanation of how to transpose from one key to another.

For the purposes of keeping this quick and easy, we're starting with three assumptions:

- We're talking only about the Western major scale, which has seven notes. We're not dealing with minors (much), half tones, Indian music, or jazz.
- We're giving you only four chords. Most of the world's songs can be played with just three, but you get an extra chord to grow on.
- You know nothing.

## SOLFÈGE

Solfège was made famous (to us) by the song "Do-Re-Mi," which might be one of the world's best family songs. We love several things about this song. First of all, it makes music essentially playful, which it is—or should be. Those squiggly notes on a G clef can be baffling to children (and adults) and can seem entirely divorced from the music they hear in their heads. But for the self-taught, ear-trained musician, solfège is an easy, friendly way to learn the notes in a major scale.

There are two kinds of solfège: "fixed do" (where do is always the note C) and "movable do" (where do is the tonic, or first note, of whatever key you happen to be in). Don't worry about this. For now, stick with the key of C, as it's friendly to the vocal ranges of both kids and adults alike. Also, it's the easiest key to play on the piano (all the white keys) and second-easiest key to play on the guitar. (The easiest key for the guitar is G, which Pete Seeger calls "the people's key.")

To talk about solfège, we have to talk about whole steps and half steps.

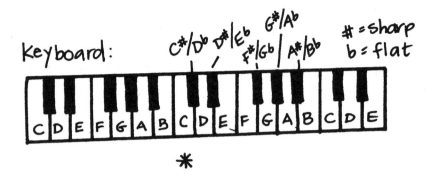

Here is a piano keyboard. The half steps are simply the steps between each of the notes, black, white, whatever. Notice that there are spaces where there are no black keys. In the key of C, these are the half steps.

In the diagram, we have marked C with a star. This is Do. So for fixed Do:

Do is C.
Re (D) is one whole step up from C.
Mi (E) is one whole step up from D.
Fa (F) is one half step up. (See how there is no black key between E and F?)
Sol (G) is one whole step up from F.
La (A) is one whole step up from G.
Ti (B) is one whole step up from A.
Do (C) is one half step up from B.

Don't worry about why. Just remember, in a Western major scale, the intervals—or distances between the notes—go like this:

Whole, Whole, Half, Whole, Whole, Whole, Half.
Do (whole), Re (whole), Mi (half), Fa (whole), Sol (whole), La (whole), Ti (half), Do.

## TRIADS

To make a simple major chord, you need three notes: do, mi, and sol. If do is C, then mi is E and sol is G. When you play these notes together on the piano, you have a C chord.

You may notice that both notes and chords have letter names. The difference is that chords are three notes composed of *triads*, and we use the first note's letter to name the whole chord. Thus, the C chord is composed of CEG; the G chord is made up of GBD; and so on. But don't worry about this. For now, just learn the shapes in the diagrams that follow.

When you play a C triad (CEG) on the piano, it looks like this:

**C CHORD**

When you play these notes on the guitar, it looks like this:

**C**

## THE BIG THREE

The "big three" chords that can make a musician out of anyone are called the I chord, the IV chord, and the V chord. (The numbers of the chords are most often written in Roman numerals, as shown

here, but you may see them elsewhere in Arabic numerals.) We will again stick with the key of C.

In the key of C, another name for C is the *tonic*, or the I chord. About 95 percent of the time, a song will begin on the I chord, and 99.9 percent of the time, it will end on the I chord as well.

Ready to move on?

The other two chords you must know for the purposes of playing three-chord songs are the IV chord and the V chord. The IV chord is four notes up from the I chord, so in the key of C, the IV chord is F. Its triad is FAC, so on the piano it looks like this:

**F CHORD**

And on the guitar, it looks like this:

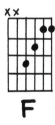

**F**

The V chord is five notes up from the I chord, so in the key of C, the V chord is G. The triad is

GBD. Count seven half steps, including the black keys:

## G CHORD

If you look at the piano, middle C is the first of the pattern of three white keys separated by two black keys. To C's left is another white key, B (see the preceding diagram). If you're moving to the right, then the "five" is up five. If you're moving to the left, "five" is actually down four.

Here is the V chord in the key of C, also known as G, on the guitar:

## G

When you play a V chord, you will have an almost irresistible urge to resolve the chord to the tonic, or play the I chord.

Try singing "Row, Row, Row Your Boat" out loud. When you get to "Life is but a dream," hold the word *a* for as long as you can before singing the word *dream*. If people are listening to you as you hold that last note (a D if you're playing in the key of C), they may want to smack you to get

you to resolve it. We must be hardwired to want resolution.

## AND A FOURTH CHORD TO GROW ON

The final chord we will teach you is the vi chord. Notice that it has a lowercase Roman numeral because it's a minor chord. Minor chords have a quirk in their triad. Instead of a regular triad, the third note (the mi of that chord) is one half step lower. So a major C triad (CEG) becomes minor when you lower the E to E♭. CE♭G is a C minor chord, which is often written "Cm." In the key of C, the relative minor, or vi chord, is A minor, often written "Am." On the guitar, it looks like this:

## Am

On the piano, it looks like this:

## Am CHORD

## TRANSPOSING FROM ONE KEY TO ANOTHER

Here is a chart to show what the I, IV, and V chords are in many different keys, since many of you won't like singing in the key of C. Changing from one key to another is called *transposing*. If you play the guitar, you can also just use a capo, which makes the entire key higher as you move the capo up the neck of the guitar.

| I | IV | V | vi* |
|---|----|----|-----|
| C | F | G | Am |
| D | G | A | Bm |
| E | A | B | C#m |
| F | B♭ | C | Dm |
| G | C | D | Em |
| A | D | E | F#m |

Chords have moods within the context of their key. The I chord feels like home, safe and familiar, like Mom or Dad. The V chord feels like adventure or a rebellious teenager, the movement away. The IV chord feels like the good kid, the one who puts his dinner plate in the dishwasher and helps carry heavy things to the car. The vi chord, or the relative minor, seems like the sad

one. Listen to Simon and Garfunkel's "The Boxer." Tap your foot along with the beat. As the song begins, you are in a major key: the tonic or I chord. But when your foot taps the seventh beat––the one over the word "told"— the chord changes to the relative minor or the vi chord. Notice how you feel when the music moves from the sunniness of that one chord to the melancholy of the vi chord. It's like Picasso's blue period. And think of the plaintive way Simon and Garfunkel sing that chorus, which starts with the Am: "Lie la lie [cymbal crash!]" That's pure minor key dramatics!

Listen to "Row, Row, Row Your Boat," which has just two chords. It's all C until the word *but* third from the end, when you move to a V chord (G). This is a great song to start with, so try this on the piano or guitar.

**C**
Row, row, row your boat,

Gently down the stream.

Merrily, merrily, merrily, merrily,
**C**    **G**    **C**
Life is but a dream.

*This is the most common "fourth" chord—the relative minor, or vi, chord.

# QUICK AND EASY GUITAR LESSON

Here are diagrams of an acoustic and an electric guitar:

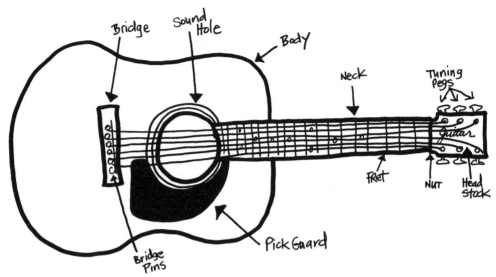

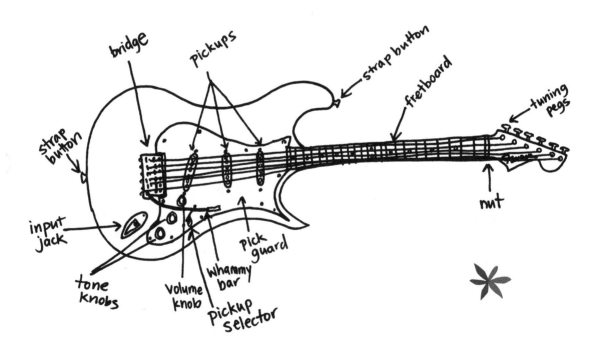

*Appendix 2*

Can you see how the little chord diagrams connect to the guitar as a whole?

The guitar is usually strung like this:

EADGBE

When you put your finger on a string and press down, each fret (the frets are the metal ridges on the neck) makes the string sound one half step higher. So if you finger the low E string on the first fret, you will play an F. If you finger the same string on the second fret, you will play an F♯.

Here are some general tips:

• If you're right-handed, you'll most likely play the chords with your left hand. Press down hard with the tips of your left fingers. You never need to use your thumb, except to support your hand on the back of the guitar neck. You will have sore fingers for a while, and that's good. Let small, circular calluses build up.

• For now, stick with first-position chords, which means play them all the way toward the nut of the guitar. Once you have mastered this, you may play barre chords (Barre chords use the index finger to make a kind of movable capo. The other three fingers then form the chord.)

• To play any chord as a barre chord, you need to understand that when you play the low string (or E string) without touching it with your left hand, you'll play the note E. (That's why it's the E string.) If you put your index finger in the middle of the first fret, you will play the note F. The next note up (on the second fret) is F♯. Next

comes G on the third fret, G♯ on the fourth, A on the fifth, B♭ on the sixth, B on the seventh, C on the eighth, C♯ on the ninth, D on the tenth, and E♭ on the eleventh. That will bring us back to do (in this case, E) on the twelfth fret. If you make a barre on a given fret and then form the E chord, whatever fret or note your barre is on on the E string informs the entire chord. Thus, a barre on the fifth fret with an E shape is the A chord. A barre on the seventh fret with an E shape is the B chord. (Barre chords are difficult. You have to hold your index finger down really hard, as though it were a capo, and then form the chord with the other three weak and formerly inadequate fingers. But it's just like lifting weights; the more you do it, the stronger you get and the easier it is to play.)

- Your right hand is your strumming/picking/fingerpicking hand. It controls the rhythm of the song. For starters, just strum with your thumb or a pick—down, down, down, down—until it's time to change chords. Try to play a song slowly enough so that you can maintain an even beat with your right hand while changing chords seamlessly with your left. This will require that you play the song much more slowly than you might like. That's all right. It's good, actually. Slow and steady wins the race, as the tortoise knows.

## QUICK AND EASY PIANO LESSON

You can actually go far on the piano playing only the black keys (see page 43) or, if you're willing to stick to the key of C, only the white keys.

## Inversions

It's extremely useful to know how to play an inversion of a triad on the piano. As we explained earlier, a regular triad is three stacked notes, such as CEG. An inversion is when you take the notes and put them in a different order. First inversion is when you take the first note and put it last (EGC). Second inversion is when you take the third note and place it first (GCE).

If you don't use inversions on the piano, you'll just be playing blocky triads awkwardly all over the keyboard. Using inversions also minimizes hand movements. Try playing a C triad in first inversion (EGC) and moving to the F triad with no inversion (FAC). See how your hand barely needs to move? Much better than if you tried to play the regular C triad (CEG) and then move to FAC.

*Appendix 2*

Here's how to play the three main chords in the key of C.

For the I chord, play a C triad in first inversion with your right hand: E (the one above middle C), G (the one above middle C), and C (the one an octave above middle C). With your left hand, just play one note: the C below middle C.

## C CHORD

For the IV chord, play an F triad with your right hand, no inversion: F (the one above middle C), A, and C (the one an octave above middle C).

## F CHORD

For the V chord, play a G triad in second inversion with your right hand: D (just above middle C), G (above middle C), and B (the one right below high C, or an octave above middle C). With your left hand, play the G below middle C.

## G CHORD

Now you have three chords. Practice playing them in quarter notes, switching every four beats from one chord to another like this:

C, C, C, C
F, F, F, F
C, C, C, C
G, G, G, G

Repeat this exercise until you can transition smoothly from one chord to another. As it gets easier, you can begin to vary your rhythm. Instead of playing those four boring beats, mix it up a little. Hold a chord for three beats, then play it again on the fourth, then switch to the next chord and do the same thing:

1, 2, 3, 4
C (hold, hold) C
F (hold, hold)F
C (hold, hold)C
G (hold, hold)G

Or do an "um-chuck" rhythm, like the one in "Organic Farm." Play the bass note on the down-beat and the triad in the right hand on the upbeat. Now you're playing microbeats: 1 and 2 and 3 and 3 and 4 and.

C (bass) C (triad) C (bass) C (triad) C (bass) C (triad) C (bass) C (triad)
   1      &      2      &      3      &      4      &

Liv-   ing   on   a   farm ———————— an

D (bass) Dm (triad) D (bass) Dm (triad) G (bass) G (triad) G (bass) G (triad)
   1      &      2      &      3      &      4      &

Or ————— gan - ic   farm ————— and

G (bass) G (triad) G (bass) G (triad) G (bass) G (triad) G (bass) G (triad)
   1      &      2      &      3      &      4      &

On ——— that ——— farm there was an

C (bass) C (triad) C (bass) C (triad) C (bass) C (triad) C (bass) C (triad)
   1      &      2      &      3      &      4      &

Or ————— gan - ic   cow   and the cow said...

And so on.

As a pianist who knows just three chords, you can still play lots of songs. Without reading music, you can play the block chords (triads and inversions) above the words of the songs in this book or many other music books geared to guitar players where just chord names are shown. You can expand to other keys too, as long as you're willing to mix a few black keys in with your white ones. Just learn the triads shown here:

When you see a ♯ (sharp), you play the black key *above* the note on the piano. When you see a ♭ (flat), you play the black key *below* the note on the piano. (See the diagram on page 228.)

Hooray! Now you can start playing all the famous three-chord songs! You'll find a list of them in Appendix 3.

| I | IV | V | vi |
|---|---|---|---|
| C | F | G | Am |
| CEG | FAC | GBD | ACE |
| D | G | A | Bm |
| DF♯A | GBD | AC♯E | BDF♯ |
| E | A | B | C♯m |
| EG♯B | AC♯E | BD♯F♯ | C♯EG♯ |
| F | B♭ | C | Dm |
| FAC | B♭DF | CEG | DFA |
| G | C | D | Em |
| GBD | CEG | DF♯A | EGB |
| A | D | E | F♯m |
| AC♯E | DF♯A | EG♯B | F♯AC♯ |

# APPENDIX 3
## Songs for Every Occassion

## EXAMPLES OF FAMILY MUSICAL CANONS

Here are our current family musical canons, as well as those with which we and our parents grew up. Our current ones are just for today, with a few hopes for the future. Even the one we grew up with, the Nields family canon of John, Gail, Nerissa, Katryna, and Abigail is in flux.

Remember, the whole idea of family musical canons is that they are works in progress. We polled our family—near and extended—and tried to limit each canon to twenty-five songs, which is roughly the number you can fit on a CD. Of course, by the time this book goes to print, CDs may well be obsolete. But twenty-five is still a good number.

## Nields Family Canon

Banks of the Ohio
Blowin' in the Wind
Blue ("I had a dog . . .")
The Blue Tail Fly

City of New Orleans
Four Green Fields
The Fox
Freedom Trilogy (Odetta)
Happy Birthday (in five-part harmony)
Irene, Goodnight
Jacob's Ladder
Last Night I Had the Strangest Dream
The Leaving of Liverpool
Lord of the Dance
Michael, Row the Boat Ashore
Miss Mary Mac
Night Rider's Lament
Oh Mary, Don't You Weep, Don't You Mourn
Puff the Magic Dragon
Rattlin' Bog
Sunny Days (from *Sesame Street*)
Sur le Pont d'Avignon
Swing Low, Sweet Chariot
There Is a Balm in Gilead
This Land Is Your Land
The Unicorn Song
When the Saints Go Marching In

Will the Circle Be Unbroken
Yellow Submarine

## Nerissa's Family Canon

ABC Song (standard and the Nields)
Allee Allee O
Blind Willie McTell
Deck the Halls
Desperado
Do-Re-Mi (and the rest of *The Sound of Music* soundtrack)
Going to Boston
Hush, Little Baby (the Nields)
Madame George (Van Morrison)
Minuet in G (J. S. Bach)
Oh, Mary
Over the Rainbow
*Peter and the Wolf*
Roy G. Biv
Sweet Baby James
Sweet Rosyanne
Tangled Up in Blue
Twinkle, Twinkle, Little Star (and its Suzuki variations)
All Beatles songs, especially Eight Days a Week, Hey Jude, Let It Be, While My Guitar Gently Weeps, and Yellow Submarine
All Dan Zanes songs, especially Fooba Wooba John, Wanderin', Waltzing Matilda, and The Sidewalks of New York (otherwise known as Sidewalks of You Nork)

All Nields songs, especially My Favorite Color, Molly, This Train, Organic Farm, Give Me a Clean Heart

## Katryna's Family Canon

A Ram Sam Sam
Angel from Montgomery
Clarinet Quintet (Mozart)
Country Life
Eshe mba iku Waye
The Fox
Girls Just Want to Have Fun (Cyndi Lauper)
Going to Boston
Hush, Little Baby
If You Want to Sing Out, Sing Out (Cat Stevens)
John the Rabbit
Jump (Van Halen)
La Bamba
*Love and China* (the CD Nerissa and I recorded when Amelia was four months old, especially the songs Tailspin and Ticket to My House)
My Generation (the Who)
Over the Rainbow
Panama (Van Halen)
*Peter and the Wolf*
Pinball Wizard (the Who)
Play with Fire (the Rolling Stones)
Ring of Fire
Smoke on the Water
Strike the Bell (Dan Zanes)
Superhero Soup
Take Me for a Ride in Your Car Car (Woody Guthrie)

We Are the World (both versions)

Wild Mountain Thyme

All the songs we made up about Amelia's stuffed animals

All Beatles songs, especially Back in the USSR, Eight Days a Week, Hey Bulldog, I Saw Her Standing There, Twist and Shout, When My Guitar Gently Weeps, and Yellow Submarine

James Taylor's greatest hits

## John's Family of Origin Family Canon

Away in a Manger

The Blue Tail Fly

Dona Nobis Pacem

The Frozen Logger

Good King Wenceslas

It Came Upon a Midnight Clear

Jacob's Ladder

Jubilate Deo

Laudate Dominum (Mozart)

Old Sam Simon

Pick a Bale of Cotton

Put on Your Old Grey Bonnet

Trumpet Concerto (Haydn)

John's father's French horn playing and whistling

## Gail's Family of Origin Family Canon

Down by the Riverside

Found a Peanut

The Fox

Frère Jacques

Last Night I Had the Strangest Dream

Mairsie Doats

Michael, Row the Boat Ashore

Ninety-Nine Bottles of Beer on the Wall

Oh, Mary

Row, Row, Row Your Boat

Sloop John B

Three Jolly Coachmen

Where Have All the Flowers Gone

## FAMOUS THREE-CHORD SONGS

Bad Moon Rising (Creedence Clearwater Revival)

Blowin' in the Wind (Bob Dylan)

La Bamba (various artists)

Louie, Louie

Mango Walk (traditional; see page 68)

Ob-La-Di, Ob-La-Da (the Beatles)

Twist and Shout (the Isley Brothers and the Beatles)

Wild Thing (Jimi Hendrix)

You Really Got Me (the Kinks)

## CALL-AND-RESPONSE SONGS

All Around the Kitchen

Cape Cod Girls

Children, Go Where I Send Thee

I'll Fly Away

Jacob's Ladder

Sipping Cider through a Straw

Swing Low, Sweet Chariot

# SOME SEASONAL SONG IDEAS

This isn't close to being the last word on seasonal songs! Rather it's the list we would make if we were appointed Deejays of the World (for this year). We hope you can use it as a jumping-off point for your own list of holiday favorites.

*New Year's:* Auld Lang Syne; New Year's Day (U2); What Are You Doing New Year's Eve?

*Martin Luther King Jr. Day:* Ain't Gonna Let Nobody Turn Me Around; If You Miss Me from the Back of the Bus; People Get Ready; Precious Lord, Take My Hand (Dr. King's favorite hymn); We Shall Overcome; and any songs from the civil rights movement

*Groundhog Day/Imbolc:* February (Dar Williams); In the Bleak Midwinter

*Valentine's Day:* All You Need Is Love; My Funny Valentine; Someone to Watch Over Me (More songs are written for Valentine's Day than for almost any other holiday. If you need an anti–Valentine's Day song, "Last Kisses" by the Nields might do.)

*March—Women's History Month:* Bread and Roses; Union Maid, I'm Gonna Be an Engineer (Peggy Seeger)

*Spring equinox:* Bright Yellow Forsythia (Pete Seeger); Southland in the Springtime (Indigo Girls)

*Easter:* For All That Dwell Below the Skies; Here Comes Peter Cottontail; Easter Parade ("In your Easter bonnet . . .")

*Passover:* Chad Gadya

*May Day:* May Day Carol; Padstow May Day Song

*Mother's Day:* Your mom's favorite song

*Memorial Day:* The Garden Song (David Mallett); John the Rabbit

*Father's Day:* Your dad's favorite song

*Summer solstice:* Summertime; Wild Mountain Thyme

*Fourth of July:* America the Beautiful; Fourth of July (Aimee Mann)

*Lughnasa:* One Man Shall Mow My Meadow

*Labor Day:* Bringing in the Sheaves; Come, Labor On

*Autumn equinox:* Harvest Moon (Neil Young); Harvest Table; Shine On, Harvest Moon; When Fall Comes to New England (Cheryl Wheeler)

*Rosh Hashana/Yom Kippur:* Shana Tovah

*Columbus Day:* Just Like Christopher Columbus (the Nields); Turning Toward the Morning (Gordon Bok)

*Halloween/Samhain:* Have You Seen the Ghost of John?; Stirring Our Brew

*Thanksgiving:* Come, Ye Thankful People, Come; Let All Things Now Living; We Gather Together

*Chanukah:* Maoz Tzur; Oh Chanakah

*Christmas:* Away in a Manger; Deck the Halls; The First Nowell; It Came Upon a Midnight Clear; Jingle Bells; your own favorites

## MORE LULLABIES

Alright for Now (Tom Petty)

All the Pretty Horses

Aunt Rhody

Golden Slumbers (traditional and the Beatles)

Good Night (the Beatles)

Irene, Goodnight

Hobo's Lullaby

Hush, Little Baby

I See the Moon

Isle au Haut (Gordon Bok)

Kumbaya

May Day Carol

May There Always Be Sunshine (traditional Russian song)

Michael, Row the Boat Ashore

Over the Rainbow

Redemption Song (Bob Marley)

The Riddle Song

The Sidewalks of New York

Stay Awake (from *Mary Poppins*)

Sweet Baby James

Sylvie

Tender Shepherd (from *Peter Pan*)

What a Wonderful World

Wild Mountain Thyme

## SONGS FOR ALL-SCHOOL SING-ALONGS

De Colores

Erie Canal

Fire Down Below

The Garden Song (David Mallett)

Going to Boston

Going to the Zoo

Had Me a Cat

I Can See Clearly Now (Johnny Nash)

If I Had a Hammer (the Weavers)

I'm a Little Airplane Now (Jonathan Richman)

If You Want to Sing Out, Sing Out (Cat Stevens)

Jamaica Farewell

John the Rabbit

Kookaburra

Lean on Me (Bill Withers)

The Leaving of Liverpool

Linstead Market

London Round

Mail Myself to You

Mr. Rabbit

The Monkey and the Kangaroo

Oh, What a Beautiful Morning

Old Mister Rabbit

One Bottle of Pop

Rattlin' Bog

Savez-Vous Plantez les Choux

Shake Your Sillies Out

Slippery Fish

Somos el Barcos

Take Me for a Ride in Your Car Car (Woody
   Guthrie)
This Land Is Your Land (Woody Guthrie)
This Little Light of Mine
Unite and Unite
When the Red Red Robin Comes Bob Bob
   Bobbin' Along
Yellow Submarine (the Beatles)

## IDEAS FOR SONGS TO PASS THE TIME IN THE CAR

A Hunting We Will Go (As a new twist on I Spy,
   rewrite this song as "To [insert your destina-
   tion] We Will Go." For the lyric, use, "Something _____ I spy / With my little eye. /
   Guess what? I bet you don't know!" Fill in the
   blank with a color or shape and have the
   other passengers guess what it is.)
Allee Allee O (Name the vehicles you see driving
   by; for example, "Oh, the Mack truck is driving on the Allee Allee O . . .")

Found a Peanut
I Had a Little Rooster (Name the vehicles—"I
   had a little school bus," "I had a little hybrid,"
   "I had a little camper"—and then imitate
   noises they might make.)
I've Been Working on the Railroad (with ABC
   variation; see page 77)
My Favorite Color (Name the colors you see out
   the window.)
Ninety-Nine Bottles of Beer on the Wall
Organic Farm

## ORCHESTRAL WORKS

*Carnival of the Animals* (Camille Saint-Saëns)
*Peter and the Wolf* (We like the Leonard Bernstein
   recording.)
*Pictures at an Exhibition* (Modest Mussorgsky)
*The Sound of Music* (Rogers and Hammerstein)
*Young Person's Guide to the Orchestra* (Benjamin
   Britten)

# NOTES

## INTRODUCTION

1. Oliver Sacks, *Musicophilia: Tales of Music and the Brain* (New York: Knopf, 2007), 42.

## CHAPTER 1

1. Brandon Keim, "Baby Got Beat: Music May Be Inborn," *Wired* magazine blog Wired Science, January 26, 2009, www.wired.com/wiredscience/2009/01/babybeats.

2. Christian Nordquist, "Music Lessons Good for Children's Brains," *Medical News Today*, September 20, 2006, www.medicalnewstoday.com/articles/52349.php.

3. Daniel Coyle, *The Talent Code: Greatness Isn't Born. It's Grown. Here's How* (New York: Bantam Dell, 2009), 5.

## CHAPTER 4

1. Nerissa learned this from a friend who learned it in a workshop with Susan Kaiser Greenland.

## CHAPTER 7

1. Michiko Yurko, *Music Mind Games Handbook* (Miami, FL: Warner Brothers Publishing, 1992), 24.

## CHAPTER 11

1. Malcom Gladwell, *Outliers: The Story of Success* (New York: Little, Brown, and Company, 2008), 39.

## CHAPTER 12

1. Daniel Siegel, *Mindsight: The New Science of Personal Transformation* (New York: Bantam, 2010), 149.

2. Melissa Healy, "Brain Booster: Learning to Play Music Sharpens the Mind, Experts Say," *Los Angeles Times*, March 23, 2010.

3. Dan Zanes, interview with the author, February 25, 2009.

## CHAPTER 13

1. Ken Robinson, "Ken Robinson Says Schools Kill Creativity," video, *TED: Ideas Worth Spreading*, February 2006, www.ted.com/talks/ ken_robinson_says_schools_kill_creativity.html.

2. Daniel Siegel, *Mindsight: The New Science of Personal Transformation* (New York: Bantam, 2010), 65–66.

3. A stands for creation, which is what we do when we begin the chant; *U* for sustaining, and this is the tone we carry on for that long, long breath; and M for dissolution, which is what happens to the tone when we close our mouths on the consonant and the "song" ends.

## APPENDIX 1

1. Julie Ayotte, Isabelle Peretz, and Krista Hyde, "Congenital Amusia: A Group Study of Adults Afflicted with a Music-Specific Disorder," *Brain* 125, no. 2 (2002): 238–251, http://brain. oxfordjournals.org/content/125/2/238.full.

# RESOURCES

## BOOKS

*Celebrate the Spring* and *Celebrate the Winter* by
Revels.org (under "Books")

*The Creative Family: How to Encourage Imagination
and Nurture Family Connections* by Amanda
Blake Soule

*Humpty Who?: A Crash Course in 80 Nursery
Rhymes* by Jennifer Griffin

*American Folk Songs for Children* by Ruth Crawford
Seeger

*The Mindful Child: How to Help Your Kid Manage
Stress and Become Happier, Kinder, and More
Compassionate* by Susan Kaiser Greenland

*Mindsight: The New Science of Personal Transforma-
tion* by Daniel Siegel

*Musicophilia: Tales of Music and the Brain* by Oliver
Sacks

*Nurtured by Love: The Classic Approach to Talent
Education* by Shinrichi Suzuki

*Outliers: The Story of Success* by Malcolm Gladwell

*Rise Up Singing: The Group Singing Songbook* by
Peter Blood, Annie Patterson, et al.

*Sally Go Round the Moon and Other Revels Songs
and Singing Games for Young Children* compiled
by Nancy and John Langstaff

*Stone Soup* by Jon Muth

*The Talent Code: Greatness Isn't Born. It's Grown.
Here's How* by Daniel Coyle

*Where Have All the Flowers Gone: A Singalong
Memoir* by Pete Seeger

## MUSIC EDUCATION

**The American Orff-Schulwerk Association:**
www.aosa.org

**Dalcroze Society of America:**
www.dalcrozeusa.org

**The Diller-Quaile School of Music:**
www.diller-quaile.org

**HooteNanny:** www.nields.com/Hoot.html

**Kindermusik:**
www.kindermusik.com/defaultb.aspx

**Marimba Magic:**
http://marimba-magic.com/classes.html

**Music Mind Games:** www.musicmindgames.com

**Music Together:** www.musictogether.com

Organization of American Kodály Educators:
https://oake.org

Suzuki Association of the Americas:
http://suzukiassociation.org

## EDUCATIONAL RESOURCES

Chordie (guitar tabs, chords, and lyrics):
www.chordie.com

Reggio-Emilio Approach to Pre-School
Education:
www.reggioemiliaapproach.net/about.php

## WEBSITES

American Sign Language: www.lifeprint.com

Boston Children's Music:
www.bostonchildrensmusic.com

Children's Music: http://kidsmusic.about.com

Cool Tunes for Kids:
http://cooltunesforkids.blogspot.com

Dadnabbit: http://dadnabbit.com

February Album Writing Month:
http://FAWM.org

Gooney Bird Kids: www.gooneybirdkids.com

Jitterbug: www.jitterbug.tv

Minivan Blues: www.minivanblues.com

The Nields Family: www.nields.com

Revels: www.revels.org

Singing in the Kitchen—our blog!
www.nields.wordpress.com

Songwriting for Kids:
www.songwritingforkids.com

Zooglobble: http://zooglobble.com

## FAMILY RADIO SHOWS AND STATIONS

Ages 3 and Up!: http://ages3andup.blogspot.com

Dadnabbit: http://dadnabbit.com

Hilltown Families radio show/podcast:
http://hilltownfamilies.wordpress.com/
category/hilltown-family-variety-show

Kids Corner: www.kidscorner.org

Kids Place Live: www.xmradio.com/kidsplacelive

Saturday Morning Cereal Bowl:
www.saturdaycerealbowl.com

Spare the Rock, Spoil the Child:
http://sparetherock.com/wordpress

Wonderground Radio: http://minnesota.public
radio.org/radio/services/wonderground

# INDEX

# ABOUT THE AUTHORS

## KATRYNA *by Nerissa*

Katryna Nields has been singing since she was verbal, at about the age of two. She grew up in Northern Virginia, and throughout her life folk music informed everything from her politics to parenthood to how she sees her role in the world. (Her first ambition was to be Chief Justice of the Supreme Court. Now she brings her wise counsel to her family and community.) At Trinity College in Hartford, Connecticut, she studied the role of music in religion and traveled to Nepal with her guitar to make and learn music with and from the people of the Himalayas. In 1991 she founded the band The Nields, along with her sister Nerissa, and has been touring North America and recording CDs (fifteen to date) ever since. She also co-created HooteNanny—an early music class for kids ages zero to five and their grown-ups—and takes great pleasure and joy in bringing family singing to communities all over her region. She is very generous and is the kind of mom every kid wishes to have: full of fun ideas, family stories, and cuddles. She lives in Western Massachusetts with her husband and children.

## NERISSA *by Katryna*

Nerissa Nields has known she wanted to be a singer and songwriter since she was about four. She didn't know she wanted to teach people music until she became a mom. Nerissa grew up in a musical family. She has played recorder, piano, violin, guitar, bass, and can harmonize to anything in the world. Her dream has always been to write songs that will be sung in the back seats of school buses. Now she turns her passion to teaching families how to make more music in the back seats of their minivans. A Yale-educated English and (almost) music major, Nerissa synthesizes her passions by envisioning a world filled with music, introspection, and creative expression. She has dedicated her life both to the doing (performing, writing, singing, recording) and to the teaching and passing on of those skills. In addition to her work with her sister, Katryna (singing with The Nields and teaching HooteNanny), she coaches writers and runs writing groups out of her house, affectionately nicknamed Big Yellow. In everything, she strives to reach her potential while helping others to reach theirs. She lives in Western Massachusetts with her husband and children.

# LIST OF AUDIO TRACKS

1. Say It Again, Cow! *(Nerissa Nields)*
2. Six Yellow Chicks *(Nerissa Nields)*
3. Clap Your Hands/Old Joan Clark *(Traditional)*
4. The Fox *(Traditional)*
5. Hi, Ho the Rattlin' Bog *(Traditional)*
6. Mango Walk *(Traditional)*
7. When the Saints Go Marching In *(Traditional, with additional lyrics by Nerissa Nields)*
8. Sugar Snap Peas *(Nerissa Nields)*
9. ABC Song *(Nerissa Nields)*
10. My Favorite Color *(Nerissa Nields)*
11. Alouette *(Traditional, arranged by the Nields)*
12. Babar the Elephant *(Nerissa Nields)*
13. The Noble Duke of York *(Traditional)*
14. Ride a Cock Horse *(Traditional)*
15. Crazy Rider *(Nerissa Nields)*
16. Three Craws *(Traditional)*
17. Sur le Pont d'Avignon *(Traditional)*
18. Organic Farm *(Nerissa Nields)*
19. Allee Allee O *(Traditional)*
20. Molly the Donkey *(Nerissa Nields)*
21. The Horse Went Around *(Traditional)*
22. A Ram Sam Sam *(Traditional)*
23. Whatever I'm Feeling Now Feels Just Fine *(Nerissa Nields)*
24. Time to Take a Bath *(Nerissa Nields)*
25. Hush, Little Baby *(Traditional, with lyrics by Nerissa Nields)*
26. The Muffin Man *(Traditional, arranged by the Nields)*
27. A Hunting We Will Go *(Traditional, arranged by the Nields)*
28. Hal an Tow *(Traditional, with additional lyrics by Nerissa Nields)*
29. In the Bleak Midwinter *(Lyrics by Christina Rossetti, music by Gustav Holst)*
30. Wild Mountain Thyme *(Traditional)*

The enclosed audio CD includes many of the songs featured in this book. You can also download the tracks listed here at www .shambhala.com/AllTogetherSigningintheKitchen.

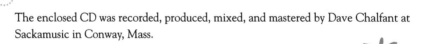

The enclosed CD was recorded, produced, mixed, and mastered by Dave Chalfant at Sackamusic in Conway, Mass.

Nerissa Nields: Acoustic guitar and vocals
Katryna Nields: Vocals and percussion
Dave Chalfant: Guitars, dobro, banjo, bass, percussion, and drums

A special thanks to the following musicians:
Dave Hower: drums on "The Muffin Man," "Alouette," and "When the Saints Go Marching In"; The Primate Fiasco: horns and banjo on "The Muffin Man" and "When the Saints Go Marching In"; Eric Lee: violin on "My Favorite Color"; Ben Demerath: mandolin and vocals on "Hi, Ho, the Rattlin' Bog" and vocals on "In the Bleak Midwinter" and "When the Saints Go Marching In"; John Nields: vocals on "When the Saints Go Marching In," "Wild Mountain Thyme," and "The Fox"; Jazer Giles: accordion on "Alouette" and "ABC Song"; William Chalfant: vocals on "Mango Walk"; Amelia Chalfant: vocals on "Mango Walk."